WITHDRAWN

The Social Philosophy of Josiah Royce

The Social Philosophy
of
JOSIAH ROYCE

Edited, with an Introductory Essay, by
STUART GERRY BROWN
Professor of Citizenship and American Culture
Maxwell School of Citizenship
Syracuse University

SYRACUSE UNIVERSITY PRESS
1950

Preface

Though Josiah Royce is one of the very few Americans who have developed and written philosophy in the grand manner, speaking, indeed, the authentic voice of modern idealism, almost all of his books have been allowed to go out of print. This book, with the generous co-operation of his son Mr. Stephen Royce, is the first of two volumes intended to make the core of his social and religious thought once more available for all students of American philosophy and culture.

The writings here collected have a certain systematic and cumulative force which I have tried to describe and evaluate in the introductory essay (reprinted here by permission of the *Journal of Ethics*). Royce wrote no full length exposition of his social philosophy. In fact he came to make social, and even political, applications of his idealism only in his later years, and his work was surely not finished when he died in 1916. However, the strict consistency of his logic and his speculation, throughout his whole career, makes it safe enough to piece together, as I have done here, his work in one broad realm of thought.

The selections which form this book are given entire. They include two essays from *Race Questions, Provincialism, and Other American Problems* (1908), the first five chapters, which form the core of that book, from *The Philosophy of Loyalty* (1908), the two central chapters from *The Hope of the Great Community* (1916), and the title essay from *War and Insurance* (1914). I have to acknowledge permission of the Macmillan Company to reprint the chapters from *Race Questions* and *The Philosophy of Loyalty*. The remainder of the book is made possible through permissions granted by Stephen Royce, to whom I wish to record not only my own obligation but that of countless other admirers of his father's work.

S. G. B.

Maxwell School of Citizenship
Syracuse University
July 1, 1950

CONTENTS

For our time shows us that individualism and collectivism are tendencies, each of which, as our social order grows, intensifies the other. The more the social will expresses itself in vast organizations of collective power, the more are individuals trained to be aware of their own personal wants and choices and ideals, and of the vast opportunities that would be theirs if they could but gain control of these social forces. The more, in sum, does their individual self-will become conscious, deliberate, cultivated, and therefore dangerously alert and ingenious.

Josiah Royce, *The Problem of Christianity*

From Provincialism To The Great Community: The Social Philosophy of Josiah Royce

The philosophers differ sadly amongst themselves. They do not at present form a literal human community of mutual enlightenment and of growth in knowledge, to any such extent as do the workers in the field of any one of the natural sciences. The philosophers are thus far individuals rather than consciously members one of another. The charity of mutual interpretation is ill developed amongst them. They frequently speak with tongues and do not edify. And they are especially disposed to contend regarding their spiritual gifts. We cannot expect them, then, at present to agree regarding any one philosophical opinion.

. . . for every estrangement that appears in the order of time, there somewhere is to be found, and will be found, the reconciling spiritual event; that for every wrong there will somewhere appear the corresponding remedy; and that for every tragedy and distraction of individual existence the universal community will find the way—how and when we know not—to provide the corresponding unity, the appropriate triumph. We are saved through and in the community. There is the victory which overcomes the world. There is the interpretation which reconciles. There is the doctrine which we teach.

Josiah Royce, *The Problem of Christianity.*

I

When Rousseau predicted, in the eighteenth century, that unless radical reforms were quickly instituted, the Western world would find itself in the future more and more torn between the poles of a dualism of man and society, orthodox philosophers of the schools either scoffed or refused to heed his warning. It was, after all, the age of Adam Smith, and the full flower of individualism was only just beginning to grow. In those pre-Marxian days, even the newly-conceived "economic man" was thought of as an individual competing freely with other individuals to produce ever more goods and widening benefits to the lasting betterment of all mankind. The true dualism, it was thought, was the dualism of man and nature, and rational philosophy and economic freedom were promising weapons for the final victory in that ageless battle. Even in the great days of liberal philosophy in Britain's Victorian age, attention to the growing problem of man as a collective being was given most frequently by radicals and reformers who could easily be discounted as failures in the individualist struggle. The voices of Carlyle and Ruskin were by no means the typical voices of their time. As late as the 1920's, such critics of literature and society as Irving Babbitt were roundly denouncing Rousseau and all his followers as enemies of the human spirit who, by insisting upon a false dualism in which the individual found himself at war with society, were obscuring the true dualism of the two natures of man. Only persuade men to bring about peace in their own hearts, to learn to control the dark impulses of the lower nature by the "higher will," and society would be composed of free individuals harmoniously competing to improve the human enterprise. But Babbitt's, by this time, was a lonely voice. When the reversal in thought came, it came suddenly and was nearly complete. After the First World War, most European thinkers were already committed to some form of collectivism, and the apparent success of Marxian communism influenced vast numbers of people even when it did not entirely convert them. The United States remained, as it does now, almost the last outpost of individualist philosophy.

Anyone who is concerned with the social condition of man in the middle of the twentieth century will do well to recall the specific reasons, not only for the development of collectivist thought in Europe, but for the survival of individualism in America. In the nearly two hundred years since Rousseau first made his dark forecast, the Old World has been almost constantly torn by a kind of civil warfare, destructive not only of individual morale and spiritual self-assurance, but of the material means to an individualist economic life. And, paradoxically enough, the long series of wars in Europe has been accompanied by vast growth in population. While in earlier ages the land could provide at least a subsistence level of life for the masses of Europe, in our time, despite the enormous achievements of the Industrial Revolution, land and industry together can neither feed, nor clothe, nor house the people on a self-sufficient basis in line with modern expectations. Dwindling resources must be conserved, and their use and distribution must be planned in the interests of all the people. It is for this reason that European thinkers are constantly reminding us in America that the issue in Europe is not socialism or communism versus democratic capitalism, but rather democratic versus undemocratic socialism. Planning there will be; nationalization there will be; the problem is whether planning and nationalization will be legislated and administered by representatives of the people through the democratic processes, or by the quicker and more dramatic devices of absolutism.

Meanwhile, on this side of the ocean, during the same two hundred years, resources of all kinds have been so abundant that they could, until recently, be wasted without seriously affecting the popular standard of living. During most of the period it was, indeed, true that the basic struggle was man against nature, and the courage, skill, and physical strength of individual men were undoubtedly necessary to win the struggle. American individualism had its roots in practice rather than theory. When Emerson cried his gospel of self-reliance in the age following the American Revolution, he was, to a great extent, only translating into terms of oratory and literature the language of plain people who were in fact living the self-reliant life, actually living that life, this is to say, on one level of Emerson's meaning. It is doubtful whether his Transcendental idealism had any more meaning for the audiences of his lectures than it does for Americans of the present day. But in social and economic life, whatever may have been happening to the spirit, the Americans were individualists, and the fruits of their individualism were plain for any man to see—fruits so rich and tasty that it would be many decades before attacks on individualism from any source and couched in any language would find sympathetic ears in this country.

But with the First World War, many Americans discovered that the United States, whatever may be the wishes of her people, is neither isolated nor immune from the currents of thought and action which run through the rest of the world. The lesson of the great depression and the Second World War has by now communicated itself to most of us, and it is difficult any longer to find an alert American who still relies upon the old slogans and practices of "rugged individualism." We have now had our New Deal, and though the Republican opposition has cried socialism and communism, that cry is dying, and all parties are more and more committed to such collectivist ideals as social insurance and social security. Even planning of a limited sort, and government control of such things as wages and prices, and the allocation of materials are generally admitted to be sometimes necessary. Individualism, in short, is rapidly disappearing from American popular philosophy, and it is time to consider whether we shall not shortly lose it entirely, with not only its evident faults but its great virtues gone from our life. It is a good moment for stock taking, since we may yet be granted a little time before we are overtaken by a collectivist revolution which, should it come upon us unawares, would not allow us to control it. In such an event, not having seen soon enough or clearly enough which freedoms must be retained to the individual and depend upon individualism and which freedoms may be safely entrusted to the collective whole, we may be in sore danger of losing them all. Whatever we may think of Rousseau's reasons and solutions, we must now grapple with the dualism he outlined. Philosophers from the beginning of thought have always recognized the centrality of the problem of the One and the Many. That problem now certainly finds its most prominent expression in the dualism of man and society. Our freedom as persons and our democratic methods of social behavior depend upon our ability to bring about a practical integration of the two terms of this dualism. If freedom and democracy are indeed worth preserving, we shall do well to seek wisdom for the solution of our common public problem wherever we can find it, and American thinkers who anticipated the present dilemma may turn out to be among our most valuable friends and aiders. Among such thinkers the long neglected social philosophy of Josiah Royce earns him a pre-eminent place.

II

Royce is generally known among students of philosophy, and to a limited extent among the general public, as a somewhat scholastic idealist whose preoccupation with a doctrine of the Absolute was neither indigenous to American thought nor widely appreciated by any but students of the technical aspects of metaphysics. My concern in these pages is by no means to revive a futile controversy in epistemology nor to recommend any Absolutist doctrine, but I am persuaded that Royce's social philosophy, which has been almost wholly ignored save for his volume on loyalty, contains a core of wisdom which is capable at once of standing independent of his metaphysical preconceptions and of serving as a rich source of insight to the student of society and morals at the present day.

In certain respects Royce was an inheritor of Emerson and carried on, in an age when idealism had become unpopular, a campaign for the Over-Soul and the Absolute against the pragmatists; he was a skillful and resourceful adversary, but was overwhelmed by the numbers of the op-

position and the popular thought of the day. In retrospect one may agree
that James, Dewey, and the others were not only more right than wrong
in the technical controversy but closer to the realities of American life.
Yet at the same time, a careful study of such books as Royce's *Philosophy
of Loyalty*, *Race Questions*, *The Problem of Christianity*, *War and
Insurance*, and *The Hope of the Great Community*, leads to the conclusion that below the surface of controversy and polemics there ran in
Royce's mind a current of thought moving more directly toward the
future and the realities of our time than could be found among his opponents. For it was precisely the dualism of man and society with which
Royce was primarily concerned when he turned his mind to social considerations. The solution which he proposed was based at once upon the
American tradition of individualism and idealistic yearning and the collective necessity which he found pressing upon him from the Old World
and present likewise in the emerging pattern of American life. His later
and last years were devoted almost entirely to a study of the community,
in the hope that he could provide some direction, for a people who were
to be organized willy-nilly into ever more and larger organizations, that
their organizations might be more than organizations, and that their virtues and ideals as individuals might be preserved in the new forms. So
great was his passion for this service that at the end he offered to unat-
tending ears a plan of world organization based upon universal insurance,
the practicality of which need not fear the criticism of our contemporary
advocates of World Federalism or Federal Union.

III

A survey of Royce's social thought properly begins, as he began, with
a consideration of provincialism. If our concern is with the virtues and
integrity of the individual man striving as best he may toward the reali-
zation of his personal ideals, it is necessary to begin with man in his im-
mediate social context—family, neighborhood, village, province. The
meaning of provincialism for Americans is well expressed in the common
question "Where are you from?", implying as it does that the answer to
the question will somehow identify the characteristics to be expected
from the individual asked. As Royce says:

> For me, then, a province shall mean any one part of a national domain,
> which is, geographically and socially, sufficiently unified to have a true
> consciousness of its own unity, to feel a pride in its own ideals and customs,

and to possess a sense of its distinction from other parts of the country. And by the term "provincialism" I shall mean, first, the tendency of such a province to possess its own customs and ideals; secondly, the totality of these customs and ideals themselves; and thirdly, the love and pride which leads the inhabitants of a province to cherish as their own these traditions, beliefs, and aspirations.[1]*

With this definition at the base of his argument, Royce offers a thesis which he puts succinctly in the following words:

My thesis is that, in the present state of the world's civilization, and of the life of our own country, the time has come to emphasize, with a new meaning and intensity, the positive value, the absolute necessity for our welfare, of a wholesome provincialism, as a saving power to which the world in the near future will need more and more appeal.[2]

and in these:

The present state of civilization, both in the world at large, and with us, in America, is such as to define a new social mission which the province alone, but not the nation, is able to fulfil. False sectionalism, which disunites, will indeed always remain as great an evil as ever it was. But the modern world has reached a point where it needs, more than ever before, the vigorous development of a highly organized provincial life.[3]

At first glance it may seem that we have here an anticipation not of a broad and unifying social philosophy, but of a kind of regionalism which was popular among literary men in the 1920's and 30's and which found its formulating reasons not so much in the hope of a better and more integrated future collective society as in nostalgia for the fragmented past. But the similarity is wholly superficial. Royce's concern is to find a practical medium in which individualism can function, in which the individual person can be a person, and be recognized as one, at a time when the tendency of social movement toward ever larger collective action and behavior is so much against the continuing recognition of men as persons. He begins with the province, as he calls it, because there if anywhere a man is known as a man and because in healthy provincialism, healthy as distinguished from diseased, nationalism may find its roots.

As our country grows in social organization, there will be, in absolute measure, more and not less provincialism amongst our people. To be sure, as I hope, there will also be, in absolute measure, more and not less patriotism, closer and not looser national ties, less and not more mutual sectional misunderstanding. But the two tendencies, the tendency toward national unity and that toward local independence of spirit, must henceforth grow

*Notes to the introduction are on page 29.

together. They cannot prosper apart. The national unity must not kill out, nor yet hinder, the provincial self-consciousness. The loyalty to the Republic must not lessen the love and the local pride of the individual community. The man of the future must love his province more than he does today.[4]

Royce's "higher provincialism" thus leads toward national collectivism and, as we shall see, international integration, but he emphasizes the province in the first instance rather than the world state toward which, in the end, he would guide us, because of his concern for the individual and the ideals of individualism.

In his analysis of the values inherent in a wise provincialism, Royce distinguishes three parallel social facts of the present day, the undesirable, or even evil, implications of which he believes can be avoided by a renewal of provincial life. The first of these tendencies he finds in one of America's most carefully cherished freedoms—the freedom of social mobility. Just at present, when many peoples of the world, under the dictates of absolute authority, are forbidden to move from place to place, to change occupation or even local residence without reasons satisfactory to the state and without numerous papers and documents, Americans are particularly solicitous of their own freedom to move where they please, limited only by their economic means. But there is, as we have seen constantly in the last generation, a cultural disadvantage in social mobility, a cultural disadvantage which sometimes develops into a downright social evil. When men become physically homeless, they often become also spiritually homeless. "To offset the social tendencies due to such frequent changes of dwelling-place," Royce says, "we need the further development and the intensification of the community spirit."[5] If our communities are firmly established, if our provincial life is vigorous, a great deal of social mobility may be exercised, many changes of dwelling-place and occupation may occur, and the individuals involved may still be readily assimilated; but if the community and provincial life deteriorates, such assimilation will become wholly quantitative and will lack the spiritual and ideal values which a genuine community can provide.

The second tendency which Royce discriminates and proposes to counter with provincialism is the "levelling" tendency.

By the levelling tendency in question I mean that aspect of modern civilization which is most obviously suggested by the fact that, because of the ease of communication amongst distant places, because of the spread of popular education, and because of the consolidation and of the centralization of industries and of social authorities, we tend all over the nation, and, in some degree, even throughout the civilized world, to read the same daily news, to share the same general ideas, to submit to the same overmastering social forces, to live in the same external fashions, to discourage individuality, and to approach a dead level of harassed mediocrity. . . . The result is a tendency to crush the individual.[6]

In elaboration of the last point, Royce continues:

> Or, in more common language, independence of spirit flourishes only when a man at least believes that he has a chance to change his fortunes if he persistently wills to do so. But the servant of some modern forms of impersonal social organization tends to lose this belief that he has a chance. Hence he tends to lose independence of spirit.[7]

How, then, can provincialism counteract the levelling tendency? It is true as Royce admits, that "Local spirit, local pride, provincial independence, influence the individual man precisely because they appeal to his imitative tendencies." But, on the other hand, "thereby they act so as to render him more or less immune in presence of the more trivial of the influence that, coming from without his community, would otherwise be likely to reduce him to the dead level of the customs of the whole nation."[8]

> For a man is in large measure what his social consciousness makes him. Give him the local community that he loves and cherishes, that he is proud to honor and to serve,—make his ideal of that community lofty,—give him faith in the dignity of his province,— and you have given him a power to counteract the levelling tendencies of modern civilization.[9]

The third tendency with which Royce concerns himself is the tendency to develop, by too rapid association of substantial numbers of people, what is known as the "mob-spirit." He refers specifically to Le Bon's study *The Crowd*, a fruitful book, but one which has long been superseded not only by the literature of social psychology, but by the experience of human beings everywhere. "The mob-spirit," as Royce says, "is no new thing. It has existed in some measure from the very beginning of social life. But there are certain modern conditions which tend to give the mob-spirit new form and power, and to lead to new social dangers that are consequent upon the presence of this spirit."[10] Although in the nature of things Royce could make no reference to such recent phenomena as the Communist or Fascist mobs, his generalized description of the mob-spirit is wholly satisfactory. He speaks of the manifestations of mob-spirit as a kind of hypnosis, after which individual members of the mob find difficulty in recalling either their speech or their behavior. He recognizes that constructive ends may sometimes be attained by hypnotic mass movement, but is constrained to emphasize that for every such desirable end achieved, there are countless social disruptions brought about by the same spirit which have evil effects in both the short and the long run. As he sees the matter, the mob or crowd attitude, even when quiescent, is one of the most serious of all threats both to the free individual and to the good life of all men. There is more than one point in his discussion at which one could introduce such illustrations as a Nazi meeting at Nuremburg, or a Red May Day in Moscow, without any violence to the text. As a counter to the mob, he opposes what he calls "the rightly constituted social group where every member feels his own responsibility for his part of the social enterprise which is in hand," and where "the result of the interaction of individuals is that the social group may show itself wiser than any of its individuals."[11] Such a group, as he says, has always "depended upon the variety and not the uniformity of its members" whereas, on the other hand, "the other sort of social group, the mob, has depended upon the emotional agreement, the sympathy, of its members. It has been powerful only in so far as they forgot who they individually were, and gave themselves up to the suggestions of the moment."[12] It follows, as he quickly adds, that "if we are to look for the source of the greatest dangers of popular government, we must expect to find them in the influence of the mob-spirit."[13] Thus the problem of the future will be to develop ever more effective groupings of that other sort in which variety is sacred, and collective judgment reflects collective thought as opposed to collective emotion.

At this point he deals carefully with the problem of sympathy. Emphasis upon sympathy which held a pre-eminent place in the humanitarian ethics of the eighteenth and nineteenth centuries, was, of course, one of the chief objects of the humanist attack led by Irving Babbitt and Paul Elmer More. As Babbitt said, "The humanist must be more selective in his embraces." At times in humanist literature sympathy appears to be almost a vice. Royce, on the other hand, deals with it as an emotion essentially neutral in its ethical significance. Sympathy evoked by the mob spirit may lead to anti-Jewish pogroms, but sympathy functioning as a part of the true community spirit may foster social insurance. Sympathy, like the other aspects of crowd psychology, does not even require any longer "the physical presence of a crowd of people in a given place. It is enough if the newspapers, if the theatre, if the other means of social communication, serve to transmit the waves of emotional enthusiasm."[14] The present-day reader would simply add motion picture, radio, television, and air transportation to Royce's list. He goes on, "A nation composed of many millions of people may fall rapidly under the hypnotic influence of a few leaders, of a few fatal phrases. And thus, as our third evil, we have not only the general levelling tendency of modern social life, but the particular tendency to emotional excitability which tends to make the social order, under certain conditions, not only monotonous and unideal, but actively dangerous."[15] Again it is the province, so Royce thinks, which is most likely to generate social groups which are not subject to the mob spirit.

> I answer that the place for fostering such groups is the province, for such groups flourish under conditions that arouse local pride, the loyalty to one's own community, the willingness to remember one's own ways and ideals, even at the moment when the nation is carried away by some levelling emotion. The lesson would then be: Keep the province awake, that the nation may be saved from the disastrous hypnotic slumber so characteristic of excited masses of mankind.[16]

The skeptic has long been waiting to enter a caveat. "What you say about this 'wise provincialism' may be well enough, but you describe only its virtues and the blessings which you assure us it can invoke upon our heads. But what of that narrower provincialism which has earned for the word itself a pejorative connotation? How in practice does the 'provincial' really differ from the 'yokel'? In order to have freedom of choice, must the civilizing influences of great urban centers or of individuals who stand apart from any group be sacrificed?" Royce is prepared for these objections. He is fully aware of the stupidity and even bigotry which false provincialism too often engenders and fosters. And so he directs his exhortations not only to persons not yet provincial, to become so, but to provincial persons as well, that they shall improve their provinces.

> Here I speak of a matter that in all our American communities has been until recently far too much neglected. Local pride ought above all to centre, so far as its material objects are concerned, about the determination to give the surroundings of the community nobility, dignity, beauty. We Americans spend far too much of our early strength and time in our newer communities upon injuring our landscapes, and far too little upon endeavoring to beautify our towns and cities. We have begun to change all that, and while I have no right to speak as an aesthetic judge concerning the growth of the love of the beautiful in our country, I can strongly insist that no community can think any creation of genuine beauty and dignity in its public buildings or in the surroundings of its towns and cities too good a thing for

its own deserts. For we deserve what in such realms we can learn how to create or to enjoy, or to make sacrifices for. And no provincialism will become dangerously narrow so long as it is constantly accompanied by a willingness to sacrifice much in order to put in the form of great institutions, of noble architecture, and of beautiful surroundings an expression of the worth that the community attaches to its own ideals.[17]

IV

As all students of philosophy know, the cornerstone of Royce's ethical theory was the principle of loyalty. Indeed, many persons who know nothing else about Royce know that he was the pre-eminent philosopher of loyalty. Yet his use of the term has often been misunderstood, and nowhere, I think, more often than in his discussion of the relation between loyalty and individualism. Just at present the term is so freely used and in so many contexts that a certain confusion is inevitable. By the same action a man may be considered disloyal by one group and loyal by another. The hierarchy of loyalties is more often than not a treacherous ladder. The measure of a man's loyalty is the highest ideal he professes to serve, and not infrequently that ideal fails to agree with the highest ideal professed by others. Thus, in the notorious Canadian spy case, a British scientist betrayed to the Soviet Union information about atomic energy belonging to the Western allies. He offered as his reason a belief that Soviet Communism was a form of international idealism transcending the professed democratic international idealism of the Western powers. To the Soviets and to Communists generally, he was no doubt a hero. On the other hand, the Russian code clerk in the Soviet Embassy who betrayed the Soviet spy ring to the Canadian authorities professed to be acting in the name of ideals of individual liberty which he opposed to the collective levelling of Communist theory and practice. In the eyes of many people in the West, the code clerk was a hero, while to the Soviets he was undoubtedly a villain. Some kind of loyalty was certainly at work in both cases, and Royce himself would in all probability have accepted such a judgment. The first concern of his argument was indeed to show that the cohesive principle of all ethical behavior is loyalty, whether the ethics practiced are good or bad for men. The first question must be, "Is a man loyal?" It is only the second question which asks, "To what is the loyal man loyal?" It is the third and final question which asks, "To what *ought* the loyal man to be loyal?"

Royce's discussion plays about these three questions and treats them in the order given. For the first, a loyal man is a man who gives himself unstintingly to a cause. As Royce puts it, "The willing and practical and thoroughgoing devotion of a person to a cause."[18] Without such loyalty, there is no moral life, and the good society cannot flourish. The second question is practical and has many answers. At the lowest level there is loyalty to self-interest,—the cause of one's own economic or social advancement, for example. Such loyalty never deliberately serves a larger cause unless the individual is persuaded that by such service he advances his personal interest. Though modern ethics has, on the whole, rejected the self-interest theory of Mandeville or Adam Smith, it is nonetheless true that loyalty to self-interest does, in fact, often serve a larger cause. The break comes when the larger cause demands a sacrifice which the individual cannot make without some detriment to what he conceives to be his best interest. The moralist steps in to point out that the individual has misconceived his self-interest, but then there arises a question of the relative value of the two judgments of the original individual's self-interest. What is the motive of the moralist in criticizing the first judgment? We shortly find ourselves, if we follow this line, floundering in a quagmire of pure relativism. But the matter is still more complicated when the question is asked, "Does the larger cause under discussion itself contribute to a still larger cause?" Is there not a breaking point at which those committed to the larger cause will refuse sacrifices for the still larger cause, as their judgment tells them that their group interest will not be served by such sacrifices? We have here a mathematical progression leading to infinity. Royce was well enough aware of these difficulties, and it was for this reason, I think, that he focussed the greater part of his attention upon loyalty as a principle rather than upon specific loyalties. His theory led him from the loyal activity of an individual man, loyal to whatever cause, to an absolute principle of loyalty to loyalty. The argument is wholly general and abstract, and the concrete application remains, as before, a question of the goods one chooses or has forced upon him. The goods which Royce chose, as I have indicated in the earlier pages of this essay, were the goods of individual freedom and democracy, and his theory of loyalty found its practical application in the terms of these goods. Thus the loyal man can serve no cause which is detrimental to the liberty or democratic right of any other man, except in so far as that other man himself wishes to sacrifice a part of his individual liberty or democratic right in the interest of securing some individual liberties or some democratic rights to larger numbers of persons. The essence of democracy is compromise, and in any compromise some interests are sacrificed in favor of others. Something that men hold dear must be given up in the interest of what they hold dearer.

How then is loyalty to individual freedom and democratic right to be fostered in the society of the present? What is the relation between such loyalty and the provincialism with which Royce's social theory begins? We have already in effect answered the question, but let us draw the implications a bit further. The individual person, taken in his narrowest context, the family, finds soon enough that his liberties are of necessity curtailed as they conflict with the liberties of the other members of his family. I wish to read; I have the time, and the skill, and the place which are required for reading. I wish to read Book A as a first choice, or Book B as a second choice. Another member of my family, having also time, skill, and place in which to read, and having a similar desire, wishes also to read Book A as a first choice, or Book B as a second choice. One of us must yield to the other if either is to read Book A. If there is any freedom or harmony at all in the family, one of us will yield to the other. The yielding is brought about by no external factor. If I yield, and accept Book B, it is my choice to do so because I prefer limited freedom to read for all the members of my family as against the failure of freedom to function at all. And so it is with neighbors, and with fellow citizens, and with communities, towns, villages, cities, states, and countries. If I had absolute power, I might read what I choose, but I cannot do so under conditions in which freedom prevails for all. Thus I make sacrifices from the lowest to the highest in the scale of values in the interests of the ideal of freedom which I serve as my cause. My loyalty to the ideal of freedom measures my action in any specific interest involving choice. So also is it with a society which functions upon the principles of democracy. The minority or opposition in a democratic situation yields to the majority, and gives its consent to rulings of which it does not approve, because it is loyal to the idea of democracy, to the method of deciding upon which rulings shall be instituted, for that method includes above all else the right of the minority or opposition to work toward becoming the majority and thereafter instituting its own rulings. This kind of loyalty to the ideals of individual liberty and democratic right and method, Royce believed, are best fostered in small environments—the family, the neighborhood, and the province. Thus loyalty is the cohesive principle, not only in ethics theoretically, but in social practice. It is loyalty which forms a bridge between any individual and any group, and it is loyalty to the ideals of freedom and democracy which forms the bridge between the free individual and the provinces of democracy.

Let us now see how Royce puts the matter in his own words. It occurs to him naturally enough that the chief opponents of his position will be professed individualists who doubt the validity of his sort of individualism, dependent as it is upon loyalty. "No impersonal moral theory can," he says, "be successful. Individualism in ethics has therefore its permanent and, as I believe, its absolute justification in the nature of things. . . . And so far, then, I myself, in defending loyalty as a good thing for the loyal, am speaking as an ethical individualist. My whole case depends upon this fact. And so, in following my argument, you need not fear that I want to set some impersonal sort of life as an ideal over against the individualism of the opponents of loyalty. . . I contend only that their opposition to loyalty, their view that one's individual purposes can be won otherwise than by and through loyalty, is due merely to their failure to comprehend what it is that the ethical individual needs, and what it is that in all, even of his blindest strivings, he is still seeking. What I hold is, that he inevitably seeks his own form of loyalty, his own cause, and his opportunity to serve that cause, and that he can actually and rationally find spiritual rest and peace in nothing else."[19] Royce goes on to assume that the ethical individualist is concerned primarily and properly with his own individual good, and he assumes that ethical individualists objecting to his theory will make certain assertions; for example, that the highest individual good is personal happiness. To this he replies that happiness is impossible without a plan, since natural desires are "countless and conflicting. What satisfies one desire defeats another. Until your desires are harmonized by means of some definite plan of life, happiness is therefore a mere accident. Now it comes and now it flies, you know not why. And the mere plan to be happy if you can is by itself no plan. You therefore cannot adopt the pursuit of happiness as your profession."[20] If this is agreed, the individualist may go on to say that he will accept as the plan of his life that way in which the social order requires him to live. But Royce immediately replies that on such a principle "you find yourself without any determinate way of expressing your own individuality. For if the social order is indeed not as chaotic in its activities as by nature you yourself are, it is quite unable of itself to do more than to make of you, in one way or another, a link in its mechanism, or a member of one of its numerous herds, in any case a mere vehicle for carrying its various influences. Against this fate, as an ethical individual, you justly revolt."[21] The third objection immediately follows that if neither personal happiness nor a plan determined by society is a suitable goal for the life of ethical individualism, then power may be the goal. Royce give three answers to this claim. First, "the attainment of power is a matter of fortune."[22] Second, "the lust for power is insatiable."[23] And third, he offers the words of Spinoza, "The power of man is infinitely surpassed by the power of external things."[24]

It follows from these considerations that "the only coherent moral independence which you can define is one that has to find its expression in a loyal life."[25] Royce readily admits that there is "endless room . . . for a rational autonomy in your choice of your cause."[26] But cause there must be, and for Royce, as for us, the cause must be liberty and democracy if we propose to preserve our way of life.

V

Thus far we have skimmed the surface of Royce's social theory. In brief summary we may put it as follows: the dearest social values are the liberty and dignity of the individual man and the democratic method of arriving at social decisions. In order to preserve and enhance these values, we must re-emphasize, re-dignify, and re-vitalize the smaller units of society which are known as provinces, for within the provincial life individual variety will most surely flourish. A democratic nation requires variety of provinces just as a democratic province requires variety of individuals; a world order which is at once free and democratic will require variety of nations. The collective tendency of social movement and development must constantly be checked by and integrated with the cultivation of the individual virtues. The great community of world democracy is to be achieved by the cultivation of the province. The road to human brotherhood in peace and democracy is the road that leads from the individual through the province to the nation and finally the world community.

But beneath the surface of Royce's thought and central in his whole conception is the distinction between organization and community, between the morally detached individual and the individual who is achieving salvation through community. In what seems to me his most important, as surely as it is his most neglected, book, *The Problem of Christianity*, Royce deals in exhaustive detail with these distinctions and the problems which they raise. Setting out upon the assumptions of a skeptical citizen of the twentieth century, Royce asks what values there may be in Christian ethics which have preserved the Church for two thousand years and which may still serve to unite mankind and foster liberty. As I am attempting in this essay to describe Royce's social philosophy independently of his metaphysical preconceptions, so Royce, in *The Problem of Christianity* and in his last book, *The Hope of the Great Community*, tries to show that what is essential and permanent in Christian ethics is in no wise dependent upon a mythology of the supernatural. And though he turns to St. Paul as the most reliable source of Christian teaching, he pays little heed to Paul's supernaturalism. It is the Pauline gospel of the community from which Royce develops his own positions. Beginning with the doctrine of original sin and concluding with the doctrine of the Church as the mystical body of Christ, Royce interprets the whole system of Pauline theology in purely ethical and human terms.

Regarding original sin, Royce argues as follows:

> The pith of the matter can be expressed, in terms of purely human psychology, thus: Man's fallen state is due to his nature as a social animal. This nature is such that you can train his conscience only by awakening his self-will. By self-will, I here mean, as Paul meant, man's conscious and active assertion of his own individual desires, worth, and undertakings, over against the will of his fellow, and over against the social will. Another name for this sort of conscious self-will is the modern term "individualism," when it is used to mean the tendency to prefer what the individual man demands to what the collective will requires. In general, and upon high levels of human intelligence, when you train individualism, you also train collectivism; that is, you train in the individual a respect for the collective will. And it belongs to Paul's very deep and searching insight to assert that these two tendencies—the tendency towards individualism, and that towards collectivism—do not exclude, but intensify and inflame each other.
>
> Training, if formally successful in producing the skilful member of human society, breeds respect, although not love, for "the law," that is, for the expression of the collective will. But training also makes the individual conscious of the "other law" in "his members," which "wars against" the law of the social will. The result may be, for his outward conduct, whatever the individual's wits and powers make it. But so far as this result is due to cultivation in intelligent conduct, it inevitably leads to an inner division of the self, a disease of self-consciousness, which Paul finds to be the curse of all merely natural human civilization.[27]

The fall from the state of grace is thus seen as an inevitable outcome of social life, and whatever one's social theory may be, whatever attempts to organize society may be undertaken on whatever principles, the elements which compose society must be sinful men. The conflict between individualism and collectivism is inherent in social life, the problem is so to integrate the individual and society as to reduce the tension between the polar extremes. Progress in social terms is therefore measured by the degree of reduction of tension achieved by social organizations.

Communities of men consist mathematically of individuals who compose them and derive their qualities from the qualities of the individuals. The individual for his part is a product of his community and derives his qualities from community life. At this point Royce is in agreement with Dewey that the social process is an interaction between individuals and groups. But the individual is more than the mere reflection of social qualities, and the community is more than the mere aggregate of its members. When a social group is simply an organization without ideal ends and purposes, it cannot command the ideal loyalty of its members and so is not a true community of the faithful either in Paul's or Royce's sense, and an individual who is merely a member of an organization cannot be ethically loyal and hence a truly free man.

> . . . his communities, to which he thus owes all his natural powers, train him by teaching him self-will, and so teach him the arts of spiritual hatred. The result is distraction,—spiritual death. Escape through any mere multitude of loves for other individuals is impossible. For such loves, unless they are united by some supreme loyalty, are capricious fondnesses for other individuals, who, by nature and by social training, are as lonely and as distracted as their lover himself. Mere altruism is no cure for the spiritual disease of cultivation.[28]

It is at this point that Royce rightly sees an agreement between early Christianity and early Buddhism regarding the condition of natural man. The natural man living in a social organization which is not a community, because it is not informed by shared ideals, must be a "morally detached individual." There would seem to be only two alternative possibilities for the salvation of such individuals: on the one hand, the alternative of Buddhism which calls for ever more intense exercise of the will to renounce the desires of the natural man, to the end that these may be finally extinguished and detachment become absolute; on the other hand, the doctrine of Christianity that sacrifice rather than extinction,—sacrifice in the name of shared ideals,—may convert a social organization into a community and that through loyalty to the community, salvation may be found. This latter was Paul's doctrine of the Church which, as he believed, was in fact the mystical body of Christ. It is this doctrine interpreted in specifically human terms which Royce adopts as the only valid alternative for modern man.

> All morality, namely, is, from this point of view, to be judged by the standards of the Beloved Community, of the ideal Kingdom of Heaven. Concretely stated, this means that you are to test every course of action *not* by

the question: What can we find in the parables or in the Sermon on the Mount which seems to us more or less directly to bear upon this special matter? The central doctrine of the Master was: "So act that the Kingdom of Heaven may come." This means: So act as to help, however you can, and whenever you can, towards making mankind one loving brotherhood, whose love is not a mere affection for morally detached individuals, but a love of the unity of its own life upon its own divine level, and a love of individuals in so far as they can be raised to communion with this spiritual community itself.[29]

Again:

Man the individual is essentially insufficient to win the goal of his own existence. Man the community is the source of salvation. And by man the community I mean, *not* the collective biological entity called the human race, and not the merely natural community which gives to us, as social animals, our ordinary moral training. Nor by man the community do I mean the series of misadventures and tragedies whereof the merely external history of what is called humanity consists. By man the community I mean man in the sense in which Paul conceived Christ's beloved and universal Church to be a community,—man viewed as one conscious spiritual whole of life. And I say that this conscious spiritual community is the sole possessor of the means of grace, and is the essential source of the salvation of the individual. This, in general, is what the Christian doctrine of life teaches. The essential problem for the modern man is the question: Is this doctrine of life true?[30]

Royce answers his own last question affirmatively. It is true, he thinks, because wherever throughout human history genuine communities have arisen, they have flourished. The Christian Church is itself the best and most continuous illustration of this fact. For all its weaknesses, failures, and sins that Church has maintained itself throughout the centuries as an approximation to true community close enough to have brought happiness and spiritual nourishment to vast numbers of human beings. In our own time, Royce finds another illustration of community in the field of science. He accepts the emphatic contemporary judgment that this is an age of science, and he finds in the fact that scientists throughout the world speak, in general, a common language, serve common ideals, and produce common results, evidence for the existence of the spirit of community. Because the Christian life is, in fact, meaningful in purely human terms, and taken in those terms is, in fact, expressed in the community of science, Royce believes that the extension and improvement of the community of science and knowledge offers a practical mode for future man's achieving the great community.

. . . as the spirit of science extends its influence, loyalty to the common insight and to the growth of knowledge will become prominent in the

consciousness of the civilized man. For the scientific spirit is indeed one of
the noblest and purest forms of loyalty.

The Christian virtues, then, will flourish in the civilization of the future,
if indeed that civilization itself flourishes. For the more complex its constitution, and the swifter and vaster its social changes, the more will that
civilization need love, and loyalty, and the grace of spiritual unity, and the
will and the conscience which the Christian ideas have defined, and counselled, and that atoning conflict with evil wherein the noblest expression of
the spirit must always be found.[31]

Now if loyalty is the cohesive principle of a community, whether
upon the scale of the province or of the world, a further perplexing
question arises. Why does true loyalty to ideal causes in fact produce
communities? It is to this question that Royce addresses himself in the
technical passages of the second volume of *The Problem of Christianity*.
He finds his answer in the discrimination of a third mode of cognition,
additional, that is to say, to perception and conception. This mode he calls
interpretation, and places it in the scale of values higher than perception
and conception because he thinks that by means of interpretation not
only is communication brought about among men, but also that synthesis of individual wills which can and sometimes does integrate society.

Royce frankly acknowledges a debt to Charles Sanders Peirce, whose
doctrine of signs first suggested to him the theory of interpretation, but
the purposes the two men had in mind were so different that the reader
might well miss the similarity if it were not specifically called to his attention. In certain respects, no doubt, Royce's theory of interpretation
belongs to the epistemological controversy of the first decade of this
century, but it is no part of my purpose to revive or agitate that controversy. I shall content myself with as brief an exposition of the doctrine as
Royce's language permits, recommending meanwhile to students of epistemology that they reconsider Royce's doctrine in the light of its social
implications.

Royce begins by posing the question whether an interpretation can be
reduced to a percept or concept:

> Now it appears that the word "interpretation" is a convenient name for a
> process which at least aims to be cognitive. And the proper object of an
> interpretation, as we usually employ the name, is either something of the
> nature of a mind, or else is a process which goes on in a mind, or, finally, is
> a sign or expression whereby some mind manifests its existence and its
> processes. Let us consider, then, more closely, whether the process of inter-
> pretation, in so far as its proper object is a mind, or is the sign of a mind,
> can be reduced to a pure perception, or to pure conception, or to any syn-
> thesis which merely involves these two.[32]

He answers the question thus posed by reference to classic dualistic epistemology of percept and concept advocated by such thinkers as James and Bergson:

> A philosophy which, like that of Bergson, defines the whole problem of knowledge in terms of the classic opposition between conception and perception, and which then declares that, if our powers of perception were unlimited, the goal of knowledge would be reached, simply misses the principal problem, both of our daily human existence and of all our higher spiritual life, as well as of the universe. And in bidding us seek the solution of our problems in terms of perception, such a doctrine simply forbids us to pass any of the great boundaries of the spiritual world, or to explore the many realms wherein the wealth of the spirit is poured out. For neither perception nor conception, nor any combination of the two, nor yet their synthesis in our practical activities, constitutes the whole of any interpretation. Interpretation, however, is what we seek in all our social and spiritual relations; and without some process of interpretation, we obtain no fulness of life.[33]

He might have added that we obtain no true communication either of thought or feeling. An interpretation above all else requires three terms, since by definition it mediates between two other terms:

> Psychologically speaking, the mental process which thus involves three members differs from perception and conception in three respects. First, interpretation is a conversation, and not a lonely enterprise. There is some one, in the realm of psychological happenings, who addresses some one. The one who addresses interprets some object to the one addressed. In the second place, the interpreted object is itself something which has the nature of a mental expression. Peirce uses the term "sign" to name this mental object which is interpreted. Thirdly, since the interpretation is a mental act, and is an act which is expressed, the interpretation itself is, in its turn, a Sign. This new sign calls for further interpretation. For the interpretation is addressed to somebody. And so,—at least in ideal,—the social process involved is endless. Thus wealthy, then, in its psychological consequences, is the formal character of a situation wherein any interpretation takes place.[34]

The richness of interpretation, as against either concept or percept, is quickly evident when these are placed in contrast.

> Conception is often denounced, in our day, as "sterile." But perception, taken by itself, is intolerably lonesome. And every philosophy whose sole principle is perception invites us to dwell in a desolate wilderness where neither God nor man exists. For where either God or man is in question, interpretation is demanded. And interpretation,—even the simplest, even the most halting and trivial interpretation of our daily life,—seeks what eye hath not seen, and ear hath not heard, and what it hath not entered into the heart of man to conceive,—namely, the successful interpretation of somebody to somebody.

Interpretation seeks an object which is essentially spiritual. The abyss of abstract conception says of this object: It is not in me. The heaven of glittering immediacies which perception furnishes answers the quest by saying: It is not in me. Interpretation says: It is nigh thee,—even in thine heart; but shows us, through manifesting the very nature of the object to be sought, what general conditions must be met if any one is to interpret a genuine Sign to an understanding mind. And withal, interpretation seeks a city out of sight, the homeland where, perchance, we learn to understand one another.[35]

Interpretation raised from the level of sheer communication to the level of insight may best be understood in terms of the rhetorical figure of comparison, and comparison itself is soon discovered to be either creative insight or what is sometimes called vision.

We often use the word "vision" for this insight which looks down upon ideas as from above, and discovers the "third," thereby uniting what was formerly estranged. If by the word "intuition" one chooses to mean this grade of insight, then one may indeed say that creative mental prowess depends, in general, upon such intuition. But such intuition is no mere perception. It is certainly not conception. And the highest order of genius depends upon reaching the stage of Peirce's "third" type of ideas. Comparison, leading to the discovery of that which mediates and solves, and to the vision of unity, is the psychological basis of poetry, as Shakespeare wrote, and of such prophecy as Paul praised when he estimated the spiritual gifts. Comparison, then, and interpretation constitute the cognitive function whereby we deal with life. Instinct and bare perception, left to themselves, can never reach this level.[36]

The bearing of this doctrine of interpretation upon the idea of community is already clear enough.

If, then, I am worthy to be an interpreter at all, we three,—you, my neighbor, whose mind I would fain interpret,—you, my kindly listener, to whom I am to address my interpretation,—we three constitute a Community. Let us give to this sort of community a technical name. Let us call it a Community of Interpretation.[37]

The most evident example of a community of interpretation in the context of this study is a scientific community in which interpretation is not only the essential mode of intercourse, but the supreme achievement of science itself. Without a community of interpretation there would be no science, only such infrequent and fortuitous invention as biological evolution might from time to time produce, as from time to time it produced men of lonely but creative powers. Through interpretation, science achieves a community which enables man to heal himself when wounded; to cure or to palliate disease; to feed, clothe, and shelter himself with a minimum of physical exertion and a maximum of comfort; to move at will not only over the face of the earth, but through the starry heavens. He needs only to extend the principle of community by which he achieves these things, and apply it to his relations with his fellow men in order to achieve a Utopia grander than anything dreamed of by Plato or St. Thomas More.

> If, then, you seek for a sign that the universe contains its own interpreter, let the very existence of the sciences, let the existence of the happy inventive power which has made their progress possible, furnish you such a sign. A being whom nature seems to have intended, in the first place, simply to be more crafty than the other animals, more skilful in war and in hunting, and in the arts of living in tribal unities, turns out to be so attuned to the whole of nature that, when he once gets the idea of scientific research, his discoveries soon relate to physical matters as remote from his practical needs as is the chemical constitution of the nebulae, or as is the origin and destiny of this earth, or as is the state of the natural universe countless ages ago in the past. In brief, man is not what he seems, a creature of a day, but is known to be an interpreter of nature. He is full of aptitudes to sound the depths of time and of space, and to invent hypotheses which it will take ages to verify, but which will, in a vast number of cases, be verified. Full of wonders is nature. But the most wonderful of all is man the interpreter,—a part and a member (if our philosophy is right) of the world's infinite Community of Interpretation.[38]

VI

By 1914, when the First World War broke out in Europe, Royce had completed the sketch of his social philosophy and filled in much of the detail. He was confident at once of its theoretical soundness and its practical usefulness. With the coming of hostilities, he immediately commenced to make public addresses in support of the Allied cause, feeling that whatever hope remained to men for liberty and democracy through true community was to be found in the triumph of Allied arms. Though, like many other neutrals, he at first supposed that the community of learning which had been so highly developed in Germany might mitigate the cruelty of the German attack, he was convinced by the sinking of the Lusitania that nothing short of the utter defeat of imperialism would enable men to make a fresh start in freedom. But though he was profoundly shocked by the barbarism of the war, he saw in the groping of various peoples in many countries toward a future international order some glimmerings of the dawn of a better day, and he resolved to make what contribution he could to the thinking through of the international problem. His contribution was in the form of the application of his theory of the community of interpretation to an already functioning international activity which he felt could be extended to become a principle of world organization. This activity was the business of insurance.

In suggesting a program for international insurance which might lead eventually to international pacification, Royce returned to his earlier analysis of the natural man as a "morally detached individual" and of quantitative social groupings as in themselves organizations without community. He found in the advance of civilization itself the chief cause of war, just as he thought he saw in the integration of the individual with society, of provinces within nations, and the variety of nations within world order, the hope of peace.

> As a fact, the advance of civilization not only brings with it motives which tend to check and to control the barbarous aspects of war, but also motives, some of them new, which tend to make war appear, to many individuals and nations, more ideal, more righteous, more significant, than ever. The modern world, wherein every great human experience of passion, of sorrow, and of love arouses a warm response in the most distant parts of the inhabited earth,—this same world echoes the warlike passions as readily as it does the humane ones, longs to imitate the powerful peoples as well as to relieve the sufferers from an earthquake, and is stirred by its far-reaching rivalries as much as by its other expressions of solidarity. Its social problems are common to all the civilized lands; but so too are the dispositions to encourage and to feel the contrasts of races, and the rivalries of commerce and of cultivation. The democracies are vast; but so too are the conflicting interests for which these democracies are ready to fight. Science brings all men near to each other; but science also originates new industrial arts, and these arts can be used for war as well as for peace. Civilization makes men more thoughtful about both social and moral issues. But such thoughtfulness, if once inspired by patriotism, and by international jealousies, can both counsel and wage war deliberately, and with a self-righteous assurance such as our elementally passionate or simply superstitious ancestors never knew.
>
> So, of themselves, neither cultivation, nor thoughtfulness, nor humane breadth of sympathies, nor the discoveries of science, nor the aspirations of the democracy, have been able to make wars cease on the earth. Modern wars may, as we now know, become more widespread, more democratic in spirit, more ideally self-righteous, than ever they were before.[39]

As we saw earlier, a community of interpretation requires at least three members, but in the social movement which leads to war Royce saw what he called a dyadic character. Just as in a family of two harmony is less easy to obtain than in a family of three or more, so among larger groups, wherever a third force exists to mediate the difference between the other two, harmony is possible because community is possible. War always engages two parties, however the opposing parties may be composed of more than one member state. The alignment is dyadic, not triadic.

> . . . here then is the fundamental principle of the philosophy of war. The deepest reason why war is so persistent is that *the nations, thus far in history, are related chiefly in pairs*—pairs of commercial rivals, pairs of borrowers and lenders, pairs of stronger and weaker nations, pairs of superiors and inferiors, pairs of plunderers who do not understand each other,—pairs of plotters, each of whom suspects his opponent.
> And the deepest reason why what is best in individual men does not destroy but often inflames the warlike spirit, lies in the fact that the best in individual men depends upon their loyalty to their own groups, upon their patriotism, and also upon their interest in groups which are not mere pairs. In such interests in groups which are larger and richer than pairs, consists men's very desire for human solidarity. For human unions can become stable and fruitful only through the establishment of relations which are very different from the dangerous dyadic relations of lovers, of rivals, and of warriors.[40]

The problem then, as Royce saw it, was to develop an international principle upon the basis of triadic relationships. In the common business of the world, he was able to discriminate at least four activities involving three elements and having something of the nature of community: the judicial community, the business or commercial community, the banking community, and the insurance community. The last of these seemed to him best suited for large-scale development in the interest of world harmony. The judicial community fails as a possibility because it functions only after conflict has arisen. The commercial community fails because too often there arises a contradiction between the commercial self-interest of one party and the commercial self-interest of another, and even the commercial self-interest of a third party which ought to serve as mediator. The banking community fails as a possibility for the same reason. Only in the case of the insurance community is there a clear and reliable motivation for continued harmony, and sacrifice in the general interest.

> . . . the insurer's community tends, far more than even the banker's community, to demand some larger union of the social molecules whereof the single community of interpretation consists. In consequence insurance very largely takes the form of mutual insurance. It brings men together in vaster and in more highly organized and articulated groups than the banker's world knows. It leads to constantly new social expressions. It contributes to

peace, to loyalty, to social unity, to active charity, as no other community of interpretation has ever done. It tends, in the long run, to carry us beyond the era of the agent and of the broker into the coming social order of the insurer. We cannot predict all that it will yet accomplish; but we can already see that *of all the business relations and of all the practical communities yet devised, the insurance relations and the insurance communities most tend to bring peace on earth, and to aid us towards the community of mankind.*[41]

Royce's little book, *War and Insurance*, proposed a practical plan for instituting an international insurance organization, a plan based upon the facts of the First World War and the probabilities, as he then saw them, of the financial settlements to be made at the peace table. We need not here concern ourselves with the details of that plan, since thirty-five years of history have in many respects altered circumstances and hence possibilities. But it is interesting to observe that if Royce's suggestion that reparations be put into an international insurance fund and that such a fund be used to underwrite an organization for the mutual insurance of nations, not only would some of the causes for the failure of democracy to survive in central Europe have been removed, but the League of Nations itself might have rested on a much firmer foundation.

The real question, of course, is whether such a concrete application of Royce's theory as mutual international insurance would be effective at the present time. I am convinced that it would be. Since Royce wrote, insurance has been almost universally adopted as a principle of social action. Most of the countries of Europe have long been accustomed not only to insurance on such risks as death, fire, theft, and the like, but also to insurance against unemployment, injury or sickness, and old age. In recent years, the United States has adopted far reaching schemes of social insurance. Social insurance is one of the cornerstones of the socialist experiments not only in democratic countries like Britain, Australia, France, and the Scandinavian nations, but also of the Soviet Union and her satellites, which are now in process of being communized. Almost alone among economic and social activities, insurance plays a major part in both capitalism and socialism as well as in both socialism and communism. If a common language among otherwise diametrically opposed social philosophies is to be found anywhere, it is to be found in the language of mutual insurance. An organization of international insurance trustees, established by the United Nations and financed by whatever nations wish to be insured, could be staffed by experts from many nations, all of whom, unlike their diplomatic colleagues, would have similar assumptions about their calling and would speak the same language of risk, loss, and probability. I should not propose, any more than Royce himself, that such an organization could undertake to insure against war in the first instance, but surely there are many untoward events and fortuitous calamities to which all or most nations are subject and against which all would like to be insured. Crop failure, or natural disaster like hurricane, are obvious examples. Were such an organization established, suitably capitalized, and staffed by insurance experts, it could quickly develop a list of such risks for which actuarial statistics are either presently available or readily obtainable. With experience, it could increase the list and enlarge the sum of liability to the policy holder. Royce hmself consulted a number of the most eminent experts of insurance in his time, and found them all in agreement on the practicality of his scheme. With the extension of the principle of insurance and with the accumulation of experience and understanding, practicality would seem to be better guaranteed at present than it was thirty years ago.

But the reasons for adopting mutual insurance as a principle for international organization in the future are not by any means exclusively practical; they are also ideal. For mutual insurance is, by its very nature, harmonizing and pacifying. All policy holders in a mutual insurance community have a common interest in the prevention of disaster, and the reduction of the cost of risks. In the long run, the self-interest of all nations might be served by the avoidance of such actions overt and covert as might bring about loss to the international insurance organization. It seems not too much to suppose that eventually an attitude which in the first instance is a matter of cold business efficiency would gradually be converted into an attitude of positive friendliness and international sympathy. However cynical the parties to such an enterprise, the enterprise itself, so long as it is practical, efficient, and financially rewarding moves toward the brotherhood of man. It is a community of interpretation, involving as it does the agency of an insurance broker, namely the international organization, but it is a community of interpretation which would be tending always to become the great or "Beloved" community, as Royce calls it, of all mankind.

VII

The whole scope of Royce's social theory is now before us, and I do not see how we can escape concluding that it has both grandeur and practicality. It is, no doubt, open to attack and criticism at various points, and I myself select three aspects which may properly be questioned. The first of these is an implication of the theory of community which Royce himself draws in some detail but which I have omitted since I do not myself accept it. This is the implication that there are not only various communities of interpretation among men, but that all mankind is a continuing community of interpretation, more or less successful and more or less happy as historical accidents permit. This does not seem to me to be a necessary conclusion logically or to make for greater edification. It is of a piece with Royce's Absolutism generally. He was, throughout his adult life, fascinated by the mystery involved in an Absolute which has existed from eternity and which is yet always striving to achieve its own perfection. Like his friend William James, I can neither understand nor sympathize with such a mystery, but I submit that such an interpretation as I have made of Royce's view suggests the direction to be followed if universal brotherhood is to be achieved, and that whatever one may make of Royce's dream of the past, one cannot help being attracted, indeed deeply moved, by his dream of the future.

The other two points about which I would raise questions are closely related. The first is his tendency to overlook the problem of the individual's relation to himself. While he seems to me eminently right in his confidence that the salvation of the individual is through community, I think he errs in neglecting the problem of individual self-mastery. There can be no lasting achievement for a province, or a country, or even a family, or a local neighborhood where individuals do not accept as necessary, and practice as rewarding, the principle of the creative restraint of natural impulses. Loyalty in itself is not enough. We must will to be loyal and in order so to will, reason, as Santayana would say, must always temper the passions in order that its life may be lived without stultification. The second point is that the principle of variety among free individuals leads Royce, by a logic which he heartily accepts, to an ultimate principle of variety among nations. This conclusion will certainly be criticized by those advocates of world government who find in national sovereignty, and even sometimes in diversity of national cultures, a principal obstacle to world peace and the acceptance of the rule of universal law. I do not myself accept this criticism. I hold rather with Royce that not only is the tendency toward extreme collectivism, with the eventual abolition of national variety, a deadly prospect, but that the brotherhood of man rightly means the harmonious and peaceful community of all sorts and conditions of men, not the endless multiplication of social, political, and spiritual twins. It may indeed be that so far from aiding the struggle of mankind to unify itself in world government, the idea of the universal state with universally accepted laws is, in fact, a major hindrance to the achievement of the community of mankind. As Royce put it in his last book, *The Hope of the Great Community*, "Therefore, while the great community of the future will unquestionably be international by virtue of the ties which will bind its various nationalities together, it will find no place for that sort of internationalism which despises the individual variety of nations, and which tries to substitute for the vices of those who at present seek merely to conquer mankind, the equally worthless desire of those who hope to see us in future as 'men without a country'. . . . There can be no true international life unless the nations remain to possess it."[42]

Royce's philosophy, leading as it does from provincialism to the great community, has a special value for Americans in these days since it suggests a practical way of meeting the collectivist drift of modern society, appropriating its best values and modifying and controlling it through the American tradition of individualism. It offers a solution in the terms of the present to the ageless problem of the One and the Many. It offers the prospect of continually reducing the tension between the poles of the social dualism of man and society. It cherishes both liberty and democracy by insisting that neither liberty nor democracy, nor both together, is enough.

> Masses of lost individuals do not become genuine freemen merely because they all have votes. The suffrage can show the way of salvation only to those who are already loyal, who already, according to their lights, live in the spirit, and are directed not by a mere disposition to give good things to everybody, or to give all their goods to feed the poor, or to give their body to be burned, but by a genuinely Pauline charity . . . .
> Liberty alone never saves us. Democracy alone never saves us. Our political freedom is but vanity unless it is a means through which we come to realize and practise charity, in the Pauline sense of that word. Hence the community of mankind will be international in the sense that it will ignore no rational and genuinely self-conscious nation. It will find the way to respect the liberty of the individual nations without destroying their genuine spiritual freedom. Its liberty and union, when attained, will be "now and forever, one and inseparable."[43]

1. *Race Questions, Provincialism, and Other American Problems*, 1908, p. 61.
2. *Ibid.*, p. 62.
3. *Ibid.*, p. 64.
4. *Ibid.*, p. 66.
5. *Ibid.*, p. 69.
6. *Ibid.*, pp. 74-75.
7. *Ibid.*, p. 78.
8. *Ibid.*, pp. 78-79.
9. *Ibid.*, p. 79.
10. *Ibid.*, p. 81.
11. *Ibid.*, p. 88.
12. *Ibid.*, p. 91.
13. *Ibid.*, p. 91.
14. *Ibid.*, pp. 94-95.
15. *Ibid.*, p. 95.
16. *Ibid.*, pp. 95-96.
17. *Ibid.*, pp. 107-108.
18. *The Philosophy of Loyalty*, 1908, pp. 16-17.
19. *Ibid.*, pp. 79-80.
20. *Ibid.*, p. 81.
21. *Ibid.*, p. 82.
22. *Ibid.*, p. 87.
23. *Ibid.*, p. 88.
24. *Ibid.*, p. 88.
25. *Ibid.*, p. 95.
26. *Ibid.*, p. 95.
27. *The Problem of Christianity*, 1913, Vol. 1, pp. 176-177.
28. *Ibid.*, p. 188.
29. *Ibid.*, pp. 356-357.
30. *Ibid.*, pp. 405-406.
31. *Ibid.*, pp. 423-424.
32. *Op. cit.*, Vol. II, p. 129.
33. *Ibid.*, pp. 135-136.
34. *Ibid.*, pp. 148-149.
35. *Ibid.*, pp. 151-152.
36. *Ibid.*, pp. 192-193.
37. *Ibid.*, p. 211.
38. *Ibid.*, pp. 417-418.
39. *War and Insurance*, 1914, pp. 8-10.
40. *Ibid.*, p. 39.
41. *Ibid.*, pp. 63-64.
42. *The Hope of the Great Community*, 1916, pp. 50-51.
43. *Ibid.*, pp. 49, 52.

Race Questions, Provincialism, and Other American Problems (1908)

RACE QUESTIONS AND PREJUDICES

The numerous questions and prejudices which are aroused by the contact of the various races of men have always been important factors in human history. They promise, however, to become, in the near future, still more important than they have ever been before. Such increased importance of race questions and prejudices, if it comes to pass, will be due not to any change in human nature, and especially not to any increase in the diversity or in the contrasting traits of the races of men themselves, but simply to the greater extent and complexity of the work of civilization. Physically speaking, great masses of men are today brought into more frequent and closer contact than was formerly possible, because of the ease with which at present the numerous means of communication can be used, because of the increase of peaceful migrations, and because of the imperial ambitions of several of the world's great peoples. Hence whatever contact, conflict, or mutual influence the races of men have had in the past, we find today more ways and places in which men find themselves in the presence of alien races, with whom they have to learn to live in the same social order. When we think of East Indian coolies now present as laborers, side by side with the native negroes, and with white men, in the British West Indies; when we remember the problem of South Africa, as it was impressed upon our minds a few years since, at a moment when Dutchmen and Englishmen fought for the land, while Kaffirs and Zulus watched the conflict; when we recall what the recent war between Japan and Russia has already meant for the future of the races of men in the far East; and when, with a few only of such typical instances in mind, we turn back to our own country, and think how many different race-problems confront us,—we then see that the earliest social problem of humanity is also the most recent problem.

This is the problem of dealing with the men who seem to us somehow very widely different from ourselves, in physical constitution, in temperament, in all their deeper nature, so that we are tempted to think of them as natural strangers to our souls, while nevertheless we find that they are stubbornly there in our world, and that they are men as much determined to live as we are, and are men who, in turn, find us as incomprehensible as we find them. Of these diverse races, what ones are the superior and what ones are the inferior races? What race or races ought to rule? What ones ought to yield to their natural masters? To which one of these races has God, or nature, or destiny, ordained the rightful and final sovereignty of the earth? Which of these types of men is really the human type? Are they by their presence and their rivalry essentially perilous to one another's interests? And if so, what one amongst them is there whose spread, or whose increase in power or in number, is most perilous to the true cause of civilization? Is it a "yellow peril," or a "black peril," or perhaps, after all, is it not rather some form of "white peril," which most threatens the future of humanity in this day of great struggles and of complex issues? Are all men equal, as the Eighteenth Century theorists insisted? Or if the actual inequality of men in power, in value, in progressiveness, is an obvious fact, then how is this fact related to racial distinctions?

Such are a few of the questions that crowd upon us when we think about the races of men, and about their various relations to civilization. I do not mean, in this brief discussion, to exhaust any of these questions, but I want to call attention to a few principles which seem to me to be serviceable to any one who wants to look at race questions fairly and humanely.

I

It will be natural for some of my readers to interpose, at this point, the suggestion that the principal guidance in any attempt to answer such questions as the foregoing must come from an appeal to the results of the modern scientific study of the races of men. Why speculate and moralize, one may say? Have not the races of men been studied in recent times with elaborate care? What can tell us how to deal with the race-problems, in case we neglect the results of anthropology and of ethnology? And if we consult those sciences, do they not already give us a basis for decision regarding all such matters—a basis which is far more valuable than any chance observations of an amateur can be?

As a fact, if I supposed that, in their present stage of progress, the sciences which deal with man had already attained to exact results regarding the mental and moral differences, prospects, and destinies, of the different stocks of the *genus homo*, nobody would be humbler than I should be in accepting, and in trying to use the verdict that would then have been obtained. But I confess that, as a student of ethics and of certain other aspects of our common human nature, I have been a good deal baffled in trying to discover just what the results of science are regarding the true psychological and moral meaning of race-differences. I shall later speak further of some of the difficulties of this scientific aspect of our topic. It is enough to say here that when I consult any of the known *Rassentheoretiker* for light, I do indeed learn that the concept of race is the key to the comprehension of all history, and that, if you only form a clear idea of the important types of men (types such, for instance, as the marvellous *Germanen* of Chamberlain's *Grundzuge des Neunzehnten Jahrhunderts*), you can then determine with exactness precisely who ought to rule and who ought to yield, and can predict the forms of civilization, the *Weltanschauungen*, and the other possessions, which will be characteristic of each type of men, so long as that type shall endure. When I observe, however, that the *Rassentheoretiker* frequently uses his science to support most of his personal prejudices, and is praised by his sympathizers almost equally for his exact knowledge and for his vigorous display of temperament, I begin to wonder whether a science which mainly devotes itself to proving that we ourselves are the salt of the earth, is after all so exact as it aims to be. It is with some modern race-theories, as it is with some forms of international yacht racing. I know nothing about yachting; but whenever any form of the exalted sport of international yachting proves to be definable as a sort of contest in which the foreigner is invariably beaten, I for my part take no interest in learning more about the rules of that particular game. And precisely so, when men marshal all the resources of their science to prove that their own race-prejudices are infallible, I can feel no confidence in what they imagine to be the result of science. Much of our modern race-theory reminds me, in its spirit, altogether too much of some of the conversations in the "Jungle Book,"—or of the type of international courtesy expressed in "The Truce of the Bear,"—too much, I say to seem like exact science. Mowgli's remarks addressed to Red Dog may have been good natural history; but scientific Zoology does not proceed in that way.

While I deeply respect, then, the actual work of the sciences which deal with man, and while I fully recognize their modern progress, I greatly doubt that these sciences as yet furnish us with the exact results which representative race-theorists sometimes insist upon. Hence I am unable to begin this little study by a mere report of what science has established regarding the mental and moral varieties of men. I must rather make my beginning with a mention of two instances which have recently been much in my mind, and which bear upon the meaning of race prejudices. One of these instances is today in everybody's mind.

II

I refer then, first, to the wonderful lesson that Japan has been teaching us regarding what human energy and devotion have done and can do, and can do also in case of a race that is indeed remote enough from our own. I remember well the Japan of the geography text-books of my childhood, text-books which were even then antiquated enough; but I believed them. Japan was a weird land, according to the old text-books,— a land from which foreigners were excluded, a land where all things were as perverse as possible, where criminals were boiled in oil, where Catholic missionaries had long ago been martyred. Whatever the Japanese were, they were plainly men of the wrong race. Later, however, I learned something of the contemporary history of Japan as it then was. The scene was now, indeed, vastly changed. The Japanese had opened their land; and hereupon, lo! in a magic way, they were imitating, so we heard, *all* of our European customs. So we next had to alter our own opinion as to their essential nature. They became in our eyes a plastic race of wonderful little children, small of stature, quick of wit, light-minded— a folk who took up any suggestion precisely as the playful children often do. They, too, were playing, it seemed, with our whole Western civilization. Plainly, then, they were a race who had no serious life of their own at all. Those of us who disliked them noted that they thus showed an ape-like unsteadiness of conduct. This, then, was their racial characteristic. Those who admired them thought of them as a new sort of pets, to be humored and instructed with all our superior condescension. Well, as time went on, and I grew to manhood, I myself came to know some of these Japanese as students. Hereupon, however, I gradually learned to see such men in a wholly new light. I found them, with all their steadfast courtesy, pleasantly, but impenetrably reserved—keepers of their own counsel, men whose life had, as I soon found, a vast background of opinions and customs that I could not fathom. When, I said, shall I ever see what is behind that Japanese smile? What is in their hearts? With an immovable self-consciousness they resisted every effort to alter, from without, any of their essential ideals. Politely, whenever you pressed them, they declined to admit that any of our Western arts or opinions were equal in value to their own most cherished national ideal treasures. And this they did even at the moment when they were present, most respectfully, as learners. They learned well; but plainly they meant to use this learning for their own purposes. An enthusiastic lady in an American university town was once seeking to draw from a Japanese visitor some admission of the importance of Christianity for the higher civilization of his country. "Confess," she insisted, "confess what a boon our missionaries have brought you in introducing Christianity into your land." "You are right," answered the Japanese, with his usual courteous smile, "you are right; the missionaries in introducing Christianity, have indeed brought us a great good. They have completed the variety of religions in Japan."

This impenetrable Japanese self-consciousness, this unconquerable polite and obstinate reserve, what did it mean? Well, Mr. Hearn and his kin have now let us know in a literary way something of the true heart of Japan. And the recent war has shown us what Japan meant by imitating our Western ways, and also what ancestral ideals have led her sons to death in battle, and still hold the nation so closely knit to their Emperor. Already I have heard some tender souls amongst us say: "It is *they* who are racially *our* superiors." Some of us may live to see Japanese customs pervading our land, and all of our professional imitators trying to be Japanese.

Well, I myself am no worshipper of any new fancy or distant civilization, merely because of its temporary prominence. But the true lesson which Japan teaches us today is, that it is somewhat hard to find out by looking at the features of a man's face, or at the color of his skin, or even at the reports of travellers who visit his land, what it is of which his race is really capable. Perhaps the Japanese are not of the right race; but we now admit that so long as we judged them merely by their race, and by mere appearances, we were judging them ignorantly, and falsely. This, I say, has been to me a most interesting lesson in the fallibility of some of our race judgments.

III

So much, then, for one lesson of experience. I have recently been much impressed by another lesson, but by one of a very different character, occurring, so to speak, at the other extremity of the world of modern race-problems. The negro has so far shown none of the great powers of the Japanese. Let us, then, provisionally admit at this stage of our discussion that the negro is in his present backward state as a race, for reasons which are not due merely to circumstances, but which are quite innate in his mental constitution. I shall indeed return to that topic later on. But, for the moment, let that view pass as if it were finally accepted. View the negro, then, for the instant merely as a backward race. But let the race-question here be our own pressing Southern question: How can the white man and the negro, once forced, as they are in our South, to live side by side, best learn to live with a minimum of friction, with a maximum of cooperation? I have long learned from my Southern friends that this end can only be attained by a firm and by a very constant and explicit insistence upon keeping the negro in his proper place, as a social inferior—who, then, as an inferior, should, of course, be treated humanely, but who must first be clearly and unmistakably taught where he belongs. I have observed that the pedagogical methods which my Southern friends of late years have found it their duty to use, to this end, are methods such as still keep awake a good deal of very lively and intense irritation in the minds not only of the pupils but also of the teachers. Now irritation, viewed merely in itself, is not an enlightening state of mind. It is, therefore, according to our modern views, not a very pedagogical state of mind. I am myself, for instance, a fairly irritable person, and I am also a teacher. But at the moments when I am irritated I am certainly not just then a good teacher. Is, however, the irritation which seems to be the accompaniment of some of the recent Southern methods of teaching the negro his place an inevitable evil, a wholly necessary accompaniment of the present transition period in the South? *Must* such increase of race-hatred first come, in order that later, whenever the negro has fully learned his lesson, and aspires no more beyond his station, peace may come? Well, concerning just this matter I lately learned what was to me, in my inexperience, a new lesson. I have had occasion three times, in recent summers, to visit British West Indies, Jamaica, and Trinidad, at a time when few tourists were there. Upon visiting Jamaica I first went round the coast of the island, visiting its various ports. I then went inland, and walked for miles over its admirable country roads. I discussed its condition with men of various occupations. I read some of its official literature. I then consulted with a new interest its history. I watched its negroes in various places, and talked with some of them, too. I have since collected such further information as I had time to collect regarding its life, as various authorities have discussed the topic, and this is the result:—

Jamaica has a population of surely not more than 14,000 or 15,000 whites, mostly English. Its black population considerably exceeds 600,000. Its mulatto population, of various shades, numbers, at the very least, some 40,000 or 50,000. Its plantation life, in the days before emancipation, was much sadder and severer, by common account, than ours in the South ever was. Both the period of emancipation and the immediately following period were of a very discouraging type. In the sixties of the last century there was one very unfortunate insurrection. The economic history of the island has also been in many ways unlucky even to the present day. Here, then, are certainly conditions which in some respects are decidedly such as would seem to tend toward a lasting state of general irritation, such as you might suppose would make race-questions acute. Moreover, the population, being a tropical one, has serious moral burdens to contend with of the sort that result from the known influences of such climates upon human character in the men of all races.

And yet, despite all these disadvantages, today, whatever the problems of Jamaica, whatever its defects, our own present Southern race-problem in the forms which we know best, simply does not exist. There is no public controversy about social race equality or superiority. Neither a white man nor a white woman feels insecure in moving about freely amongst the black population anywhere on the island. The colony has a Legislative Assembly, although one of extremely limited legislative powers. For the choice to this assembly a suffrage determined only by a decidedly low rate-qualification is free to all who have sufficient property, but is used by only a very small portion of the negro population. The negro is, on the whole, neither painfully obtrusive in his public manners, nor in need of being sharply kept in his place. Within the circles of the black population itself there is meanwhile a decidedly rich social differentiation. There are negroes in government service, negroes in the professions, negroes who are fairly prosperous peasant proprietors, and there are also the poor peasants; there are the thriftless, the poor in the towns,—yes, as in any tropical country, the beggars. In Kingston and in some other towns there is a small class of negroes who are distinctly criminal. On the whole, however, the negroes and colored population, taken in the mass, are orderly, law-abiding, contented, still backward in their education, but apparently advancing. They are generally loyal to the government. The best of them are aspiring, in their own way, and wholesomely self-conscious. Yet there is no doubt whatever that English white men are the essential controllers of the destiny of the country. But these English whites, few as they are, control the country as present, with extraordinarily little friction, and wholly without those painful emotions, those insistent complaints and anxieties, which at present are so prominent in the minds of many of our own Southern brethren. Life in Jamaica is not ideal. The economical aspect of the island is in many ways unsatisfactory. But the negro race-question, in our present American sense of that term, seems to be substantially solved.

How? By race-mixture?

The considerable extent to which race-mixture went in the earlier history of Jamaica is generally known. Here, as elsewhere, however, it has been rather the social inequality of the races, than any approach to equality, which has been responsible for the mixture, in so far as such has occurred. It was the social inequality of the plantation days that began the process of mixture. If the often-mentioned desire to raise the "color" of their children, has later led the colored population to seek a further amalgamation of the two stocks, certainly that tendency, so far as it is effective, has been due to the social advantages of the lighter color—and not due to any motive which has decreased the ancient disadvantages under which the darker race has had to suffer. If race-amalgamation is indeed to be viewed as always an evil, the best way to counteract the growth of that evil must everywhere be the cultivation of racial self-respect and not of racial degradation. As a fact, it is not the amalgamation of the stocks, so far as that has occurred, which has tended to reduce the friction between the races in Jamaica. As to the English newcomers to the island, they probably do not tend to become amalgamated with the colored stocks in Jamaica, more than in any other region where the English live. The English stock tends, here as elsewhere, to be proud of itself, and to keep to itself. How then has the solution of what was once indeed a grave race-question been brought about in Jamaica?

I answer, by the simplest means in the world—the simplest, that is, for English viz.: by English administration, and by English reticence. When once the sad period of emancipation and of subsequent occasional disorder was passed, the Englishman did in Jamaica what he has so often and so well done elsewhere. He organized his colony; he established good local courts, which gained by square treatment the confidence of the blacks. The judges of such courts were Englishmen. The English ruler also provided a good country constabulary, in which native blacks also found service, and in which they could exercise authority over other blacks. Black men, in other words, were trained, under English management, of course, to police black men. A sound civil service was also organized; and in that educated negroes found in due time their place, while the chiefs of each branch of the service were and are, in the main, Englishmen. The excise and the health services, both of which are very highly developed, have brought the law near to the life of the humblest negro, in ways which he sometimes finds, of course, restraining, but which he also frequently finds beneficent. Hence he is accustomed to the law; he sees its ministers often, and often, too, as men of his own race; and in the main, he is fond of order, and learns to be respectful toward the established ways of society. The Jamaica negro is described by those who know him as especially fond of bringing his petty quarrels and personal grievances into court. He is litigious just as he is vivacious. But this confidence in the law is just what the courts have encouraged. That is one way, in fact, to deal with the too forward and strident negro. Encourage him to air his grievances in court, listen to him patiently, and fine him when he deserves fines. That is a truly English type of social pedagogy. It works in the direction of making the negro a conscious helper toward good social order.

Administration, I say, has done the larger half of the work of solving Jamaica's race-problem. Administration has filled the island with good roads, has reduced to a minimum the tropical diseases by means of an excellent health-service, has taught the population loyalty and order, has led them some steps already on the long road "up from slavery," has given them, in many cases, the true self-respect of those who themselves officially cooperate in the work of the law, and it has done this without any such result as our Southern friends nowadays conceive when they think of what is called "negro domination." Administration has allayed ancient irritations. It has gone far to offset the serious economic and tropical troubles from which Jamaica meanwhile suffers.

Yes, the work has been done by administration,—and by reticence. For the Englishman, in his official and governmental dealings with backward peoples, has a great way of being superior without very often publicly saying that he is superior. You well know that in dealing, as an individual, with other individuals, trouble is seldom made by the fact that you are actually the superior of another man in any respect. The trouble comes when you tell the other man, too stridently, that you are his superior. Be my superior, quietly, simply showing your superiority in your deeds, and very likely I shall love you for the very fact of your superiority. For we all love our leaders. But tell me that I am your inferior, and then perhaps I may grow boyish, and may throw stones. Well, it is so with races. Grant then that yours is the superior race. Then you can afford to say little about that subject in your public dealings with the backward race. Superiority is best shown by good deeds and by few boasts.

IV

So much for the lesson that Jamaica has suggested to me. The widely different conditions of Trinidad suggest, despite the differences, a somewhat similar lesson. Here also there are great defects in the social order; but again, our Southern race-problem does not exist. When, with such lessons in mind, I recall our problem, as I hear it from my brethren of certain regions of our Union, I see how easily we can all mistake for a permanent race-problem a difficulty that is essentially a problem of quite another sort. Mr. Thomas Nelson Page in his recent book on the "Southerners' Problem" speaks, in one notable passage, of the possibility which he calls Utopian, that perhaps some day the negro in the South may be made to cooperate in the keeping of order by the organization under State control of a police of his own race, who shall deal with blacks. He even mentions that the English in the East Indies use native constabulary. But this possibility is not Utopian. When I hear the complaint of the Southerner, that the race-problem is such as constantly to endanger the safety of his home, I now feel disposed to say: "The problem that endangers the sanctity of your homes and that is said sometimes to make lynching a necessity, is not a race-problem. It is an administrative problem. You have never organized a country constabulary. Hence, when various social conditions, amongst which the habit of irritating public speech about race-questions is indeed one, though only one, condition, have tended to the producing and to the arousing of extremely dangerous criminals in your communities, you have no adequate means of guarding against the danger. When you complain that such criminals, when they flee from justice, get sympathy from some portion of their ignorant fellows and so are aided to get away, you forget that you have not first made your negro countryman familiar with, and fond of, the law, by means of a vigorous and well-organized and generally beneficent administration constantly before his eyes, not only in the pursuit of criminals, but in the whole care of public order and health. If you insist that in some districts the white population is too sparse or too poor, or both, to furnish an efficient country constabulary constantly on duty, why, then, have you not long since trained black men to police black men? Sympathy with the law grows with responsibility for its administration. If it is revolting to you to see black men possessed of the authority of a country constabulary, still, if you will, you can limit their authority to a control over their own race. If you say all this speech of mine is professorial, unpractical, Utopian, and if you still cry out bitterly for the effective protection of your womankind, I reply merely, look at Jamaica. Look at other English colonies.

In any case, the Southern race-problem will never be relieved by speech or by practices such as increase irritation. It will be relieved when administration grows sufficiently effective, and when the negroes themselves get an increasingly responsible part in this administration in so far as it relates to their own race. That may seem a wild scheme. But I insist: It is the English way. Look at Jamaica, and learn how to protect your own homes.

I have reviewed two very different lessons which I have recently had brought home to me regarding race-problems. What is there which is common to these two lessons? Is it not this: In estimating, in dealing with races, in defining what their supposedly unchangeable characteristics are, in planning what to do with them, we are all prone to confuse the accidental with the essential. We are likely to take for an essential race-characteristic what is a transient incident, or a product of special social conditions. We are disposed to view as a fatal and overwhelming race-problem what is a perfectly curable accident of our present form of administration. If we are indeed of a superior race ourselves, we shall, however, best prove the fact by learning to distinguish the accidental from the essential in our relations with other races. I speak with no lack of sympathy for the genuine and bitter trials of our Southern brethren when I say that I suppose the mistake which I now point out, the mistake of confusing the essential and the accidental, is the mistake that they are now making in many of their sincerest expressions of concern over their race-problem.

So much for the two lessons that have led me to the present discussion. But now let me pass to a somewhat wider view of race-problems. Let me ask a little more generally, What, if anything, can be known to be essential about the characteristics of a race of men and consequently an essentially important consideration in our dealings with alien races? Speaking so far as we can, apart from prejudice, what can we say about what it is which distinguishes the various races of men from one another?

V

The term "race" is popularly used in a very vague way. The newspapers not long ago said, during trouble in Poland, that the Russian soldiers then in Warsaw showed "race-antipathy" in their conflicts with the people. We all know, however, that the mutual hatred of Russians and Poles is due mainly to political and to religious causes. Frenchmen of the northern provinces, who are anthropologically wholly indistinguishable, as Professor Ripley tells us, from the inhabitants of many western German districts, still have what they call a "race-antipathy" for the men across the border. Thus almost any national or political or religious barrier, if it is old enough, may lead to a consciousness of difference of race. On the other hand, there are, of course, unquestionable physical varieties of mankind, distinguished by well-known physical contrasts. But the anthropologists still almost hopelessly disagree as to what the accurate classification of these true races may be. Such a classification, however, does not concern us here. We are now interested in the minds of men. We want to know what the races of men are socially good for. And not in the study of skulls or of hair, or of skin color, and not in the survey of all these bewildering complications with which physical anthropology deals, shall we easily find an answer to our more practical questions, viz., to our questions regarding the way in which these various races of men are related to the interests of civilization, and regarding the spirit in which we ought to estimate and practically to deal with these racial traits of mankind.

For after all, it is a man's mind, rather than his skull, or his hair, or his skin, that we most need to estimate. And if hereupon we ask ourselves just how these physical varieties of the human stock, just how these shades of color, these types of hair, these forms of skull, or these contours of body, are related to the mental powers and to the moral characteristics of the men in question, then, if only we set prejudice wholly aside, and appeal to science to help us, we find ourselves in the present state of knowledge almost hopelessly at sea. We know too little as yet about the natural history of the human mind, our psychology is far

too infantile a science, to give any precise information as to the way in
which the inherited, the native, the constitutional aspects of the minds
of men really vary with their complexions or with their hair. Yet that, of
course, is just what we most want to know. It is easy to show that an
Australian is just now far below our mental level. But how far is his
degradation due to the inherited and unchangeable characters of his race,
and how far to his long struggle with the dreary desert? How far is he,
as we now find him, a degenerate, whose ancestors were on some far
higher level? In other words, is his type of mind a true variety of the
human mind, inbred and unchangeable? How far is it, so to speak, a mere
incident? Upon what level were the minds of our own ancestors in the
early stone age of Europe? How did their minds then compare with the
minds of those ancestors of the Australian who were then their con-
temporaries? Who shall answer such questions? Yet just such questions
we should have to answer before we could decide upon the true relations of race and of mind.

To be sure, anthropology has made a beginning, and a very important
beginning, in the study of the mental types of primitive man. By various
comparative and archaeological methods we can already learn a good
deal about the minds of our own ancestors. We can also study various
races as they are to-day. We know, about the early stages of human
culture, far more than we knew a little while since. But one result may
forthwith be stated regarding what we have so far learned concerning
the early history of the human mind, whether it is the mind of our ancestors, or of other races. Of course, we cannot doubt that, just as now we
widely differ in mental life, so always there must have been great contrasts
between the minds of the various stocks of men. No doubt, if the science
of man were exact, it would indeed include a race-psychology. But my
present scepticism concerns the present state of science, and the result of
such study as we have yet made of the racial psychology of man is distinctly disappointing to those who want to make their task easy by insisting that the physical varieties of mankind are in our present state of
knowledge sufficient guides to an interpretation of the whole inner contrast of the characters and of the mental processes of men. For what
anthropology thus far shows us is, that, so soon as you go back beyond
those stages of cultivation where history is possible, and so soon as you
view men as they are apart from the higher culture—well, then, all men,
so far as we can yet study them, appear to us not, of course, the same in
mind, but yet surprisingly alike in their minds, in their morals, and in

their arts. Widely as the primitive men differ, in certain broad features they remain, for our present knowledge, notably similar. And these common features are such as are by no means altogether flattering to our racial pride, when we think that our own ancestors, too, were, not very long since, comparatively, primitive men like the rest.

All the more primitive men, namely, are largely alike in the grossness and in the unpromising stupidity of their superstitions, and in their moral defects and virtues. Very many of them, belonging to the most various races, resemble one another in possessing customs which we now, for the most part, profoundly abhor, and which we are at present prone to view as characteristic of essentially debased minds. Such customs as cannibalism, or as human sacrifice, or as the systematic torturing of prisoners of war, such horrors as those of the witchcraft from whose bondage Europeans escaped only since the seventeenth century—such things, I say, are characteristic of no one race of men. To surround one's life with a confused mass of spiritual horrors, to believe in ghosts, or in vampires, in demons, in magic, in witchcraft, and in hostile gods of all sorts, to tangle up one's daily activities in a net of superstitious customs, to waste time in elaborate incantations, to live in fantastic terrors of an unseen world, to be terrified by tabus of all kinds, so that numerous sorts of useful deeds are superstitiously forbidden, to narrate impossible stories and believe in them, to live in filth, to persecute, to resist light, to fight against progress, to be mentally slothful, dull, sensuous, cruel, to be the prey of endless foolishness, to be treacherous, to be destructive—well, these are the mental traits of no one or two races of men. These are simply the common evil, traits of primitive humanity, traits to which our own ancestors were very long ago a prey, traits against which civilized man has still constantly to fight. Any frenzied mob of civilized men may relapse in an hour to the level of a very base savagery. All the religions of men, without exception, and however lofty the heights that they have since climbed, appear to have begun with much the same chaos of weird customs and of unreasonable delusions. Man's mental burdens have thus been, in all races, of very much the same sort, except, to be sure, that civilization, side by side with the good that it has created, has invented some new mental burdens, such as our increasing percentage of insanity in recent times illustrates.

The souls of men, then, if viewed apart from the influences of culture, if viewed as they were in primitive times, are by no means as easy to classify as the woolly-haired and the straight-haired races at first appear to be.

If you study the thoughts of the various peoples, as the anthropologist Bastian has loved to mass them together in his chaotic and learned monographs, or as Fraser has surveyed some of them in his "Golden Bough," well, these primitive thoughts appear, in all their own chaos, and in all their vast varieties of detail, to be the outcome not of racial differences so much as of a few essentially human, although by no means always very lofty, motives. These fundamental motives appear, with almost monotonous regularity, in the superstitions, the customs, the legends, of all races. Esquimaux and Australians, negroes and Scotch Highlanders of former days, ancient Japanese and Hindoos, Polynesians and early Greeks,—all these appear side by side, in such comparative studies of the primitive mind of man, side by side as brothers in error and in ignorance, so soon as you proceed to study by the comparative method their early magic, their old beliefs, their early customs. Yet only by such a study could you hope to distinguish what really belongs to the mind of a race of men, as distinct from what belongs to culture.

If, then, it is the mind and the heart of man that you really want to know, you will find it hard, so soon as you leave civilization out of account, to tell what the precise meaning of the term "race of men" is, when that term is conceived as characterizing a distinct hereditary variety of human mental constitution. A race-psychology is still a science for the future to discover.

Perhaps, however, as you may say, I have not been just, in this very summary statement, to what, after all, may prove to be the best test of the true racial differences amongst the various types of the human mind. Some races, namely, have proved themselves to be *capable of civilization.* Other races have stubbornly refused civilization, or have remained helplessly degraded even when surrounded by civilization. Others still have perished at the first contact with civilization. The Germanic ancestors of the present western Europeans were barbarians, although of a high type. But when they met civilization, they first adopted, and then improved it. Not so was it with the Indians, with the Polynesians. Here, then, is the test of a true mental difference amongst races. Watch them when they meet civilization. Do they show themselves first teachable and then originative? Then they are mentally higher races. Do they stagnate or die out in the presence of civilization? Then they are of the lower types. Such differences, you will say, are deep and ineradicable, like the differences between the higher and the lower sorts of individual men. And such differences will enable us to define racial types of mind.

I fully agree that this test is an important one. Unfortunately, the test has never been so fairly applied by the civilized nations of men that it can give us any exact results. Again, the facts are too complex to be estimated with accuracy. Our Germanic ancestors accepted civilization when they met with it. Yes, but they met civilization under conditions peculiarly favorable to their own education. They had been more or less remotely influenced by its existence, centuries before they entered the field of history. When they entered this field, they met civilization first as formidable foes; they were long in contact with it without being themselves enslaved; and then later, in numerous cases, they met civilization as conquerors, who, in the course of their very efforts to conquer, found thus the opportunity and later something of the leisure to learn, and who had time to discover by centuries of hard experience, how great were the advantages the cultivation of the Roman empire had to offer them. But suppose that Caesar in the first century B. C. had already had the opportunity to undertake the civilization of Germany by means of our own modern devices. Suppose that he had then possessed unlimited supplies of rum, of rifles, and of machine guns. Suppose in brief that, by the aid of such gentle arts as we now often use, he had very greatly abbreviated the period of probation and of schooling that was open to the German barbarians to learn the lessons that the cultivated peoples had to teach. Suppose that Roman syndicates had been ready to take possession, at once, of the partly depopulated lands of the north, and to keep the few surviving natives thenceforth in their place, by showing them how cultivated races can look down upon savage folk. Well, in that case, the further history of civilization might have gone on without the aid of the Germanic peoples. The latter would then have quickly proved their natural inferiority once for all. They would have furnished one instance more for the race-partisans to cite in order to show how incapable the lower races are of ascending from barbarism to civilization. Dead men not only tell no tales; they also, strange to say, attend no schools, and learn no lessons. And hereby they prove themselves in the eyes of certain students of race-questions to have been always of a much lower mental type than the cultivated men who killed them. Their surviving descendants, if sufficiently provided with the means of corruption, and if sufficiently downtrodden, may remain henceforth models of degradation. For man, whatever his race, is an animal that you unquestionably can debase to whatever level you please, if you only have power, and if you then begin early enough, and devote yourself persistently enough to the noble and civilized task of proving him to be debased.

I do not doubt, then, that some races are more teachable than others. But I do very much doubt our power to estimate how teachable a race is, or what can be made of them, or what hereditary mental powers they have until we have given them centuries of opportunity to be taught. Fortune and the defects of the Roman Empire gave to the Germanic peoples an extraordinary opportunity to learn. So the world found out how teachable they were. Let their descendants not boast unduly until they, too, have given to other races, not indeed the opportunities of conquerors, but some equal opportunity to show of what sort of manhood they are capable.

Yet, you may insist, civilization itself had an origin. Were not the races that first won civilized rank superior in mental type to those that never showed themselves capable of such originality? Well, I reply, we do not know as yet precisely where, and still less how, civilization originated. But this seems clear, viz.: first, that physical environment and the forms of social aggregation which this environment determined, had a very great share in making the beginnings of civilization possible; while, secondly, whatever part race-qualities played in early civilization, certainly no one race has the honor of beginning the process. Neither Chinese nor Egyptian, neither Caucasian nor Mongol, was the sole originator of civilization. The African of the tropical swamps and forests, the Australian of the desert, the Indian of our prairies, was sufficiently prevented by his physical environment from being the originator of a great civilization. What each of these races would have done in another environment, we cannot tell. But the Indian of Central America, of Mexico, and of Peru, shows us that race alone did not predetermine how remote from the origination of a higher civilization a stock must needs remain. Chinese civilization, and, in recent times, Japanese civilization, have shown us that one need not be a Caucasian in order to originate a higher type of wisdom.

In brief, then, there is hardly any one thing that our actual knowledge of the human mind enables us to assert, with any scientific exactness, regarding the permanent, the hereditary, the unchangeable mental characteristics which distinguish even the most widely sundered physical varieties of mankind. There is, to be sure, one exception to this rule, which is itself instructive. It is the case where we are dealing with physical and social degeneracy, the result of circumstances and of environment, and where such degeneracy has already gone so far that we have before us highly diseased human types, such as can no longer be reclaimed. But such types are not racial types. They are results of alcohol, of infection, or in some instances, of the long-continued pressure of physical environment. In such cases we can sometimes say, Here is a hopelessly degraded stock of men. But, then, civilization can create such stocks, out of any race of men, by means of a sufficient amount of oppression and of other causes of degradation, if continued through generations.

No race of men, then, can lay claim to a fixed and hereditary type of mental life such as we can now know with exactness to be unchangeable. We do not scientifically know what the true racial varieties of mental types really are. No doubt there are such varieties. The judgment day, or the science of the future, may demonstrate what they are. We are at present very ignorant regarding the whole matter.

VI

What, then, in the light of these considerations, is there which can be called fundamentally significant about our numerous modern race-problems? I answer, scientifically viewed, these problems of ours turn out to be not so much problems caused by anything which is essential to the existence or to the nature of the races of men themselves. Our so-called race-problems are merely the problems caused by our antipathies.

Now, the mental antipathies of men, like the fears of men, are very elemental, widespread, and momentous mental phenomena. But they are also in their fundamental nature extremely capricious, and extremely suggestible mental phenomena. Let an individual man alone, and he will feel antipathies for certain other human beings very much as any young child does—namely, quite capriciously—just as he will also feel all sorts of capricious likings for people. But train a man first to give names to his antipathies, and then to regard the antipathies thus named as sacred merely because they have a name, and then you get the phenomena of racial hatred, of religious hatred, of class hatred, and so on indefinitely. Such trained hatreds are peculiarly pathetic and peculiarly deceitful, because they combine in such a subtle way the elemental vehemence of the hatred that a child may feel for a stranger, or a cat for a dog, with the appearance of dignity and solemnity and even of duty which a name gives. Such antipathies will always play their part in human history. But what we can do about them is to try not to be fooled by them, not to take them too seriously because of their mere name. We can remember that they are childish phenomena in our lives, phenomena on a level with a dread of snakes, or of mice; phenomena that we share with the cats and with the dogs, not noble phenomena, but caprices of our complex nature.

Upon the theoretical aspects of the problem which such antipathies present, psychology can already throw some light. Man, as a social being, needs and possesses a vast range of simply elemental tendencies to be socially sensitive when in the presence of other men. These elemental tendencies appear, more or less untrained, in the bashfulness of childhood, in the stage fright of the unskilled, in the emotional disturbances of young people who are finding their way in the world, in the surprises of early love, in the various sorts of anthropophobia which beset nervous patients, in the antipathies of country folk toward strangers, in the excitement of mobs, in countless other cases of social stress or of social novelty. Such sensitiveness may arise in advance of or apart from any individual experience which gives a conscious reason why one should feel thus. A common feature of all such experiences is the fact that one human being finds other human beings to be *portentous*, even when the socially sensitive being does not in the least know why they should be so. That such reactions have an instinctive basis is unquestionable. Their general use is that they prepare one, through interest in men, to be ready for social training, and to be submissively plastic. In milder forms, or upon the basis of agreeable social relations, such instinctive emotions easily come to be moulded into the most fascinating of human interests; and the social life is impossible without this basis of the elemental concerns which man feels merely because of the fact that other men are there in his world. If decidedly intense, however, such instinctively determined experiences are apt, like other intense disturbances, to be prevailingly painful. And since novelty, oddity, and lack of social training on the part of the subject concerned are motives which tend to make such social reflexes intense, a very great number of the cruder and more childish social reactions involve antipathies; for a social antipathy is merely a painful, and so, in general, an overintense, reflex disturbance in the presence of another human being. No light need be thrown, by the mere occurrence of such an antipathy, upon any permanently important social character of the hated object. The chance intensity of the passing experience may be alone significant. And any chance association may serve to secure, in a given case, the intensity of disturbance which makes the object hated. Oddities of feature or of complexion, slight physical variations from the customary, a strange dress, a scar, a too steady look, a limp, a loud or deep voice, any of these peculiarities, in a stranger, may be, to one child, or nervous subject, or other sensitive observer, an object of fascinated curiosity; to another, slightly less stable observer, an intense irritation, an object of terror, or of violent antipathy. The significant fact is that we are all instinctively more or less sensitive to such features, simply because we are by heredity doomed to be interested in all facts which may prove to be socially important. Whether we are fascinated, or horror-stricken, or angry, is, apart from training, largely a matter of the momentary subjective intensity of the disturbance.

But all such elemental social experiences are *ipso facto*, highly suggestible. Our social training largely consists in the elimination or in the intensification or in the systematizing of these original reactions through the influence of suggestion and of habit. Hence the antipathy, once by chance aroused, but then named, imitated, insisted upon, becomes to its victims a sort of sacred revelation of truth, sacred merely because it is felt, a revelation merely because it has won a name and a social standing.

What such sacred revelations, however, really mean, is proved by the fact that the hungry traveller, if deprived of his breakfast long enough, by means of an accidental delay of his train, or the tired camper in the forest, may readily come to feel whatever racial antipathy you please toward his own brother, if the latter then wounds social susceptibilities which the abnormal situation has made momentarily hyperaesthetic.

I have said little or nothing, in this paper, of human justice. I have spoken mainly of human illusions. We all have illusions, and hug them. Let us not sanctify them by the name of science.

For my part, then, I am a member of the human race, and this is a race which is, as a whole, considerably lower than the angels, so that the whole of it very badly needs race-elevation. In this need of my race I personally and very deeply share. And it is in this spirit only that I am able to approach our problem.

PROVINCIALISM

I propose, in this address, to define certain issues which, as I think, the present state of the world's civilization, and of our own national life, make both prominent and critical.

I

The word "provincialism," which I have used as my title, has been
chosen because it is the best single word that I have been able to find to
suggest the group of social tendencies to which I want to call your
especial attention. I intend to use this word in a somewhat elastic sense,
which I may at once indicate. When we employ the word "provincialism" as a concrete term, speaking of "a provincialism," we mean, I suppose, any social disposition, or custom, or form of speech or of civilization, which is especially characteristic of a province. In this sense one
speaks of the provincialisms of the local dialect of any English shire, or of
any German country district. This use of the term in relation to the dialects of any language is very common. But one may also apply the term
to name, not only the peculiarities of a local dialect, but the fashions, the
manners, and customs of a given restricted region of any country. One
also often employs the word "provincialism" as an abstract term, to name
not only the customs or social tendencies themselves, but that fondness
for them, that pride in them, which may make the inhabitants of a
province indisposed to conform to the ways of those who come from
without, and anxious to follow persistently their own local traditions.
Thus the word "provincialism" applies both to the social habits of a given
region, and to the mental interest which inspires and maintains these
habits. But both uses of the term imply, of course, that one first knows
what is to be meant by the word "province." This word, however, is one
of an especially elastic usage. Sometimes, by a province, we mean a region as restricted as a single English county, or as the smallest of the old
German principalities. Sometimes, however, one speaks of the whole
of New England, or even of the Southern states of our Union, as con-
stituting one province; and I know of no easy way of defining how large
a province may be. For the term, in this looser sense, stands for no determinate political or legal division of a country. Meanwhile we all, in
our minds, oppose the term "province" to the term "nation," as the part
is opposed to the whole. Yet we also often oppose the terms "provincial"
and "metropolitan," conceiving that the country districts and the smaller
towns and cities belong even to the province, while the very great cities
belong rather to the whole country, or even to the world in general.
Yet here the distinction that we make is not the same as the former
distinction between the part of a country and the whole country. Nevertheless, the ground for such an identification of the provincial with that

which pertains to country districts and to smaller cities can only lie in the supposed tendency of the great city to represent better the interests of the larger whole than do the lesser communities. This supposition, however, is certainly not altogether well founded. In the sense of possessing local interests and customs, and of being limited to ideas of their own, many great cities are almost as distinctly provincial as are certain less populous regions. The plain people of London or of Berlin have their local dialect; and it seems fair to speak of the peculiarities of such dialects as provincialisms. And almost the same holds true of the other social traditions peculiar to individual great cities. It is possible to find, even amongst the highly cultivated classes of ancient cities, ideas and fashions of behavior as characteristically local, as exclusive in their indifference to the ways of outsiders, as are the similarly characteristic ways and opinions of the country districts of the same nationality. And so the opposition of the provincial to the metropolitan, in manners and in beliefs, seems to me much less important than the other opposition of the province, as the more or less restricted part, to the nation as the whole. It is this latter opposition that I shall therefore emphasize in the present discussion. But I shall not attempt to define how large or how well organized, politically, a province must be. For my present purpose a county, a state, or even a large section of the country, such as New England, might constitute a province. For me, then, a province shall mean any one part of a national domain, which is, geographically and socially, sufficiently unified to have a true consciousness of its own unity, to feel a pride in its own ideals and customs, and to possess a sense of its distinction from other parts of the country. And by the term "provincialism" I shall mean, first, the tendency of such a province to possess its own customs and ideals; secondly, the totality of these customs and ideals themselves; and thirdly, the love and pride which leads the inhabitants of a province to cherish as their own these traditions, beliefs, and aspirations.

II

I have defined the term used as my title. But now, in what sense do I propose to make provincialism our topic? You will foresee that I intend to discuss the worth of provincialism, i. e. to consider, to some extent, whether it constitutes a good or an evil element in civilization. You will properly expect me, therefore, to compare provincialism with other social tendencies; such tendencies as patriotism, the larger love of hu-

manity, and the ideals of higher cultivation. Precisely these will constitute, in fact, the special topics of my address. But all that I have to say will
group itself about a single thesis, which I shall forthwith announce. My
thesis is that, in the present state of the world's civilization, and of the
life of our own country, the time has come to emphasize, with a new
meaning and intensity, the positive value, the absolute necessity for our
welfare, of a wholesome provincialism, as a saving power to which the
world in the near future will need more and more to appeal.

The time was (and not very long since), when, in our own country,
we had to contend against very grave evils due to false forms of provincialism. What has been called sectionalism long threatened our national
unity. Our Civil War was fought to overcome the ills due to such influences. There was, therefore, a time when the virtue of true patriotism
had to be founded upon a vigorous condemnation of certain powerful
forms of provincialism. And our national education at that time depended both upon our learning common federal ideals, and upon our
looking to foreign lands for the spiritual guidance of older civilizations.
Furthermore, not only have these things been so in the past, but similar
needs will, of course, be felt in the future. We shall always be required to
take counsel of the other nations in company with whom we are at work
upon the tasks of civilization. Nor have we outgrown our spiritual dependence upon older forms of civilization. In fact we shall never out-
grow a certain inevitable degree of such dependence. Our national unity,
moreover, will always require of us a devotion that will transcend in
some directions the limits of all our provincial ideas. A common sympathy between the different sections of our country will, in future, need
a constantly fresh cultivation. Against the evil forms of sectionalism we
shall always have to contend. All this I well know, and these things I need
not in your presence emphasize. But what I am to emphasize is this: The
present state of civilization, both in the world at large, and with us, in
America, is such as to define a new social mission which the province
alone, but not the nation, is able to fulfil. False sectionalism, which disunites, will indeed always remain as great an evil as ever it was. But the
modern world has reached a point where it needs, more than ever before,
the vigorous development of a highly organized provincial life. Such a
life, if wisely guided, will not mean disloyalty to the nation; and it need
not mean narrowness of spirit, nor yet the further development of jealousies between various communities. What it will mean, or at least may
mean,—this, so far as I have time, I wish to set forth in the following dis-

cussion. My main intention is to define the right form and the true office of provincialism,—to portray what, if you please, we may well call the Higher Provincialism,—to portray it, and then to defend it, to extol it, and to counsel you to further just such provincialism.

Since this is my purpose, let me at once say that I address myself, in the most explicit terms, to men and women who, as I hope and presuppose, are and wish to be, in the wholesome sense, provincial. Every one, as I maintain, ought, ideally speaking, to be provincial,—and that no matter how cultivated, or humanitarian, or universal in purpose or in experience he may be or may become. If in our own country, where often so many people are still comparative strangers to the communities in which they have come to live, there are some of us who, like myself, have changed our provinces during our adult years, and who have so been unable to become and to remain in the sense of European countries provincial; and if, moreover, the life of our American provinces everywhere has still too brief a tradition,—all that is our misfortune, and not our advantage. As our country grows in social organization, there will be, in absolute measure, more and not less provincialism amongst our people. To be sure, as I hope, there will also be, in absolute measure, more and not less patriotism, closer and not looser national ties, less and not more mutual sectional misunderstanding. But the two tendencies, the tendency toward national unity and that toward local independence of spirit, must henceforth grow together. They cannot prosper apart. The national unity must not kill out, nor yet hinder, the provincial self-consciousness. The loyalty to the Republic must not lessen the love and the local pride of the individual community. The man of the future must love his province more than he does today. His provincial customs and ideals must be more and not less highly developed, more and not less self-conscious, well-established, and earnest. And therefore, I say, I appeal to you as to a company of people who are, and who mean to be, provincial as well as patriotic,—servants and lovers of your own community and of its ways, as well as citizens of the world. I hope and believe that you all intend to have your community live its own life, and not the life of any other community, nor yet the life of a mere abstraction called humanity in general. I hope that you are fully aware how provincialism, like monogamy, is an essential basis of true civilization. And it is with this presupposition that I undertake to suggest something toward a definition and defence of the higher provincialism and of its office in civilization.

III

With this programme in mind, let me first tell you what seem to me to be in our modern world, and, in particular, in our American world, the principal evils which are to be corrected by a further development of a true provincial spirit, and which cannot be corrected without such a development.

The first of these evils I have already mentioned. It is a defect incidental, partly to the newness of our own country, but partly also to those world-wide conditions of modern life which make travel, and even a change of home, both attractive and easy to dwellers in the most various parts of the globe. In nearly every one of our American communities, at least in the northern and in the western regions of our country, there is a rather large proportion of people who either have not grown up where they were born, or who have changed their dwelling-place in adult years. I can speak all the more freely regarding this class of our communities, because, in my own community, I myself, as a native of California, now resident in New England, belong to such a class. Such classes, even in modern New England, are too large. The stranger, the sojourner, the newcomer, is an inevitable factor in the life of most American communities. To make him welcome is one of the most gracious of the tasks in which our people have become expert. To give him his fair chance is the rule of our national life. But it is not on the whole well when the affairs of a community remain too largely under the influence of those who mainly feel either the wanderer's or the new resident's interest in the region where they are now dwelling. To offset the social tendencies due to such frequent changes of dwelling-place we need the further development and the intensification of the community spirit. The sooner the new resident learns to share this spirit, the better for him and for his community. A sound instinct, therefore, guides even our newer communities, in the more fortunate cases, to a rapid development of such a local sentiment as makes the stranger feel that he must in due measure conform if he would be permanently welcome, and must accept the local spirit if he is to enjoy the advantages of his community. As a Californian I have been interested to see both the evidences and the nature of this rapid evolution of the genuine provincial spirit in my own state. How swiftly, in that country, the Californians of the early days seized upon every suggestion that could give a sense of the unique importance of their new provincial life. The associations that soon clustered about the tales of the life of Spanish missionaries and Mexican colonists in the years before 1846,—these our American Californians cherished from the outset. This, to us often half-legendary past, gave us a history of our own. The wondrous events of the early mining life,—how earnestly the pioneers later loved to rehearse that story; and how proud every young Californian soon became of the fact that his father had had his part therein. Even the Californian's well-known and largely justified glorification of his climate was, in his own mind, part of the same expression of his tendency to idealize whatever tended to make his community, and all its affairs, seem unique, beloved, and deeply founded upon some significant natural basis. Such a foundation was, indeed, actually there; nature had, indeed, richly blessed his land; but the real interest that made one emphasize and idealize all these things, often so boastfully, was the interest of the loyal citizen in finding his community an object of pride. Now you, who know well your own local history, will be able to observe the growth amongst you of this tendency to idealize your past, to glorify the bounties that nature has showered upon you, all in such wise as to give the present life of your community more dignity, more honor, more value in the eyes of yourselves and of strangers. In fact, that we all do thus glorify our various provinces, we well know; and with what feelings we accompany the process, we can all observe for ourselves. But it is well to remember that the special office, the principal use, the social justification, of such mental tendencies in ourselves lies in the aid that they give us in becoming loyal to our community, and in assimilating to our own social order the strangers that are within our gates. It is the especial art of the colonizing peoples, such as we are, and such as the English are, to be able by devices of this sort rapidly to build up in their own minds a provincial loyalty in a new environment. The French, who are not a colonizing people, seem to possess much less of this tendency. The Chinese seem to lack it almost altogether. Our own success as possessors of new lands depends upon this one skill in making the new lands where we came to dwell soon seem to us glorious and unique. I was much impressed, some years ago, during a visit to Australia and New Zealand, with the parallel developments in the Australasian colonies. They too have already their glorious past history, their unique fortunes, their romances of the heroic days,— and, in consequence, their provincial loyalty and their power to assimilate their newcomers. So learn to view your new community that every stranger who enters it shall at once feel the dignity of its past, and the unique privilege that is offered to him when he is permitted to belong to its company of citizens,—this is the first rule of the people of every colonizing nation when they found a new province.

Thus, then, I have pointed out the first evil with which our provincialism has to deal—the evil due to the presence of a considerable number of not yet assimilated newcomers in most of our communities. The newcomers themselves are often a boon and welcome indeed. But their failure to be assimilated constitutes, so long as it endures, a source of social danger, because the community needs well-knit organization. We meet this danger by the development of a strong provincial spirit amongst those who already constitute the centralized portion of the community. For thus a dignity is given to the social order which makes the newcomer long to share in its honors by deserving its confidence. But this aspect of provincialism, this usefulness of local pride, is indeed the best known aspect of my topic. I pass at once to the less frequently recognized uses of the provincial spirit, by mentioning the second of the evils with which a wise provincialism is destined to contend.

IV

This second modern evil arises from, and constitutes, one aspect of the levelling tendency of recent civilization. That such a levelling tendency exists, most of us recognize. That it is the office of the province to contend against some of the attendant evils of this tendency, we less often observe. By the levelling tendency in question I mean that aspect of modern civilization which is most obviously suggested by the fact that, because of the ease of communication amongst distant places, because of the spread of popular education, and because of the consolidation and of the centralization of industries and of social authorities, we tend all over the nation, and, in some degree, even throughout the civilized world, to read the same daily news, to share the same general ideas, to submit to the same overmastering social forces, to live in the same external fashions, to discourage individuality, and to approach a dead level of harassed mediocrity. One of the most marked of all social tendencies is in any age that toward the mutual assimilation of men in so far as they are in social relations with one another. One of the strongest human predispositions is that toward imitation. But our modern conditions have greatly favored the increase of the numbers of people who read the same books and newspapers, who repeat the same phrases, who follow the same social fashions, and who thus, in general, imitate one another in constantly more and more ways. The result is a tendency to crush the individual.

Furthermore there are modern economic and industrial developments, too well known to all of you to need any detailed mention here, which lead toward similar results. The independence of the small trader or manufacturer becomes lost in the great commercial or industrial combination. The vast corporation succeeds and displaces the individual. Ingenuity and initiative become subordinated to the discipline of an impersonal social order. And each man, becoming, like his fellow, the servant of masters too powerful for him to resist, and too complex in their undertakings for him to understand, is, in so far, disposed unobtrusively to conform to the ways of his innumerable fellow-servants, and to lose all sense of his unique moral destiny as an individual.

I speak here merely of tendencies. As you know, they are nowhere unopposed tendencies. Nor do I for an instant pretend to call even these levelling tendencies wholly, or principally, evil. But for the moment I call attention to what are obviously questionable, and in some degree are plainly evil, aspects of these modern tendencies. Imitation is a good thing. All civilization depends upon it. But there may be a limit to the number of people who ought to imitate precisely the same body of ideas and customs. For imitation is not man's whole business. There ought to be some room left for variety. Modern conditions have often increased too much what one might call the purely mechanical carrying-power of certain ruling social influences. There are certain metropolitan newspapers, for instance, which have far too many readers for the good of the social order in which they circulate. These newspapers need not always be very mischievous ones. But when read by too vast multitudes, they tend to produce a certain monotonously uniform triviality of mind in a large proportion of our city and suburban population. It would be better if the same readers were divided into smaller sections, which read different newspapers, even if these papers were of no higher level. For then there would at least be a greater variety in the sorts of triviality which from day to day occupied their minds. And variety is the beginning of individual independence of insight and of conviction. As for the masses of people who are under the domination of the great corporations that employ them, I am here not in the least dwelling upon their economic difficulties. I am pointing out that the lack of initiative in their lives tends to make their spiritual range narrower. They are too little disposed to create their own world. Now every man who gets into a vital relation to God's truth becomes, in his own way, a creator. And if you deprive a man of all incentive to create, you in so far tend to cut him off from God's truth. Or, in more common language, independence of spirit flourishes only when a man at least believes that he has a chance to change his fortunes if he persistently wills to do so. But the servant of some modern forms of impersonal social organization tends to lose this belief that he has a chance. Hence he tends to lose independence of spirit.

Well, this is the second of the evils of the modern world which, as I have said, provincialism may tend to counteract. Local spirit, local pride, provincial independence, influence the individual man precisely because they appeal to his imitative tendencies. But thereby they act so as to render him more or less immune in presence of the more trivial of the influences that, coming from without his community, would otherwise be likely to reduce him to the dead level of the customs of the whole nation. A country district may seem to a stranger unduly crude in its ways; but it does not become wiser in case, under the influence of city newspapers and of summer boarders, it begins to follow city fashions merely for the sake of imitating. Other things being equal, it is better in proportion as it remains self-possessed,—proud of its own traditions, not unwilling indeed to learn, but also quite ready to teach the stranger its own wisdom. And in similar fashion provincial pride helps the individual man to keep his self-respect even when the vast forces that work toward industrial consolidation, and toward the effacement of individual initiative, are besetting his life at every turn. For a man is in large measure what his social consciousness makes him. Give him the local community that he loves and cherishes, that he is proud to honor and to serve,— make his ideal of that community lofty,—give him faith in the dignity of his province,—and you have given him a power to counteract the levelling tendencies of modern civilization.

V

The third of the evils with which a wise provincialism must contend is closely connected with the second. I have spoken of the constant tendency of modern life to the mutual assimilation of various parts of the social order. Now this assimilation may occur slowly and steadily, as in great measure it normally does; or, on the other hand, it may take more sudden and striking forms, at moments when the popular mind is excited, when great emotions affect the social order. At such times of emotional disturbance, society is subject to tendencies which have recently received a good deal of psychological study. They are the tendencies to constitute what has often been called the spirit of the crowd or of the mob. Modern readers of the well-known book of Le Bon's on "The Crowd" well know what the tendencies to which I refer may accomplish. It is true that the results of Le Bon are by no means wholly acceptable. It is true that the psychology of large social masses is still insufficiently understood, and that a great many hasty statements have been made about the fatal tendency of great companies of people to go wrong. Yet in the complex world of social processes there can be no doubt that there exist such processes as the ones which Le Bon characterizes. The mob-spirit is a genuine psychological fact which occasionally becomes important in the life of all numerous communities. Moreover, the mob-spirit is no new thing. It has existed in some measure from the very beginning of social life. But there are certain modern conditions which tend to give the mob-spirit new form and power, and to lead to new social dangers that are consequent upon the presence of this spirit.

I use the term "mob-spirit" as an abbreviation for a very large range of phenomena, phenomena which may indeed be classed with all the rest of the imitative phenomena as belonging to one genus. But the mob-phenomena are distinguished from the other imitative phenomena by certain characteristic emotional tendencies which belong to excited crowds of people, and which do not belong to the more strictly normal social activities. Man, as an imitative animal, naturally tends, as we have seen, to do whatever his companions do, so long as he is not somehow aroused to independence and to individuality. Accordingly, he easily shares the beliefs and temperaments of those who are near enough to him to influence him. But now suppose a condition of things such as may readily occur in any large group of people who have somehow come to feel strong sympathy with one another, and who are for any reason in a relatively passive and impressible state of mind. In such a company of people let any idea which has a strong emotional coloring come to be suggested, by the words of the leader, by the singing of a song, by the beginning of any social activity that does not involve clear thinking, that does not call upon a man to assert his own independence. Such an idea forthwith tends to take possession in an extraordinarily strong degree of every member of the social group in question. As a consequence, the individual may come to be, as it were, hypnotized by his social group. He may reach a stage where he not merely lacks a disposition to individual initiative, but becomes for the time simply unable to assert himself, to think his own thoughts, or even to remember his ordinary habits and principles of conduct. His judgment for the time becomes one with that of the mass. He may not himself observe this fact. Like the hypnotized subject, the member of the excited mob may feel as if he were very independently expressing himself. He may say: "This idea is my own idea," when as a fact the ruling idea is suggested by the leaders of the mob, or even by the accident of the momentary situation. The individual may be led to acts of which he says: "These things are my duty, my sacred privilege, my right," when as a fact the acts in question are forced upon him by the suggestions of the social mass of which at the instant he is merely a helpless member. As the hypnotized subject, again, thinks his will free when an observer can see that he is obliged to follow the suggestions of the hypnotizer, so the member of the mob may feel all the sense of pure initiative, although as a fact he is in bondage to the will of another, to the motives of the moment.

All such phenomena are due to very deep-seated and common human tendencies. It is no individual reproach to any one of us that, under certain conditions, he would lose his individuality and become the temporary prey of the mob-spirit. Moreover, by the word "mob" itself, or by the equivalent word "crowd," I here mean no term that reflects upon the personal characters or upon the private intelligence of the individuals who chance to compose any given mob. In former ages when the defenders of aristocratic or of monarchical institutions used to speak with contempt of the mob, and oppose to the mob the enlightened portion of the community, the wise who ought to rule, or the people whom birth and social position secured against the defects of the mob, the term was used without a true understanding of the reason why crowds of people are upon occasion disposed to do things that are less intelligent than the acts of normal and thoughtful people would be. For the modern student of the psychology of crowds, a crowd or a mob means not in any wise a company of wicked, of debased, or even of ignorant persons. The term means merely a company of people who, by reason of their sympathies, have for the time being resigned their individual judgment. A mob might be a mob of saints or of cutthroats, of peasants or of men of science. If it were a mob it would lack due social wisdom whatever its membership might be. For the members of the mob are sympathizing rather than criticising. Their ruling ideas then, therefore, are what Le Bon calls atavistic ideas; ideas such as belong to earlier and cruder periods of civilization. Opposed to the mob in which the good sense of individuals is lost in a blur of emotion, and in a helpless suggestibility,—opposed to the mob, I say, is the small company of thoughtful individuals who are tak-

ing counsel together. Now our modern life, with its vast unions of people, with its high development of popular sentiments, with its passive
and sympathetic love for knowing and feeling whatever other men
know and feel, is subject to the disorders of larger crowds, of more dangerous mobs, than have ever before been brought into sympathetic union.
One great problem of our time, then, is how to carry on popular government without being at the mercy of the mob-spirit. It is easy to give
this mob-spirit noble names. Often you hear of it as "grand popular
enthusiasm." Often it is highly praised as a loyal party spirit or as patriotism. But psychologically it is the mob-spirit whenever it is the spirit of a
large company of people who are no longer either taking calm counsel
together in small groups, or obeying an already established law or custom but who are merely sympathizing with one another, listening to
the words of leaders, and believing the large print headings of their
newspapers. Every such company of people is, in so far, a mob. Though
they spoke with the tongues of men and of angels, you could not then
trust them. Wisdom is not in them nor in their mood. However highly
trained they may be as individuals, their mental processes, as a mob, are
degraded. Their suffrages, as a mob, ought not to count. Their deeds
come of evil. The next mob may undo their work. Accident may render
their enthusiasm relatively harmless. But, as a mere crowd, they cannot be
wise. They cannot be safe rulers. Who, then, are the men who wisely
think and rightly guide? They are, I repeat, the men who take counsel
together in small groups, who respect one another's individuality, who
meanwhile criticise one another constantly, and earnestly, and who sus-
pect whatever the crowd teaches. In such men there need be no lack of
wise sympathy, but there is much besides sympathy. There is individuality, and there is a willingness to doubt both one another and themselves.
To such men, and to such groups, popular government ought to be in-
trusted.

Now these principles are responsible for the explanation of the well-
known contrast between those social phenomena which illustrate the
wisdom of the enlightened social order, and the phenomena which, on
the contrary, often seem such as to make us despair for the moment of
the permanent success of popular government. In the rightly constituted social group where every member feels his own responsibility for
his part of the social enterprise which is in hand, the result of the interaction of individuals is that the social group may show itself wiser than
any of its individuals. In the mere crowd, on the other hand, the social

group may be, and generally is, more stupid than any of its individual members. Compare a really successful town meeting in a comparatively small community with the accidental and sometimes dangerous social phenomena of a street mob or of a great political convention. In the one case every individual may gain wisdom from his contact with the social group. In the other case every man concerned, if ever he comes again to himself, may feel ashamed of the absurdity of which the whole company was guilty. Social phenomena of the type that may result from the higher social group, the group in which individuality is respected, even while social loyalty is demanded,—these phenomena may lead to permanent social results which as tradition gives them a fixed character may gradually lead to the formation of permanent institutions, in which a wisdom much higher than that of any individual man may get embodied. A classic instance of social phenomena of this type, and of the results of such social activities as constantly make use of individual skill, we find in language. However human language originated, it is certain that it was never the product of the mob-spirit. Language has been formed through the efforts of individuals to communicate with other individuals. Human speech is, therefore, in its structure, in its devices, in its thoughtfulness, essentially the product of the social activities of comparatively small groups of persons whose ingenuity was constantly aroused by the desire of making some form of social cooperation definite, and some form of communication amongst individuals effective. The consequence is that the language of an uncultivated people, who have as yet no grammarians to guide them and no literature to transmit the express wisdom of individual guides from generation to generation, may, nevertheless, be on the whole much more intelligent than is any individual that speaks the language.

Other classic instances of social processes wherein the group appears wiser than the individual are furnished to us by the processes that resulted through centuries of development in the production of the system of Roman law or of the British constitution. Such institutions embody more wisdom than any individual who has taken part in the production of these institutions has ever possessed. Now the common characteristic of all such social products seems to me to be due to the fact that the social groups in which they originated were always such as encouraged and as in fact necessitated an emphasis upon the contrasts between various individuals. In such groups what Tarde has called "the universal opposition" has always been an effective motive. The group has depended upon the variety and not the uniformity of its members. On the other hand, the other sort of social group, the mob, has depended upon the emotional agreement, the sympathy, of its members. It has been powerful only in so far as they forgot who they individually were, and gave themselves up to the suggestions of the moment.

It follows that if we are to look for the source of the greatest dangers of popular government, we must expect to find them in the influence of the mob-spirit. Le Bon is right when he says that the problem of the future will become more and more the problem how to escape from the domination of the crowd. Now I do not share Le Bon's pessimism when he holds, as he seems to do, that all popular government necessarily involves the tendency to the prevalence of the mob-spirit. So far as I can see Le Bon and most of the other writers who in recent times have laid so much stress upon the dangers of the mob, have ignored, or at least have greatly neglected, that other social tendency, that tendency to the formation of smaller social groups, which makes use of the contrasts of individuals, and which leads to a collective wisdom greater than any individual wisdom. But why I do insist upon this is that the problem of the future for popular government must involve the higher development, the better organization, the more potent influence, of the social groups of the wiser type, and the neutralization through their influence of the power of the mob-spirit. Now the modern forms of the mob-spirit have become so portentous because of a tendency that is in itself very good, even as may be the results to which it often leads. This tendency is that toward a very wide and inclusive human sympathy, a sympathy which may be as undiscriminating as it often is kindly. Sympathy, however, as one must recollect, is not necessarily even a kindly tendency. For one may sympathize with any emotion,—for instance, with the emotions of a cruelly ferocious mob. Sympathy itself is a sort of neutral basis for more rational mental development. The noblest structures may be reared upon its soil. The basest absurdities may, upon occasion, seem to be justified, because an undiscriminating sympathy makes them plausible. Now modern conditions have certainly tended, as I have said, to the spread of sympathy. Consider modern literature with its disposition to portray any form of human life, however ignoble or worthless, or on the other hand, however lofty or inspiring,—to portray it not because of its intrinsic worth but because of the mere fact that it exists. All sorts and conditions of men,—yes, all sorts and conditions of emotion, however irrational, have their hearing in the world of art to-day, win their expression, charm their audience, get, as we say, their recognition. Never were men so busy as now with the mere eagerness to sympathize with, to feel whatever is the lot of any portion of humanity. Now, as I have said, this spread of human sympathy, furthered as it is by all the means at the disposal of modern science, so far as that science deals with humanity, is a good thing just in so far as it is a basis upon which a rational philanthropy and a more intelligent social organization can be founded. But this habit of sympathy disposes us more and more to the influence of the mob. When the time of popular excitement comes, it finds us expert in sharing the emotions of the crowd, but often enervated by too frequent indulgence in just such emotion. The result is that modern mobs are much vaster, and in some respects more excitable than ever they were before. The psychological conditions of the mob no longer need include the physical presence of a crowd of people in a given place. It is enough if the newspapers, if the theatre, if the other means of social communication, serve to transmit the waves of emotional enthusiasm. A nation composed of many millions of people may fall rapidly under the hypnotic influence of a few leaders, of a few fatal phrases. And thus, as our third evil, we have not only the general levelling tendency of modern social life, but the particular tendency to emotional excitability which tends to make the social order, under certain conditions, not only monotonous and unideal, but actively dangerous.

Yet, as we have seen, this evil is not, as Le Bon and the pessimists would have it, inherent in the very fact of the existence of a social order. There are social groups that are not subject to the mob-spirit. And now if you ask how such social groups are nowadays to be fostered, to be trained, to be kept alive for the service of the nation, I answer that the place for fostering such groups is the province, for such groups flourish under conditions that arouse local pride, the loyalty to one's own community, the willingness to remember one's own ways and ideals, even at the moment when the nation is carried away by some levelling emotion. The lesson would then be: Keep the province awake, that the nation may be saved from the disastrous hypnotic slumber so characteristic of excited masses of mankind.

VI

I have now reviewed three types of evils against which I think it is the office of provincialism to contend. As I review these evils, I am reminded somewhat of the famous words of Schiller in his "Greeting to the New

Century," which he composed at the outset of the nineteenth century. In his age, which in some respects was so analogous to our own, despite certain vast differences, Schiller found himself overwhelmed as he contemplated the social problem of the moment by the vast national conflict, and the overwhelming forces which seemed to him to be crushing the more ideal life of his nation, and of humanity. With a poetic despair that we need indeed no longer share, Schiller counsels his reader, in certain famous lines, to flee from the stress of life into the still recesses of the heart, for, as he says, beauty lives only in song, and freedom has departed into the realm of dreams. Now Schiller spoke in the romantic period. We no longer intend to flee from our social ills to any realm of dreams. And as to the recesses of the heart, we now remember that out of the heart are the issues of life. But so much my own thesis and my own counsel would share in common with Schiller's words. I should say today that our national unities have grown so vast, our forces of social consolidation have become so paramount, the resulting problems, conflicts, evils, have been so intensified, that we, too, must flee in the pursuit of the ideal to a new realm. Only this realm is, to my mind, so long as we are speaking of social problems, a realm of real life. It is the realm of the province. There must we flee from the stress of the now too vast and problematic life of the nation as a whole. There we must flee, I mean, not in the sense of a cowardly and permanent retirement, but in the sense of a search for renewed strength, for a social inspiration, for the salvation of the individual from the overwhelming forces of consolidation. Freedom, I should say, dwells now in the small social group, and has its securest home in the provincial life. The nation by itself, apart from the influence of the province, is in danger of becoming an incomprehensible monster, in whose presence the individual loses his right, his self-consciousness, and his dignity. The province must save the individual.

But, you may ask, in what way do I conceive that the wise provincialism of which I speak ought to undertake and carry on its task? How is it to meet the evils of which I have been speaking? In what way is its influence to be exerted against them? And how can the province cultivate its self-consciousness without tending to fall back again into the ancient narrowness from which small communities were so long struggling to escape? How can we keep broad humanity and yet cultivate provincialism? How can we be loyally patriotic, and yet preserve our consciousness of the peculiar and unique dignity of our own community? In what form are our wholesome provincial activities to be carried on?

I answer, of course, in general terms, that the problem of the wholesome provincial consciousness is closely allied to the problem of any individual form of activity. An individual tends to become narrow when he is what we call self-centered. But, on the other hand, philanthropy that is not founded upon a personal loyalty of the individual to his own family and to his own personal duties is notoriously a worthless abstraction. We love the world better when we cherish our own friends the more faithfully. We do not grow in grace by forgetting individual duties in behalf of remote social enterprises. Precisely so, the province will not serve the nation best by forgetting itself, but by loyally emphasizing its own duty to the nation and therefore its right to attain and to cultivate its own unique wisdom. Now all this is indeed obvious enough, but this is precisely what in our days of vast social consolidation we are some of us tending to forget.

Now as to the more concrete means whereby the wholesome provincialism is to be cultivated and encouraged, let me appeal directly to the loyal member of any provincial community, be it the community of a small town, or of a great city, or of a country district. Let me point out what kind of work is needed in order to cultivate that wise provincialism which, as you see, I wish to have grow not in opposition to the interests of the nation, but for the very sake of saving the nation from the modern evil tendencies of which I have spoken.

First, then, I should say a wholesome provincialism is founded upon the thought that while local pride is indeed a praiseworthy accompaniment of every form of social activity, our province, like our own individuality, ought to be to all of us rather an ideal than a mere boast. And here, as I think, is a matter which is too often forgotten. Everything valuable is, in our present human life, known to us an an ideal before it becomes an attainment, and in view of our human imperfections, remains to the end of our short lives much more a hope and an inspiration than it becomes a present achievement. Just because the true issues of human life are brought to a finish not in time but in eternity, it is necessary that in our temporal existence what is most worthy should appear to us as an ideal, as an Ought, rather than as something that is already in our hands. The old saying about the bird in hand being worth two in the bush does not rightly apply to the ideal goods of a moral agent working under human limitations. For him the very value of life includes the fact that its goal as something infinite can never at any one instant be attained. In this fact the moral agent glories, for it means that he has something to do.

Hence the ideal in the bush, so to speak, is always worth infinitely more to him than the food or the plaything of time that happens to be just now in his hands. The difference between vanity and self-respect depends largely upon this emphasizing of ideals in the case of the higher forms of self-consciousness, as opposed to the emphasis upon transient temporal attainments in the case of the lower forms. Now what holds true of individual self-consciousness ought to hold true of the self-consciousness of the community. Boasting is often indeed harmless and may prove a stimulus to good work. It is therefore to be indulged as a tribute to our human weakness. But the better aspect of our provincial consciousness is always its longing for the improvement of the community.

And now, in the second place, a wise provincialism remembers that it is one thing to seek to make ideal values in some unique sense our own, and it is quite another thing to believe that if they are our own, other people cannot possess such ideal values in their own equally unique fashion. A realm of genuinely spiritual individuality is one where each individual has his own unique significance, so that none could take another's place. But for just that very reason all the unique individuals of the truly spiritual order stand in relation to the same universal light, to the same divine whole in relation to which they win their individuality. Hence all the individuals of the true spiritual order have ideal goods in common, as the very means whereby they can win each his individual place with reference to the possession and the employment of these common goods. Well, it is with provinces as with individuals. The way to win independence is by learning freely from abroad, but by then insisting upon our own interpretation of the common good. A generation ago the Japanese seemed to most European observers to be entering upon a career of total self-surrender. They seemed to be adopting without stint European customs and ideals. They seemed to be abandoning their own national independence of spirit. They appeared to be purely imitative in their main purposes. They asked other nations where the skill of modern sciences lay, and how the new powers were to be gained by them. They seemed to accept with the utmost docility every lesson, and to abandon with unexampled submissiveness, their purpose to remain themselves. Yet those of us who have watched them since, or who have become acquainted with representative Japanese students, know how utterly superficial and illusory that old impression of ours was regarding the dependence, or the extreme imitativeness, or the helpless docility, of the modern Japanese. He has now taught us quite another lesson. With a curious and on the whole not unjust spiritual wiliness, he has learned indeed our lesson, but he has given it his own interpretation. You always feel in intercourse with a Japanese how unconquerable the spirit of his nation is, how inaccessible the recesses of his spirit have remained after all these years of free intercourse with Europeans. In your presence the Japanese always remains the courteous and respectful learner so long as he has reason to think that you have anything to teach him. But he remains as absolutely his own master with regard to the interpretation, the use, the possession of all spiritual gifts, as if he were the master and you the learner. He accepts the gifts, but their place in his national and individual life is his own. And we now begin to see that the feature of the Japanese nationality as a member of the civilized company of nations is to be something quite unique and independent. Well, let the Japanese give us a lesson in the spirit of true provincialism. Provincialism does not mean a lack of plasticity, an unteachable spirit; it means a determination to use the spiritual gifts that come to us from abroad in our own way and with reference to the ideals of our own social order.

And therefore, thirdly, I say in developing your provincial spirit, be quite willing to encourage your young men to have relations with other communities. But on the other hand, encourage them also to make use of what they thus acquire for the furtherance of the life of their own community. Let them win aid from abroad, but let them also have, so far as possible, an opportunity to use this which they acquire in the service of their home. Of course economic conditions rather than deliberate choice commonly determine how far the youth of a province are able to remain for their lifetime in a place where they grow up. But so far as a provincial spirit is concerned, it is well to avoid each of two extremes in the treatment of the young men of the community,—extremes that I have too often seen exemplified. The one extreme consists in maintaining that if young men mean to be loyal to their own province, to their own state, to their own home, they ought to show their loyalty by an unwillingness to seek guidance from foreign literature, from foreign lands, in the patronizing of foreign or distant institutions, or in the acceptance of the customs and ideas of other communities than their own. Against this extreme let the Japanese be our typical instance. They have wandered far. They have studied abroad. They have assimilated the lore of other communities. And they have only gained in local consciousness, in independence of spirit, by the ordeal. The other extreme is the one expressed in that tendency to wander and to encourage wandering, which has led so many of our communities to drive away the best and most active of their young men. We want more of the determination to find, if possible, a place for our youth in their own communities.

Finally, let the province more and more seek its own adornment. Here I speak of a matter that in all our American communities has been until recently far too much neglected. Local pride ought above all to centre, so far as its material objects are concerned, about the determination to give the surroundings of the community nobility, dignity, beauty. We Americans spend far too much of our early strength and time in our newer communities upon injuring our landscapes, and far too little upon endeavoring to beautify our towns and cities. We have begun to change all that, and while I have no right to speak as an aesthetic judge concerning the growth of the love of the beautiful in our country, I can strongly insist that no community can think any creation of genuine beauty and dignity in its public buildings or in the surroundings of its towns and cities too good a thing for its own deserts. For we deserve what in such realms we can learn how to create or to enjoy, or to make sacrifices for. And no provincialism will become dangerously narrow so long as it is constantly accompanied by a willingness to sacrifice much in order to put in the form of great institutions, of noble architecture, and of beautiful surroundings an expression of the worth that the community attaches to its own ideals.

The Philosophy of Loyalty (1908)

THE NATURE AND NEED OF LOYALTY

One of the most familiar traits of our time is the tendency to revise tradition, to reconsider the foundations of old beliefs, and sometimes mercilessly to destroy what once seemed indispensable. This disposition, as we all know, is especially prominent in the realms of social theory and of religious belief. But even the exact sciences do not escape from the influence of those who are fond of the reexamination of dogmas. And the modern tendency in question has, of late years, been very notable in the field of Ethics. Conventional morality has been required, in company with religion, and also in company with exact science, to endure the fire of criticism. And although, in all ages, the moral law has indeed been exposed to the assaults of the wayward, the peculiar moral situation of our time is this, that it is no longer either the flippant or the vicious who are the most pronounced or the most dangerous opponents of our moral traditions. Devoted reformers, earnest public servants, ardent prophets of a coming spiritual order,—all these types of lovers of humanity are represented amongst those who today demand great and deep changes in the moral standards by which our lives are to be governed. We have become accustomed, during the past few generations,—during the period of Socialism and of Individualism, of Karl Marx, of Henry George, of Ibsen, of Nietzsche, of Tolstoi,—to hear unquestionably sincere lovers of humanity sometimes declaring our traditions regarding the rights of property to be immoral, and sometimes assailing, in the name of virtue, our present family ties as essentially unworthy of the highest ideals. Individualism itself, in many rebellious forms, we often find asserting that it speaks in the name of the true morality of the future. And the movement begun in Germany by Nietzsche—the tendency towards what that philosophical rhapsodist called the "transmutation of all moral values"— has in recent years made popular the thesis that all the conventional morality of the past, whatever may have been its inevitableness, or its temporary usefulness, was in principle false, was a mere transition stage of evolution, and must be altered to the core. "Time makes ancient good uncouth": in this well-known word one might sum up the spirit of this modern revolt against moral traditions.

Now when we review the recent moral controversies that express this sort of questioning, some of us find ourselves especially troubled and bewildered. We all feel that if the foundations of the exact sciences are to be criticised by the restless spirit of our reforming age, the exact sciences are indeed well able to take care of themselves. And as for religion,—if its fortunes have indeed, of late, deeply troubled and perplexed many gentle hearts, still both believers and doubters have now generally come to view with a certain resignation this aspect of the fate of our time, whether they regard religious doubt as the result of God's way of dealing with a wayward world, or as a sign of man's transition to a higher stage of enlightenment.

But restlessness regarding the very foundations of morality—that seems to many of us especially discouraging. For that concerns both the seen and the unseen world, both the truths that justify the toil spent upon exact science, and the hopes for the love of which the religions of men have seemed dear. For what is science worth, and what is religion worth, if human life itself, for whose ennoblement science and religion have both labored, has no genuine moral standards by which one may measure its value? If, then, our moral standards themselves are questioned, the iron of doubt—so some of us feel—seems to enter our very hearts.

I

In view, then, of the fact that the modern tendency to revise traditions has inevitably extended itself, in new ways, to the region of morals, I suppose that a study of some of the foundations of the moral life is a timely undertaking. It is such an undertaking that I propose as the task of the present course of lectures. My purpose, in these discussions, is both a philosophical and a practical purpose. I should indeed be glad, if there were time, to attempt, in your company, a systematic review of all the main problems of philosophical ethics. That is, I should like, were that possible, to discuss with you at length the nature, the foundation, and the truth of the moral law, approaching that problem from all those various sides which interest philosophers. And, as a fact, I shall indeed venture to say something, in the course of these lectures, regarding each of these topics. But I well know that there is no space, in eight lectures, for any adequate treatment of that branch of philosophy which is called ethics. Nor do you come here merely or mainly for the sake of hearing what a student of philosophy chances to think about the problems of his own calling. Accordingly, I shall not try, in this place, to state to you any system of moral philosophy. Rather is it the other aspect of my purpose in appealing to you—the practical aspect, which I must especially try to bear in mind throughout these lectures.

Our age, as I have said, is a good deal perplexed regarding its moral ideals and its standards of duty. It has doubts about what is really the best plan of human life. This perplexity is not wholly due to any peculiar waywardness of our time, or to any general lack of moral seriousness. It is just our moral leaders, our reformers, our prophets, who most perplex us. Whether these revolutionary moral teachers are right or wrong, they beset us, they give us no rest, they call in doubt our moral judgments, they undertake to "transmute values." And the result, for many of us, is a practical result. It tends to deprive us of that confidence which we all need in order to be ready to do good works. It threatens to paralyze the effectiveness of many conscientious people. Hence any effort to reason calmly and constructively about the foundations of the moral life may serve, not merely to clarify our minds, but to give vigor to our deeds. In these lectures, then, I shall ask you to think indeed about moral problems, but to think for the sake of action. I shall try to give you some fragments of a moral philosophy; but I shall try to justify the philosophy through its application to life. I do not much care whether you agree with the letter of any of my philosophical formulas; but I do want to bring to your consciousness, by means of these formulas, a certain spirit in terms of which you may henceforth be helped to interpret the life that we all in common need to live. Meanwhile, I do not want merely to refute those reformers and prophets of whose perplexing assaults upon moral traditions I have just spoken, nor yet do I want to join myself with them in perplexing you still further. I want, as far as I can, to indicate some ways whereby we may clarify and simplify our moral situation.

I indeed agree with the view that, in many ways, our traditional moral standards ought to be revised. We need a new heaven and a new earth. We do well to set out to seek for both, however hard or doubtful may be the quest. In so far as our restlessness about moral matters—our unsettlement—implies a sense of this need, it is a good thing. To use a comparison suggested by modern Biblical criticism—our conventional morality is indeed a sort of Pentateuch, made up of many ancient documents. It has often been edited afresh. It needs critical re-examination. I am a student of philosophy. My principal business has always been criticism. I shall propose nothing in this course which I have not tried to submit to critical standards, and to revise repeatedly.

But, on the other hand, I do not believe that unsettlement is finality. Nor to my mind is the last word of human wisdom this: that the truth is inaccessible. Nor yet is the last word of wisdom this: that the truth is merely fluent and transient. I believe in the eternal. I am in quest of the eternal. As to moral standards, in particular, I do not like that mere homesickness and spiritual estrangement, and that confusion of mind about moral ideals, which is nowadays too common. I want to know the way that leads our human practical life homewards, even if that way prove to be infinitely long. I am discontented with mere discontent. I want, as well as I can, not merely to help you to revise some of your moral standards, but to help you to give to this revision some definitive form and tendency, some image and hint of finality.

Moreover, since moral standards, as Antigone said, are not of today or yesterday, I believe that revision does not mean, in this field, a mere break with the past. I myself have spent my life in revising my opinions. And yet, whenever I have most carefully revised my moral standards, I am always able to see, upon reviewing my course of thought, that at best I have been finding out, in some new light, the true meaning that was latent in old traditions. Those traditions were often better in spirit than the fathers knew. We who revise may sometimes be able to see this better meaning that was latent in forms such as are now antiquated, and perhaps, in their old literal interpretation, even mischievous. Revision does not mean mere destruction. We can often say to tradition: That which thou sowest is not quickened except it die. But we can sometimes see in the world of opinion a sort of resurrection of the dead,—a resurrection wherein what was indeed justly sown in dishonor is raised in honor,—glorified,—and perhaps incorruptible. Let us bury the natural body of tradition. What we want is its glorified body and its immortal soul.

II

I have entitled these lectures, "The Philosophy of Loyalty." I may as well confess at once that my title was suggested to me, early last summer, by a book that I read—a recent work by a distinguished ethnologist, Dr. Rudolf Steinmetz of The Hague, entitled "The Philosophy of War." War and loyalty have been, in the past, two very closely associated ideas. It will be part of the task of these lectures to break up, so far as I can, in your own minds, that ancient and disastrous association, and to show how much the true conception of loyalty has been obscured by viewing the warrior as the most typical representative of rational loyalty. Steinmetz, however, accepts, in this respect, the traditional view. According to him, war gives an opportunity for loyal devotion so notable and important that, if war were altogether abolished, one of the greatest goods of civilization would thereby be hopelessly lost. I am keenly conscious of the sharp contrast between Steinmetz's theory of loyalty and my own. I agree with Steinmetz, as you will later see, regarding the significance of loyalty as a central principle of the moral life. I disagree with him very profoundly as to the relation of war both to true loyalty and to civilization in general. The very contrast has suggested to me the adoption of the form of title which Steinmetz has used.

The phrase, "Philosophy of Loyalty," is intended to indicate first, that we are here to consider loyalty as an ethical principle. For philosophy deals with first principles. And secondly, my title means to suggest that we are to view the matter critically and discriminatingly, as well as practically. For philosophy is essentially a criticism of life. Not everything, then, that calls itself loyalty, and not every form of loyalty, shall be put in our discussion on the same level with every other moral quality that uses or that deserves the ancient name in question. Moreover, the term "loyalty" comes to us as a good old popular word, without any exact definition. We are hereafter to define our term as precisely as possible, yet so as to preserve the spirit of the former usage. In estimating the place of loyalty in the moral life, we are, moreover, to follow neither traditional authority nor the voice of private prejudice. We are to use our reason as best we can; for philosophy is an effort to think out the reasons for our opinions. We are not to praise blindly, nor to condemn according to our moods. Where loyalty seems to be a good, we are to see why; when what men call loyalty leads them astray, we are to find wherein the fault lies. Since loyalty is a relative term, and always implies that there is some object, some cause, to which any given loyalty is to be shown, we must consider what are the fitting objects of loyalty. In attempting an answer to these various questions, our philosophy of loyalty must try to delve down to the roots of human conduct, the grounds for our moral standards, as far as our time permits.

But when all these efforts have been made towards a philosophical treatment of our topic, when certain discriminations between true and mistaken loyalty have been defined, when we have insisted upon the fitting objects of loyalty, and have throughout indicated our reasons for our theses, there will then stand out one great practical lesson, which I shall try to illustrate from the start, and to bring to its fruition as our lectures close. And the lesson will be this: *In loyalty, when loyalty is properly defined, is the fulfilment of the whole moral law.* You can truthfully centre your entire moral world about a rational conception of loyalty. Justice, charity, industry, wisdom, spirituality, are all definable in terms of enlightened loyalty. And, as I shall maintain, this very way of viewing the moral world—this deliberate centralization of all the duties and of all the virtues about the one conception of rational loyalty—is of great service as a means of clarifying and simplifying the tangled moral problems of our lives and of our age.

Thus, then, I state the task which our title is intended to set before us. The rest of this opening lecture must be devoted to clearing our way— and to a merely preliminary and tentative view of our topic. I must first attempt a partial and provisional definition of the term "loyalty" as I shall use that term. I wish that I could begin with a final and adequate definition; but I cannot. Why I cannot, you will see in later lectures. At the moment I shall try to direct your minds, as well as I can, merely to some of the features that are essential to my conception of loyalty.

III

Loyalty shall mean, according to this preliminary definition: *The willing and practical and thoroughgoing devotion of a person to a cause.* A man is loyal when, first, he has some *cause* to which he is loyal; when, secondly, he *willingly* and *thoroughly* devotes himself to this cause; and when, thirdly, he expresses his devotion in some *sustained and practical way*, by acting steadily in the service of his cause. Instances of loyalty are: The devotion of a patriot to his country, when this devotion leads him actually to live and perhaps to die for his country; the devotion of a martyr to his religion; the devotion of a ship's captain to the requirements of his office when, after a disaster, he works steadily for his ship and for the saving of his ship's company until the last possible service is accomplished, so that he is the last man to leave the ship, and is ready if need be to go down with his ship.

Such cases of loyalty are typical. They involve, I have said, the willingness of the loyal man to do his service. The loyal man's cause is his cause by virtue of the assent of his own will. His devotion is his own. He chooses it, or, at all events, approves it. Moreover, his devotion is a practical one. He does something. This something serves his cause. Loyalty is never mere emotion. Adoration and affection may go with loyalty, but can never alone constitute loyalty. Furthermore, the devotion of the loyal man involves a sort of restraint or submission of his natural desires to his cause. Loyalty without self-control is impossible. The loyal man serves. That is, he does not merely follow his own impulses. He looks to his cause for guidance. This cause tells him what to do, and he does it. His devotion, furthermore, is entire. He is ready to live or to die as the cause directs.

And now for a further word about the hardest part of this preliminary definition of loyalty: A loyal man, I have said, has a cause. I do not yet say that he has a good cause. He might have a bad one. I do not say, as yet, what makes a cause a good one, and worthy of loyalty. All that is to be considered hereafter. But this I now premise: If one is loyal, he has a cause which he indeed personally values. Otherwise, how could he be devoted to it? He therefore takes interest in the cause, loves it, is well pleased with it. On the other hand, loyalty never means the mere emotion of love for your cause, and never means merely following your own pleasure, viewed *as* your private pleasure and interest. For if you are loyal, your cause is viewed by you as something outside of you. Or if, like your country, your cause includes yourself, it is still much larger than your private self. It has its own value, so you as a loyal person believe. This essential value it would keep (so you believe) even if your private interest were left out of account. Your cause you take, then, to be something objective—something that is not your private self. It does

not get its value merely from your being pleased with it. You believe, on
the contrary, that you love it just because of its own value, which it has
by itself, even if you die. That is just why one may be ready to die for his
cause. In any case, when the loyal man serves his cause, he is not seeking
his own private advantage.

Moreover, the cause to which a loyal man is devoted is never something *wholly* impersonal. It concerns other men. Loyalty is social. If one
is a loyal servant of a cause, one has at least possible fellow-servants. On
the other hand, since a cause, in general, tends to unite the many fellow-
servants in one service, it consequently seems to the loyal man to have a
sort of impersonal or superpersonal quality about it. You can love an individual. But you can be loyal only to a tie that binds you and others into
some sort of unity, and loyal to individuals only through the tie. The
cause to which loyalty devotes itself has always this union of the personal and the seemingly superindividual about it. It binds many individuals into one service. Loyal lovers, for instance, are loyal not merely
to one another as separate individuals, but to their love, to their union,
which is something more than either of them, or even than both of them
viewed as distinct individuals.

So much for a preliminary view of what loyalty is. Our definition is
not complete. It raises rather than solves problems about the nature of
loyalty. But thus indeed we get a first notion of the general nature of
loyalty.

IV

But now for a next step. Many people find that they have a need of
loyalty. Loyalty is a good thing for them. If you ask, however, why
loyalty may be needed by a given man, the answer may be very complex.
A patriot may, in your opinion, need loyalty, first because his country
needs his service, and, as you add, he actually owes this service, and so
needs to do his duty, viz. to be loyal. This first way of stating a given
man's need of a given loyalty, turns upon asserting that a specific cause
rightly requires of a certain man a certain service. The cause, as one holds,
is good and worthy. This man actually ought to serve just that cause.
Hence he stands in need of loyalty, and of just this loyalty.

But in order thus to define this man's need of loyalty, you have to determine what causes are worthy of loyalty, and why this man ought to
serve his own cause. To answer such questions would apparently pre-

suppose a whole system of morals,—a system which at this stage of our argument we have not yet in sight.

But there is another,—a simpler, and, at the outset, a lower way of estimating the value of loyalty. One may, for the time, abstract from all questions as to the value of causes. Whether a man is loyal to a good cause or to a bad cause, his own personal attitude, when he is loyal, has a certain general quality. Whoever is loyal, whatever be his cause, is devoted, is active, surrenders his private self-will, controls himself, is in love with his cause, and believes in it. The loyal man is thus in a certain state of mind which has its own value for himself. To live a loyal life, whatever be one's cause, is to live in a way which is certainly free from many well-known sources of inner dissatisfaction. Thus hesitancy is often corrected by loyalty; for the cause plainly tells the loyal man what to do. Loyalty, again, tends to unify life, to give it centre, fixity, stability.

Well, these aspects of loyalty are, so far as they go, good for the loyal man. We may therefore define our need of loyalty in a certain preliminary way. We may take what is indeed a lower view of loyalty, regarding it, for the moment, in deliberate abstraction from the cause to which one is loyal. We may thus regard loyalty, for the moment, just as a personal attitude, which is good for the loyal man himself.

Now this lower view of our need of loyalty is the one to which in the rest of this lecture I want you to attend. All that I now say is preliminary. Results belong later. Let us simply abstract from the question whether a man's cause is objectively worthy of his loyalty or not. Let us ask: What does a man gain by being loyal? Suppose that some cause, outside of and also inclusive of his private self, so appeals to a man that he believes it to be worthy, and becomes heartily loyal to it. What good does he get personally out of his loyalty? In order to answer this question, even in this preliminary way, I must indeed go rather far afield, and define for you, still very tentatively, one of the best-known and hardest of the problems of our personal life.

V

What do we live for? What is our duty? What is the true ideal of life? What is the true difference between right and wrong? What is the true good which we all need? Whoever begins seriously to consider such questions as these soon observes certain great truths about the moral life which he must take into account if his enterprise is to succeed, that is, if he is ever to answer these questions.

The first truth is this: We all of us first learned about what we ought to do, about what our ideal should be, and in general about the moral law, through some authority external to our own wills. Our teachers, our parents, our playmates, society, custom, or perhaps some church,—these taught us about one or another aspect of right and wrong. The moral law came to us from without. It often seemed to us, in so far, something other than our will, something threatening or socially compelling, or externally restraining. In so far as our moral training is still incomplete, the moral law may at any moment have to assume afresh this air of an external authority merely in order to win our due attention. But if we have learned the moral law, or any part of it, and if we do not ask any longer how we first learned, or how we may still have to learn afresh our duty, but if, on the contrary, we rather ask: "What reason can I now give to myself why a given act is truly right? What reason can I give why my duty is my duty?"—then, indeed, we find that no external authority, viewed merely as external, can give one any reason why an act is truly right or wrong. Only a calm and reasonable view of what it is that I myself really will,—only this can decide such a question. My duty is simply my own will brought to my clear self-consciousness. That which I can rightly view as good for me is simply the object of my own deepest desire set plainly before my insight. For your own will and your own desire, once fully brought to self-consciousness, furnish the only valid reason for you to know what is right and good.

This comment which I now make upon the nature of the moral law is familiar to every serious student of ethics. In one form or another this fact, that the ultimate moral authority for each of us is determined by our own rational will, is admitted even by apparently extreme partisans of authority. Socrates long ago announced the principle in question when he taught that no man is willingly base. Plato and Aristotle employed it in developing their ethical doctrines. When St. Augustine, in a familiar passage in his Confessions, regards God's will as that in which, and in which alone, our wills can find rest and peace, he indeed makes God's will the rule of life; but he also shows that the reason why each of us, if enlightened, recognizes the divine will as right, is that, in Augustine's opinion, God has so made us for himself that our own wills are by nature inwardly restless until they rest in harmony with God's will. Our restlessness, then, so long as we are out of this harmony, gives us the reason why we find it right, if we are enlightened, to surrender our self-will.

If you want to find out, then, what is right and what is good for you, bring your own will to self-consciousness. Your duty is what you yourself will to do in so far as you clearly discover who you are, and what your place in the world is. This is, indeed, a first principle of all ethical inquiry. Kant called it the Principle of the Autonomy or self-direction of the rational will of each moral being.

But now there stands beside this first principle a second principle, equally inevitable and equally important. This principle is, that I can never find out what my own will is by merely brooding over my natural desires, or by following my momentary caprices. For by nature I am a sort of meeting place of countless streams of ancestral tendency. From moment to moment, if you consider me apart from my training, I am a collection of impulses. There is no one desire that is always present to me. Left to myself alone, I can never find out what my will is.

You may interpose here the familiar thesis that there is one desire which I always have, namely, the desire to escape from pain and to get pleasure. But as soon as you try to adjust this thesis to the facts of life, it is a thesis which simplifies nothing, and which at best simply gives me back again, under new names, that chaos of conflicting passions and interests which constitutes, apart from training, my natural life. What we naturally desire is determined for us by our countless instincts and by whatever training they have received. We want to breathe, to eat, to walk, to run, to speak, to see, to hear, to love, to fight, and, amongst other things, we want to be more or less reasonable. Now, if one of these instinctive wants of ours drives us at any moment to action, we normally take pleasure in such action, in so far as it succeeds. For action in accordance with desire means relief from tension; and that is usually accompanied with pleasure. On the other hand, a thwarted activity gives us pain. But only under special circumstances does this resulting pleasure or pain of the successful or of the hindered activity come to constitute a principal object of our desire. We all do like pleasure, and we all do shun pain. But a great deal of what we desire is desired by instinct, apart from the memory or the expectation of pleasure and pain, and often counter to the warnings that pleasure and pain have given to us. It is normal to desire food because one is hungry, rather than because one loves the pleasures of the table. It is water that the thirsty man in the desert longs for, rather than pleasure, and rather than even mere relief from pain as such. For much of the pain appears to his consciousness as largely due to his longing for water. Pain, then, is indeed an evil, but it is in part secondary to thwarted desire; while, when pain appears as a brute fact of our feelings, which we indeed hate, such pain is even then only one amongst the many ills of life, only one of the many undesirable objects. The burnt child, indeed, dreads the fire; but the climbing child, instinctively loving the ways of his remote arboreal ancestors, is little deterred by the pain of an occasional fall.

Furthermore, if I even admitted that I always desire pleasure and relief from pain, and nothing else, I should not learn from such a principle what it is that, on the whole, I am to will to do, in order to express my desire for pleasure, and in order to escape from pain. For no art is harder than the art of pleasure seeking. I can never learn that art alone by myself. And so I cannot define my own will, and hence cannot define my duty, merely in terms of pleasure and pain.

VI

So far, then, we have a rather paradoxical situation before us. Yet it is the moral situation of every one of us. If I am to know my duty, I must consult my own reasonable will. I alone can show myself why I view this or this as my duty. But on the other hand, if I merely look within myself to find what it is that I will, my own private individual nature, apart from due training, never gives me any answer to the question: What do I will? By nature I am a victim of my ancestry, a mass of world-old passions and impulses, desiring and suffering in constantly new ways as my circumstances change, and as one or another of my natural impulses comes to the front. By nature, then, apart from a specific training, I have no personal will of my own. One of the principal tasks of my life is to learn to have a will of my own. To learn your own will,—yes, to create your own will, is one of the largest of your human undertakings.

Here, then, is the paradox. I, and only I, whenever I come to my own, can morally justify to myself my own plan of life. No outer authority can ever give me the true reason for my duty. Yet I, left to myself, can never find a plan of life. I have no inborn ideal naturally present within myself. By nature I simply go on crying out in a sort of chaotic self-will, according as the momentary play of desire determines.

Whence, then, can I learn any plan of life? The moral education of any civilized person easily reminds you how this question is, in one respect, very partially, but, so far as ordinary training goes, constantly answered. One gets one's various plans of life suggested through the models that are set before each one of us by his fellows. Plans of life first come to us in connection with our endless imitative activities. These imitative processes begin in our infancy, and run on through our whole life. We learn to play, to speak, to enter into our social realm, to take part in the ways and so in the life of mankind. This imitative social activity is itself due to our instincts as social beings. But in turn the social activities are the ones that first tend to organize all of our instincts, to give unity to our passions and impulses, to transform our natural chaos of desires into some sort of order—usually, indeed, a very imperfect order. It is our social existence, then, as imitative beings,—it is this that suggests to us the sorts of plans of life which we get when we learn a calling, when we find a business in life, when we discover our place in the social world. And so our actual plans of life, namely, our callings, our more or less settled daily activities, come to us from without. We in so far learn what our own will is by first imitating the wills of others.

Yet no,—this, once more, is never the whole truth about our social situation, and is still less the whole truth about our moral situation. By ourselves alone, we have said, we can never discover in our own inner life any one plan of life that expresses our genuine will. So then, we have said, all of our plans get suggested to us by the social order in which we grow up. But on the other hand, our social training gives us a mass of varying plans of life,—plans that are not utterly chaotic, indeed, but imperfectly ordered,—mere routine, not ideal life. Moreover, social training tends not only to teach us the way of other people, but to heighten by contrast our vague natural sense of the importance of having our own way. Social training stimulates the will of the individual self, and also teaches this self customs and devices for self-expression. We never merely imitate. Conformity attracts, but also wearies us. Meanwhile, even by imitation, we often learn how to possess, and then to carry out, our own self-will. For instance, we learn speech first by imitation; but henceforth we love to hear ourselves talk; and our whole plan of life gets affected accordingly. Speech has, indeed, its origin in social conformity. Yet the tongue is an unruly member, and wags rebelliously. Teach men customs, and you equip them with weapons for expressing their own personalities. As you train the social being, you make use of his natural submissiveness.

But as a result of your training he forms plans; he interprets these plans with reference to his own personal interests; he becomes aware who he is; and he may end by becoming, if not original, then at least obstreperous. And thus society is constantly engaged in training up children who may, and often do, rebel against their mother. Social conformity gives us social power. Such power brings to us a consciousness of who and what we are. Now, for the first time, we begin to have a real will of our own. And hereupon we may discover this will to be in sharp conflict with the will of society. This is what normally happens to most of us, for a time at least, in youth.

You see, so far, how the whole process upon which man's moral life depends involves this seemingly endless play of inner and outer. How shall my duty be defined? Only by my own will, whenever that will is brought to rational self-consciousness. But what is my will? By nature I know not; for by birth I am a mere eddy in the turbulent stream of inherited human passion. How, then, shall I get a will of my own? Only through social training. That indeed gives me plans, for it teaches me the settled ways of my world. Yet no,—for such training really teaches me rather the arts whereby I may express myself. It makes me clever, ambitious, often rebellious, and in so far it teaches me how to plan opposition to the social order. The circular process thus briefly indicated goes on throughout the lives of many of us. It appears in new forms at various stages of our growth. At any moment we may meet new problems of right and wrong, relating to our plans of life. We hereupon look within, at what we call our own conscience, to find out what our duty is. But, as we do so, we discover, too often, what wayward and blind guides our own hearts so far are. So we look without, in order to understand better the ways of the social world. We cannot see the inner light. Let us try the outer one. These ways of the world appeal to our imitativeness, and so we learn from the other people how we ourselves are in this case to live. Yet no,—this very learning often makes us aware of our personal contrast with other people, and so makes us self-conscious, individualistic, critical, rebellious; and again we are thrown back on ourselves for guidance. Seeing the world's way afresh, I see that it is not my way. I revive. I assert myself. My duty, I say, is my own. And so, perhaps, I go back again to my own wayward heart.

It is this sort of process which goes on, sometimes in a hopelessly circular way, when, in some complicated situation, you are morally perplexed, and after much inner brooding give up deciding by yourself and appeal to friends for advice. The advice at first pleases you, but soon may arouse your self-will more than before. You may become, as a result, more wayward and sometimes more perplexed, the longer you continue this sort of inquiry. We all know what it is to seek advice, just with the result of finding out what it is that we do not want to do.

Neither within nor without, then, do I find what seems to me a settled authority,—a settled and harmonious plan of life,—unless, indeed, one happy sort of union takes place between the inner and the outer, between my social world and myself, between my natural waywardness and the ways of my fellows. This happy union is the one that takes place whenever my mere social conformity, my docility as an imitative creature, turns into exactly that which, in these lectures, I shall call loyalty. Let us consider what happens in such cases.

VII

Suppose a being whose social conformity has been sufficient to enable him to learn many skilful social arts,—arts of speech, of prowess in contest, of influence over other men. Suppose that these arts have at the same time awakened this man's pride, his self-confidence, his disposition to assert himself. Such a man will have in him a good deal of what you can well call social will. He will be no mere anarchist. He will have been trained into much obedience. He will be no natural enemy of society, unless, indeed, fortune has given him extraordinary opportunities to win his way without scruples. On the other hand, this man must acquire a good deal of self-will. He becomes found of success, of mastery, of his own demands. To be sure, he can find within himself no one naturally sovereign will. He can so far find only a general determination to define some way of his own, and to have his own way. Hence the conflicts of social will and self-will are inevitable, circular, endless, so long as this is the whole story of the man's life. By merely consulting convention, on the one hand, and his disposition to be somebody, on the other hand, this man can never find any one final and consistent plan of life, nor reach any one definition of his duty.

But now suppose that there appears in this man's life some one of the greater social passions, such as patriotism well exemplifies. Let his country be in danger. Let his elemental passion for conflict hereupon fuse with his brotherly love for his own countrymen into that fascinating and blood-thirst form of humane but furious ecstasy, which is called the war-spirit. The mood in question may or may not be justified by the passing circumstances. For that I now care not. At its best the war-spirit is no very clear or rational state of anybody's mind. But one reason why men may love this spirit is that when it comes, it seems at once to define a plan of life,—a plan which solves the conflicts of self-will and conformity. This plan has two features: (1) it is through and through a social plan, obedient to the general will of one's country, submissive; (2) it is through and through an exaltation of the self, of the inner man, who now feels glorified through his sacrifice, dignified in his self-surrender, glad to be his country's servant and martyr,—yet sure that through this very readiness for self-destruction he wins the rank of hero.

Well, if the man whose case we are supposing gets possessed by some such passion as this, he wins for the moment the consciousness of what I call loyalty. This loyalty no longer knows anything about the old circular conflicts of self-will and of conformity. The self, at such moments, looks indeed *outwards* for its plan of life. "The country needs me," it says. It looks, meanwhile, *inwards* for the inspiring justification of this plan. "Honor, the hero's crown, the soldier's death, the patriot's devotion—these," it says, "are my will. I am not giving up this will of mine. It is my pride, my glory, my self-assertion, to be ready at my country's call." And now there is no conflict of outer and inner.

How wise or how enduring or how practical such a passion may prove, I do not yet consider. What I point out is that this war-spirit, for the time at least, makes obedience to the country's call seem to be the proudest sort of display of one's own powers. Honor now means submission, and to obey means to have one's way. Power and service are at one. Conformity is no longer opposed to having one's own will. One has no will but that of the country.

As a mere fact of human nature, then, there are social passions which actually tend to do at once two things: (1) to intensify our self-consciousness, to make us more than ever determined to express our own will and more than ever sure of our own rights, of our own strength, of our dignity, of our power, of our value; (2) to make obvious to us that this our will has no purpose but to do the will of some fascinating social power. This social power is the cause to which we are loyal.

Loyalty, then, fixes our attention upon some one cause, bids us look without ourselves to see what this unified cause is, shows us thus some one plan of action, and then says to us, "In this cause is your life, your will, your opportunity, your fulfilment."

Thus loyalty, viewed merely as a personal attitude, solves the paradox of our ordinary existence, by showing us outside of ourselves the cause which is to be served, and inside of ourselves the will which delights to do this service, and which is not thwarted but enriched and expressed in such service.

I have used patriotism and the war-spirit merely as a first and familiar illustration of loyalty. But now, as we shall later see, there is no necessary connection between loyalty and war; and there are many other forms of loyalty besides the patriotic forms. Loyalty has its domestic, its religious, its commercial, its professional forms, and many other forms as well. The essence of it, whatever forms it may take, is, as I conceive the matter, this: Since no man can find a plan of life by merely looking within his own chaotic nature, he has to look without, to the world of social conventions, deeds, and causes. Now, a loyal man is one who has found, and who sees, neither mere individual fellow-men to be loved or hated, nor mere conventions, nor customs, nor laws to be obeyed, but some social cause, or some system of causes, so rich, so well knit, and, to him, so fascinating, and withal so kindly in its appeal to his natural self-will, that he says to his cause: "Thy will is mine and mine is thine. In thee I do not lose but find myself, living intensely in proportion as I live for thee." If one could find such a cause, and hold it for his lifetime before his mind, clearly observing it, passionately loving it, and yet calmly understanding it, and steadily and practically serving it, he would have one plan of life, and this plan of life would be his own plan, his own will set before him, expressing all that his self-will has ever sought. Yet this plan would also be a plan of obedience, because it would mean living for the cause.

Now, in all ages of civilized life there have been people who have won in some form a consciousness of loyalty, and who have held to such a consciousness through life. Such people may or may not have been right in their choice of a cause. But at least they have exemplified through their loyalty one feature of a rational moral life. They have known what it was to have unity of purpose.

And again, the loyal have known what it was to be free from moral doubts and scruple. Their cause has been their conscience. It has told them what to do. They have listened and obeyed, not because of what they took to be blind convention, not because of a fear of external authority, not even because of what seemed to themselves any purely private and personal intuition, but because, when they have looked first outwards at their cause, and then inwards at themselves, they have found themselves worthless in their own eyes, except when viewed as active, as confidently devoted, as willing instruments of their cause. Their cause has forbidden them to doubt; it has said: "You are mine, you cannot do otherwise." And they have said to the cause: "I am, even of my own will, thine. I have no will except thy will. Take me, use me, control me, and even thereby fulfil me and exalt me." That is again the speech of the devoted patriots, soldiers, mothers, and martyrs of our race. They have had the grace of this willing, this active loyalty.

Now, people loyal in this sense have surely existed in the world, and, as you all know, the loyal still exist amongst us. And I beg you not to object to me, at this point, that such devoted people have often been loyal to very bad causes; or that different people have been loyal to causes which were in deadly war with one another, so that loyal people must often have been falsely guided. I beg you, above all, not to interpose here the objection that our modern doubters concerning moral problems simply cannot at present see to what one cause they ought to be loyal, so that just herein, just in our inability to see a fitting and central object of loyalty, lies the root of our modern moral confusion and distraction. All those possible objections are indeed perfectly fair considerations. I shall deal with them in due time; and I am just as earnestly aware of them as you can be. But just now we are getting our first glimpse of our future philosophy of loyalty. All that you can say of the defects of loyalty leaves still untouched the one great fact that, if you want to find a way of living which surmounts doubts, and centralizes your powers, it must be some such a way as all the loyal in common have trodden, since first loyalty was known amongst men. What form of loyalty is the right one, we are hereafter to see. But unless you can find some sort of loyalty, you cannot find unity and peace in your active living. You must find, then, a cause that is really worthy of the sort of devotion that the soldiers, rushing cheerfully to certain death, have felt for their clan or for their country, and that the martyrs have shown on behalf of their faith. This cause must be indeed rational, worthy, and no object of a false devotion. But once found, it must become your conscience, must tell you the truth about your duty, and must unify, as from without and from above, your motives, your special ideals, and your plans. You ought, I say, to find such a cause, if indeed there be any ought at all. And this is my first hint of our moral code.

But you repeat, perhaps in bewilderment, your question: "Where, in our distracted modern world, in this time when cause wars with cause, and when all old moral standards are remorsely criticised and doubted, are we to find such a cause—a cause, all-embracing, definite, rationally compelling, supreme, certain, and fit to centralize life? What cause is there that for us would rationally justify a martyr's devotion?" I reply: "A perfectly simple consideration, derived from a study of the very spirit of loyalty itself, as this spirit is manifested by all the loyal, will soon furnish to us the unmistakable answer to this question." For the moment we have won our first distant glimpse of what I mean by the general nature of loyalty, and by our common need of loyalty.

INDIVIDUALISM

In my opening lecture I undertook to define the personal attitude which I called loyalty, and to show that, for our own individual good, we all need loyalty, and need to find causes to which we can be loyal. This was but the beginning of our philosophy of loyalty. Before I take my next step, I must ask you briefly to review the results that we have already reached.

I

By loyalty, as you remember, I mean in this preliminary view of loyalty, the willing and practical and thoroughgoing devotion of a person to a cause. By a cause that is adapted to call forth loyalty I mean, for the first, something which seems to the loyal person to be larger than his private self, and so to be, in some respect, external to his purely individual will. This cause must, in the second place, unite him with other persons by some social tie, such as a personal friendship, or his family, or the state may, in a given case, represent. The cause, therefore, to which the loyal man is devoted, is something that appears to him to be at once personal (since it concerns both himself and other people), and impersonal, or rather, if regarded from a purely human point of view, superpersonal, because it links several human selves, perhaps a vast number of selves, into some higher social unity. You cannot be loyal to a merely impersonal abstraction; and you also cannot be loyal simply to a collection of various separate persons, viewed merely as a collection. Where there is an object of loyalty, there is, then, a union of various selves into one life. This union constitutes a cause to which one may indeed be loyal, if such is his disposition. And such a union of many in one, if known to anybody for whom a person means merely a human person, appears to be something impersonal or superpersonal, just because it is more than all those separate and private personalities whom it joins. Yet it is also intensely personal, because the union is indeed a union of selves, and so not a merely artificial abstraction.

That such causes and that a thoroughgoing, willing, practical devotion to them, such as our definition of loyalty demands—that, I say, such things exist in the world, I tried at the last time to illustrate to you. My illustrations were inadequate; for it is simply impossible to show you briefly how Protean the forms of human loyalty are, and yet how similar, amidst all this endless variety of forms, the spirit of loyalty remains, whatever the causes in question may be, and whoever the loyal people are. We began, of course, with marked, traditional, and familiar illustrations. The loyal captain, steadfastly standing by his sinking ship until his last possible duty for the service to which he belongs has been accomplished; the loyal patriot, eager to devote every power to living, and, if need be, to dying for his endangered country; the loyal religious martyr, faithful unto death,—these are indeed impressive and typical instances of loyalty; but they are not the only possible instances. Anybody who, for a time, is in charge of the lives of others (for instance, any one who takes a party of children on a pleasure trip) may have the opportunity to possess and to show as genuine a loyalty as does the true-hearted captain of the sinking ship. For danger is everywhere, and to be in charge of life is always an occasion for loyalty. Anybody who has friends may devote his life to some cause which his friendship defines for him and makes, in his eyes, sacred. Anybody who has given his word in a serious matter may come to think himself called upon to sacrifice every private advantage in order to keep his word. Thus, then, anything which can link various people by fixed social ties may suggest to somebody the opportunity for a lifelong loyalty. The loyal are, therefore, to be found in all orders of society. They may be of very various degrees of intelligence, of power, of effectiveness. Wherever there are mothers and brethren, and kindred of any degree, and social organizations of any type; wherever men accept offices, or pledge their word, or, as in the pursuit of science or of art, cooperate in the search for truth and for beauty,— there are to be found causes which may appeal to the loyal interest of somebody. Loyalty may thus exist amongst the lowliest and amongst the loftiest of mankind. The king and the peasant, the saint and the worldling, all have their various opportunities for loyalty. The practical man of the world and the seemingly lonely student of science may be equally loyal.

But whatever the cause to which one is loyal, and whoever it be that is loyal, the spirit of loyalty is always the one which our preliminary definition set forth, and which our former discussion attempted more precisely to describe. Whenever a cause, beyond your private self, greater than you are,—a cause social in its nature and capable of linking into one the wills of various individuals, a cause thus at once personal and, from the purely human point of view, superpersonal,—whenever, I say, such a cause so arouses your interest that it appears to you worthy to be served with all your might, with all your soul, with all your strength, then this cause awakens in you the spirit of loyalty. If you act out this spirit, you become, in fact, loyal. And upon the unity of this spirit, amidst all its countless varieties, our future argument will depend. It is essential to that argument to insist that the humblest, as well as the wisest and mightiest of men, may share in this one spirit.

Now, loyalty, thus defined, is, as we have maintained, something which we all, as human beings, need. That is, we all need to find causes which shall awaken our loyalty. I tried to indicate to you at the last time the grounds for this our common need for loyalty. In order to do so, I began with a confessedly lower view of loyalty. I have asked you, for the time, in this opening study, to abstract altogether from the cause to which any man is loyal, to leave out of account whether that cause is or is not in your opinion worthy, and to begin by considering what good the loyal man gets out of the personal attitude of loyalty, whatever be his cause. Only by thus beginning can we prepare the way for a higher view of loyalty.

Loyalty, I have said, be the cause worthy or unworthy, is for the loyal man a good, just as, even if his beloved be unworthy, love may in its place still be a good thing for a lover. And loyalty is for the loyal man not only a good, but for him chief amongst all the moral goods of his life, because it furnishes to him a personal solution of the hardest of human practical problems, the problem: "For what do I live? Why am I here? For what am I good? Why am I needed?"

The natural man, more or less vaguely and unconsciously, asks such questions as these. But if he looks merely within his natural self, he cannot answer them. Within himself he finds vague cravings for happiness, a chaos of desires, a medley of conflicting instincts. He has come—

> "Into this universe, the why not knowing,
> Now whence, like water, willy-nilly flowing."

He must, then, in any case consult society in order to define the purpose of his life. The social order, however, taken as it comes, gives him customs, employment, conventions, laws, and advice, but no one overmastering ideal. It controls him, but often by the very show of authority it also inflames his self-will. It rebukes and amuses; it threatens and praises him by turns; but it leaves him to find out and to justify the sense of his own life as he can. It solves for him no ultimate problems of life, so long as his loyalty is unawakened.

Only a cause, then, an absorbing and fascinating social cause, which by his own will and consent comes to take possession of his life, as the spirits that a magician summons might by the magician's own will and consent take control of the fortunes of the one who has called for their aid,—only a cause, dignified by the social unity that it gives to many human lives, but rendered also vital for the loyal man by the personal affection which it awakens in his heart, only such a cause can unify his outer and inner world. When such unity comes, it takes in him the form of an active loyalty. Whatever cause thus appeals to a man meets therefore one of his deepest personal needs, and in fact the very deepest of his moral needs; namely, the need of a life task that is at once voluntary and to his mind worthy.

II

So far the former discussion led us. But already, at this point, an objection arises,—or rather, there arise a whole host of objections,—whereof I must take account before you will be ready to comprehend the philosophy of loyalty which I am to propose in later lectures. These objections, familiar in the present day, come from the partisans of certain forms of individualism which in our modern world are so prevalent. I shall devote this lecture to a study of the relations of the spirit of loyalty to the spirit of individualism. Individualism is as Protean as loyalty. Hence my task involves meeting various very different objections.

Somewhat more than a year since, I was attempting to state in the presence of a company of young people my arguments for loyalty. I was trying to tell that company, as I am trying to tell you, how much we all need some form of loyalty as a centralizing motive in our personal lives. I was also deploring the fact that, in our modern American life, there are so many social motives that seem to take away from people the true spirit of loyalty, and to leave them distracted, unsettled as to their moral standards, uncertain why or for what they live. After I had said my work, my hearers were invited to discuss the question. Amongst those who responded was a very earnest youth, the son of a Russian immigrant. My words had awakened my young friend's righteous indignation. "Loyalty," so he in effect said, "has been in the past one of humanity's most disastrous failings and weaknesses. Tyrants have used the spirit of loyalty as their principal tool. I am glad," he went on, "that we are outgrowing loyalty, whatever its forms or whatever the causes that it serves. What we want in the future is the training of individual judgment. We want enlightenment and independence. Let us have done with loyalty."

I need hardly remark that my opponent's earnestness, his passion for the universal triumph of individual freedom, his plainness of speech, his hatred of oppression, were themselves symptoms of a very loyal spirit. For he had his cause. That was plain. It was a social cause,—the one need of the many for release from the oppressor. He spoke like a man who was devoted to that cause. I honored his loyalty to humanity, in so far as he understood the needs of his fellows. His spirit, then, as he spoke, simply illustrated my own thesis. He was awake, resolute, eager. He had his ideal. And his loyalty to the cause of the oppressed had given to him this fine self-possession. He was a living instance of my view of the value of loyalty to the loyal man.

So, in fact, he was not my opponent. But he thought that he was. And his view of loyalty, his conception that loyalty is by its nature, as a spirit of devotion and of self-sacrifice for a cause, necessarily a spirit of subservience, of slavish submission,—this view, I say, although it was clearly refuted by the very existence of his own loyalty to the cause of the relief of the people from the oppressor, was still a misunderstanding of himself and of life,—a misunderstanding such as is nowadays only too common. Here, then, is one form which current objections to the spirit of loyalty often take.

Another and a decidedly different objection to my own views about loyalty was expressed to me, also within the past year, by a friend high in official position in a distant community,—a teacher who has charge of many youth, and who is profoundly concerned for their moral welfare. "I wish," he said, "that, if you address the youth who are under my charge, you would tell them that loyalty to their various organizations, to their clubs, to their secret societies, to their own student body generally, is no excuse for mischief-makers, and gives to loyal students no right to encourage one another to do mischief, and then to stand together to shield offenders for the sake of loyalty. Loyalty hereabouts," he in substance went on, speaking of his own community, "is a cloak to cover a multitude of sins. What these youth need is the sense that each individual has his own personal duty, and should develop his own conscience, and should not look to loyalty to excuse him from individual responsibility."

The objection which was thus in substance contained in my friend's words, was of course partly an objection to the special causes to which these students were loyal; that is, it was an objection to their clubs, and to their views about the special rights of the student body. In so far, of course, this objection does not yet concern us; for I am not now estimating the worth of men's causes, but am considering only the inner value of the loyal spirit to the man who has that spirit, whatever be the cause to which this man is loyal. In part, however, this objection was founded upon a well-known form of ethical individualism, and is an objection that does here concern us. For his own good, so my critic seemed to hold, each man needs to develop his own individual sense of personal duty and of responsibility. Loyalty, as my critic further held, tends to take the life out of a young man's conscience, because it makes him simply look outside of himself to see what his cause requires him to do. In other words, loyalty seems to be opposed to the development of that individual autonomy of the moral will which, as I told you in the last lecture, Kant insists upon, and which all moralists must indeed emphasize as one of our highest goods. If I look to my cause to tell me what to do, am I not resigning my moral birthright? Must I not always judge my own duty? Now, does not loyalty tend to make me ask my club or my other social cause simply to tell me what to do?

And yet, as you see, even the objector who pointed out this difficulty about loyalty cannot have been as much my opponent as he seemed to believe that he was. For he himself, by virtue of his own autonomous choice of his career, is a very loyal teacher, devoted to his office, and loyal to the true welfare of his students as he sees that welfare. I am sure that his spirit must be the very loyalty which I have been describing to you. He is an independent sort of man, who has chosen his cause and is now profoundly loyal. Otherwise, how could he love, as he does, the hard tasks of his office and live, as he does, in his devotion to that office, accepting its demands as his own? He works like a slave at his own task,—and of course he works lovingly. Yet he seemed to condemn the loyalty of his students to their clubs as essentially slavish. Is there not some misunderstanding here?

But yet another, and once more a very different form of individualism I find, at times, opposed by my objectors to the loyalty whose importance I am maintaining. The objection here in question is familiar. It may be stated thus: The modern man—yes, the modern woman also, as we sometimes are told—can be content only with the completest possible self-development and the fullest self-expression which the conditions of our social life permit. We all of us have individual rights, so such an objector vigorously insists. Duties, perhaps, as he adds, we also occasionally have, under rather exceptional, perhaps abnormal and annoying, conditions. But whether or no the duties get in our way and hinder our growth, the rights at least are ours. Now, there is no good equal to winning what is your right; namely, this free self-expression, this untrammelled play of the spirit. You have opinions; utter them. They are opposed to current moral traditions; then so much the better; for when you utter them you know, because of their unconventional sound, that they must be your own. Even so, your social ties prove irksome. Break them. Form new ones. Is not the free spirit eternally young? From this point of view loyalty does indeed appear to be slavish. Why sacrifice the one thing that you have,—your chance to be yourself, and nobody else?

I need not further pursue, at the moment, the statement of the case for this special type of modern individualism. In this form individualism does not stand, like the enthusiasm of my young Russian, for sympathy with the oppressed, but rather for the exuberance of the vitality of certain people who, as I shall hereafter try to show, have not yet found out what to do with themselves. In any case, individualism of this sort, as I have said, is familiar enough. You know it well in recent literature. Plays, romances, essays, embody its teachings. You know this form of individualism also in real life. You read of its doings in the current newspapers. As you go about your own daily business, it sometimes, to show its moral dignity, jostles you more than even our modern congestion of population makes necessary; or it passes you by all too swiftly and perilously, in its triumphant and intrepid—self-assertion. In brief, the people who have more rights than duties have gained a notable and distinguished ethical position in our modern world. The selfish we had always with us. But the divine right to be selfish was never more ingeniously defended, in the name of the loftiest spiritual dignity, than it is sometimes defended and illustrated today.

But even now I have not done with stating the case of my objectors. Still another form of modern individualism exists, and this form is again very different from any of the foregoing forms. Yet once more I must let a friend of mine state the case for this sort of individualism. This is no longer the enthusiastic revolt against the oppressor which my young Russian expressed; nor is it the interest in moral independence of judgment which the teacher of youth emphasized; nor is it the type of self-assertion which prefers rights to duties; it is, on the contrary, the individualism of those who seek, and who believe that they find, an interior spiritual light which guides them and which relieves them of the need of any loyalty to externally visible causes. Such people might themselves sometimes speak of their fidelity to their inner vision as a sort of loyalty. But they would not define their loyalty in the terms which I have used in defining the loyal spirit. The friend of whom I have spoken stated the case for such people by saying: "Loyalty, such as you define, is not a man's chief good. Spirituality, contemplative self-possession, rest in the light of the truth, interior peace—these constitute, if one can attain to them, man's chief good. Good works for other men, and what externally appears as loyal conduct—such things may and will result from the attainment of inner perfection, but will so result merely because the good soul overflows, just as, to adapt the famous metaphor of Plotinus, just as the sun shines. The true good is to be at one with yourself within. Then you are at the centre of your world, and whatever good deeds you ought to do will result from the mere fact that you are thus self-possessed, and are therefore also in possession of light and peace. It is, then, spirituality rather than loyalty which we principally need." Thus, then, my friend's objection was stated.

I have thus let four different kinds of individualism state their case, as against my own thesis that loyalty is man's chief moral good. Perhaps the foregoing objections are the principal ones which my thesis in the present day has to meet; although, as I said, a host of special objections can be made merely by varying the form of these. The objections, as you will have observed, are founded upon very various and mutually conflicting principles. Yet each one of them seems somewhat formidable, especially at this stage of my argument, where I am maintaining, not that loyalty is good because or in so far as its cause is objectively and socially a good cause, but that loyalty is a centrally significant good for the loyal man himself, apart from the cause to which he is loyal, and so apart from the usefulness to other people which his loyalty may possess.

III

The scholastic philosopher, Thomas Aquinas, in his famous theological treatise, the Summa, always, in each one of the articles into which his work is divided, gives his opponents the word before he states his own case. And after thus setting forth in order the supposed reasons for the very views which he intends to combat, and immediately before beginning his detailed argument for the theses that he proposes to defend, he confronts his various opponents with some single counter-consideration, —a Scriptural passage, a word from the Fathers, or whatever brief assertion will serve his purpose,—as a sort of indication to all of his opponents together that they somehow must be in the wrong. This brief opening of his confutation is always formally introduced by the set phrase: *Sed contra est*, "But on the contrary stands the fact that," etc.

And so now, having sketched various objections, due to equally various forms of individualism, I may venture my own *Sed contra est* before I go on to a better statement of my case. Against all my four opponents stands the following fact:—

A little while since the Japanese won much admiration from all of us by the absolute loyalty to their own national cause which they displayed during their late war. Hereupon we turned for information to our various authorities upon things Japanese, and came to know something of that old moral code Bushido which Nitobe in his little book has called the Soul of Japan. Well, whatever our other views regarding Japanese life and policy, I think that we have now come to see that the ideal of Bushido, the ancient Japanese type of loyalty, despite the barbarous life of feuds and of bloodshed in which it first was born, had very many elements of wonderful spiritual power about it. Now, Bushido did indeed involve many anti-individualistic features. But it never meant to those who believed in it any sort of mere slavishness. The loyal Japanese Samurai, as he is described to us by those who know, never lacked his own sort of self-assertion. He never accepted what he took to be tyranny. He had his chiefs; but as an individual, he was proud to serve them. He often used his own highly trained judgment regarding the applications of the complex code of honor under which he was reared. He was fond of what he took to be his rights as a man of honor. He made much, even childlike, display of his dignity. His costume, his sword, his bearing, displayed this sense of his importance. Yet his ideal at least, and in large part his practice, as his admirers depict him, involved a great deal of elaborate cultivation of a genuine spiritual serenity. His whole early training involved a repression of private emotions, a control over his moods, a deliberate cheer and peace of mind, all of which he conceived to be a necessary part of his knightly equipment. Chinese sages, as well as Buddhistic traditions, influenced his views of the cultivation of this interior self-possession and serenity of soul. And yet he was also a man of the world, a warrior, an avenger of insults to his honor; and above all, he was loyal. His loyalty, in fact, consisted of all these personal and social virtues together.

This Japanese loyalty of the Samurai was trained by the ancient customs of Bushido to such freedom and plasticity of conception and expression that, when the modern reform came, the feudal loyalties were readily transformed, almost at a stroke, into that active devotion of the individual to the whole nation and to its modern needs and demands,— that devotion, I say, which made the rapid and wonderful transformation of Japan possible. The ideal of Bushido, meanwhile, spread from the old military class to a great part of the nation at large. It is plainly not the only Japanese ideal. And I am not disposed to exaggerate what I hear of the part that the old Japanese loyalty actually plays in determining the present morality of the plain people of that country. But there can be no doubt that Bushido has been an enviable spiritual possession of vast numbers of Japanese. It is indeed universally agreed that this ideal of loyalty has been conceived in Japan as requiring a certain impersonalism, a certain disregard of the central importance of the ethical individual. And I myself do not believe, in fact, that the Japanese have rightly conceived the true worth of the individual. And yet, after all, is not this Japanese ideal of loyalty a sort of counter-instance which all the various opponents of loyalty, whose cases have heretofore been stated, ought to consider?

For Japanese loyalty has not been a mere tool for the oppressors to use. Herein it has indeed strongly differed from that blind and pathetic loyalty of the ignorant Russian peasant, which my young friend had in mind when he condemned loyalty. Japanese loyalty has led, on the contrary, to a wonderful and cordial solidarity of national spirit. If it has discouraged strident self-assertion, it has not suppressed individual judgment. For the modern transformation of Japan has surely depended upon a vast development of personal ingenuity and plasticity, not only intellectual but moral. This loyalty has not made machines out of men. It has given rise to a wonderful development of individual talent. Japanese loyalty, furthermore, if indeed strongly opposed to the individualism which knows its rights rather than its duties, has expressed itself in an heroic vigor of life which the most energetic amongst those who love to assert themselves might well envy. And meanwhile this loyalty, in some at least of its representatives, has included, has used, has elaborately trained an inner serenity of individual self-control, a spiritual peace and inner perfection which I find enviable, and which many of our own nervous wanderers upon the higher plane might find indeed restful if they could attain to it. There is, then, not so much opposition between the good which the loyal may win, and the various personal goods which our partisans of individualism emphasized. I do not believe that the Japanese ought to be our models. Our civilization has its own moral problems, and must meet them in its own way. But I am sure that our various partisans of ethical individualism, when they conceive that they are opponents of the spirit of loyalty, ought to consider those aspects of Japanese loyalty which most of us do indeed find enviable. This counter-instance serves to show that, at least in some measure, the various personal goods which the different ethical individualists seek, have been won, and so can be won, by means of the spirit of loyalty.

IV

With this counter-instance once before you, I may now go on to a closer analysis of the rational claims of ethical individualism.

Whether he takes account of the physical or of the natural world, every man inevitably finds himself as apparently occupying the centre of his own universe. The starry heavens form to his eyes a sphere, and he himself, so far as he can ever see, is at the centre of that sphere. Yes, the entire and infinite visible world, to be even more exact, seems to each of you to have its centre about where the bridge of your own nose chances to be. What is very remote from us we all of us find it difficult to regard as real in the same warm and vital sense in which the world near to us is real. It is for us all a little hard to see how the people who live far from our own dwelling-place, say, the Australians or the Siberians, can really fail to observe how distant they are from the place where, after all, it is from our point of view most natural to have one's abiding-place. And the people of alien races must surely feel, if they share our so natural insight regarding them, that they are indeed a strange sort of folk.

This inevitable illusion of perspective is, of course, responsible for what is called our natural selfishness. But on the other hand, this illusion is no mere illusion. It suggests, even while it distorts, the true nature of things. The real world has a genuine relation to the various personalities that live in it. The truth is diversified by its relation to these personalities. Values do indeed alter with the point of view. The world as interpreted by me is a fact different from the world as interpreted by you; and these different interpretations have all of them their basis in the truth of things. So far as moral values are concerned, it is therefore indeed certain that no ethical doctrine can be right which neglects individuals, and which disregards, I will not say their right, but their duty to centralize their lives, and so their moral universe, about their own purposes. As we seem to be at the centre of the starry heavens, so each of us is indeed at the centre of his own realm of duty. No impersonal moral theory can be successful. Individualism in ethics has therefore its permanent and, as I believe, its absolute justification in the nature of things. And the first principle of a true individualism in ethics is indeed that moral autonomy of any rational person which I mentioned at the last time, and which Kant so beautifully defended. Only your own will, brought to a true knowledge of itself, can ever determine for you what your duty is. And so far, then, I myself, in defending loyalty as a good thing for the loyal, am speaking as an ethical individualist. My whole case depends upon this fact. And so, in following my argument, you need not fear that I want to set some impersonal sort of life as an ideal over against the individualism of the opponents of loyalty whose various cases I have just been stating. I contend only that their opposition to loyalty, their view that one's individual purposes can be won otherwise than by and through loyalty, is due merely to their failure to comprehend what it is that the ethical individual needs, and what it is that in all, even of his blindest strivings, he is still seeking. What I hold is, that he inevitably seeks his own form of loyalty, his own cause, and his opportunity to serve that cause, and that he can actually and rationally find spiritual rest and peace in nothing else. Let me indicate to you my reasons for this view; and then, as I hope, you will see that my opponents do not at heart mean to oppose me. As the matter stands, they merely oppose themselves, and this through a mere misapprehension.

To my opponent, wherever he is, I therefore say: Be an individual; seek your own individual good; seek that good thoroughly, unswervingly, unsparingly, with all your heart and soul. But I persist in asking: Where, in heaven above and in earth beneath, have you to look for this your highest good? Where can you find it?

V

The first answer to this question might very naturally take the form of saying: "I seek, as my highest individual good, my own happiness." But, as I pointed out to you in my opening discussion, this answer only gives you your problem back again, unsolved. Happiness involves the satisfaction of desires. Your natural desires are countless and conflicting. What satisfies one desire defeats another. Until your desires are harmonized by means of some definite plan of life, happiness is therefore a mere accident. Now it comes and now it flies, you know not why. And the mere plan to be happy if you can is by itself no plan. You therefore cannot adopt the pursuit of happiness as your profession. The calling that you adopt will in any case be something that the social order in which you live teaches you; and all plans will in your mind be practically secondary to your general plan to live in some sort of tolerable relation to you social order. For you are indeed a social being.

If, next, you simply say: "Well, then, I will live as my social order requires me to live,"—again, as we have seen, you find yourself without any determinate way of expressing your own individuality. For if the social order is indeed not as chaotic in its activities as by nature you yourself are, it is quite unable of itself to do more than to make of you, in one way or another, a link in its mechanism, or a member of one of its numerous herds, in any case a mere vehicle for carrying its various influences. Against this fate, as an ethical individual, you justly revolt. If this chance social existence furnishes to you your only plan of life, you therefore live in a sad but altogether too common wavering between blind submission and incoherent rebellion. As Kant says of the natural human being, your state so far remains this, that you can neither endure your fellow-man nor do without him. You do your daily work perhaps, but you complain of your employer. You earn your bread, but you are bitter because of hard times, and because of the social oppressions that beset you. You are insufferably dreary when alone, but are bored when in company. Your neighbors determine your customs; but in return for the art of life thus acquired, you persistently criticise your neighbors for their offences against custom. Imitation and jealousy, slavish conventionality, on the one hand, secret or open disorder, on the other, bickerings that inflame, and gayeties that do not cheer—these, along with many joys and sorrows that come by accident, constitute upon this level the chronicle of your life. It is such a chronicle that the daily newspapers, in the most of their less violently criminal reports, constantly rehearse to us, so far as they are not taken up with reporting the really greater social activities of mankind. Thus the merely social animal escapes from the chaos of his natural desires, only to sink to the pettiness of a hewer of wood and drawer of water for his lord, the social order. He may become fairly happy for a longer or shorter time; but that is so far mere chance. He may even think himself fairly contented, but that is, upon this level, mere callousness.

But if, indeed, you are a genuine individualist, you cannot accept this fate. If you are an effective individualist, you do not remain a prey to that fate. You demand your liberation. You require your birthright of the social order which has brought your individuality into being. You seek the salvation of yourself from this intolerable bondage. Now, I have already counselled you to seek such liberty in the form of loyalty; that is, of a willing and whole-souled devotion to a fascinating social cause. But perhaps this does not yet seem to you the solution. And therefore you may next turn to a very familiar form of individualism. You may say, "Well, then, my ideal shall be Power. I seek to be master of my fate."

That the highest good for the individual is to be defined in terms of Power,—this, I say, is a well-known doctrine. It is very old. It is in each generation renewed, for the young men define it ever afresh. In our time it has been emphasized by Nietzsche's view that the central principle of ethical individuality is *Der Wille zur Macht*—the will to be mighty.

If this is now your doctrine, the power that you seek will, of course, not be mere brute force. Those have ill interpreted Nietzsche,—that heavily burdened invalid, doomed to solitude by his sensitiveness, and yet longing amidst his sufferings for an influence over his fellow-men of which he never became conscious before the end came to him,—those have ill interpreted him who have found in his passionate aphorisms only a glorification of elemental selfishness. No,—power for Nietzsche, as for all ethical individualists of serious significance, is power idealized through its social efficacy, and conceived in terms of some more or less vague dream of a completely perfected and ideal, but certainly social, individual man. And Nietzsche's particular dream of power has all the pathos of the hopeless invalid's longing for escape from his disease. The tragedy of his personal life was one only of the countless tragedies to which the seekers after power have fallen victims.

Well, if it is power that you seek, your ideal may not be expressed as Nietzsche expressed his, but in any case you will be seeking some socially idealized type of power. Warriors, statesmen, artists, will be before your mind as examples of what power, if attained, would be. In your sphere you will be seeking to control social conditions, and to centre them about your individual interests. Our present question is: Can you hope to attain the highest individual good by such a quest for power as this?

When we remember that the principal theme of heroic tragedy in all ages has been the fate of the seekers after individual power, and that one of the favorite topics of comedy, from the beginning of comedy until to-day, has been the absurdity of the quest of these very lovers of power, our question begins to suggest its own answer. Regarding few topics have the sages, the poets, and the cynical critics of mankind more agreed than regarding the significance of the search for power, whenever power is sought otherwise than as a mere means to some more ideal goal. Let us then merely recall the well-known verdict that tragedy and comedy, and the wisdom of the ages, have passed upon the lust of power.

The objections to defining your individual good in terms merely of power are threefold. First, the attainment of power is a matter of fortune. Set your heart upon power, make it your central good in life, and you have staked the worth of your moral individuality upon a mere venture. In the end old age and death will at best make a mockery of whatever purely individual powers your life as a human being can possess for yourself alone. While life lasts, the attainment of power is at best but a little less uncertain than the attainment of a purely private individual happiness. This is the first objection to power as the highest individual good. It is an objection as sound as it is old; and in this objection the poets and the sages are at one; and the cynics join in the verdict.

Secondly, the lust for power is insatiable. To say, I seek merely power, not as a means to an end, but as my chief good, is to say that, for my own sake alone, I condemn myself to a laborious quest that is certain, from my own point of view and however fortune favors me, to give me a constantly increasing sense that I have not found what I need. Thus, then, I condemn myself to an endless disappointment. This objection is also well known; and it is easily illustrated. After fortune had long seemed to be actually unable to thwart Napoleon, he went on to destroy himself, merely because his lust for power grew with what it fed upon, until the fatal Russian campaign became inevitable.

Thirdly, in the often quoted words of Spinoza, "The power of man is infinitely surpassed by the power of external things;" and hence the seeker after merely individual power has undertaken a battle with the essentially irresistible forces of the whole universe. Therefore, to adapt other word of Spinoza, when such a seeker after power "ceases to suffer, he ceases also to be." The larger one's powers, the more are the places in which he comes in contact with the world that he would conquer, and the more are the ways in which he feels its force. It is with the seeker after individual power as it has lately been with some of our corporations. The vaster the capital of these corporations, and the more widely spread the interests that they control, the more numerous are their enemies, the harder the legislative enactments that they have to fear, the greater their fines if they are convicted of misdoing. Power means increasing opportunities for conflict. Hence the mere seeker for power not only, by the accidents of fortune, may meet his downfall, but also, himself, actively pursues his own destruction.

Whoever pursues power, and only power, wars therefore with unconquerable fate. But you may retort: "Are the loyal also not subject to fortune, like others?" And, in reply, I call at once attention to the fact that precisely such fate is what the loyal also unhesitatingly face; but they meet it in a totally different spirit. They, too, are indeed subject to fortune; their loyalty, also, is an insatiable passion to serve their cause; they also know what it is to meet with tasks that are too vast for mortals to accomplish. Only their very loyalty, since it is a willing surrender of the self to the cause, is no hopeless warfare with this fate, but is a joyous acceptance in advance of the inevitable destiny of every individual human being. In such matters, as you well know, "the readiness is all." Loyalty discounts death, for it is from the start a readiness to die for the cause. It defies fortune; for it says: "Lo, have I not surrendered my all? Did I ever assert that just I must be fortunate?" Since it views life as service of the cause, it is content with an endless quest. Since nothing is too vast to undertake for the cause, loyalty regards the greatness of its tasks as mere opportunity. But the lust of power, on the contrary, has staked its value not upon the giving up of self-will, but upon the attainment of private possessions, upon the winning of the hopeless fight of the individual with his private fate. Hence, in a world of wandering and of private disasters and unsettlement, the loyal indeed are always at home. For however they may wander or lose, they view their cause as fixed and as worthy. To serve the cause is an honor; and this honor they have in their own possession. But in this same world the seekers for power are never at home. If they have conquered Western Europe, power lies still hidden in the Far East, and they wander into the snows of a Russian winter in pursuit of that ghost of real life which always beckons to them from the dark world beyond. Napoleon's loyal soldiers won, indeed, their goal when they died in his service. But he lost. They were more fortunate than was their leader. They had their will, and then slept. He lived on for a while, and failed.

Such considerations may suffice to show wherein consists the blindness of those who in our day seem to themselves to have more rights than duties. This homily of mine about the vanity of the lust for power is, of course, a very old story. You may think these remarks but wearisome moral platitudes. But we all have to learn this sort of lesson sometime afresh, and for ourselves. And if the story of the fate of the lust for power is old, it is none the less true. And it is a story that we in America seem to need to have told to us anew today. Any financial crisis with its tragedies can serve by way of illustration.

But perhaps this is not the form of individualism which is asserted by the ethical individualist whom I am now addressing. Perhaps you say: "It is not mere power that I want. I demand moral autonomy, personal independence of judgment. I want to call my soul my own. The highest good is an active self-possession." Well, in this case I wholly agree with your demand, precisely in so far as you make that demand positive. I only undertake to supplement your own statement of your demand, and to oppose your denial of the supreme value of loyalty. For what end, I insist, is your moral independence good? Do you find anything finally important in the mere fact that you are unlike anybody else, or that you think good what another man condemns? What worth could you find in an independence that should merely isolate you, that should leave you but a queer creature, whose views are shared by nobody? No,—you are still a social being. What you really mean is, that you want to be heard and respected as regards your choice of your own cause. What you actually intend is, that nobody else shall determine, apart from this your own choice, the special loyalty that shall be yours.

Now, I, who have defined loyalty as the willing devotion of a self to a cause, am far from demanding from you any unwilling devotion to any cause. You are autonomous, of course. You can even cut loose from all loyalty if you will. I only plead that, if you do so, if you wholly decline to devote yourself to any cause whatever, your assertion of moral independence will remain but an empty proclaiming of a moral sovereignty over your life, without any definite life over which to be sovereign. For the only definite life that you can live will be a social life. This social life may indeed be one of enmity to society. But in that case your social order will crush you, and then your moral independence will die without any of the comfort of the loyal man's last glimpse of the banner for which he sheds his blood. For the loyal man's cause survives him. Your independence will die with you, and while it lives, nobody else will find its life worth insuring. Your last word will then be simply the empty phrase: "Lo, I asserted myself." But in the supposed case of your enmity to society, you will never know what it was that you thus asserted when you asserted yourself. For a man's self has no contents, no plans, no purposes, except those which are, in one way or another, defined for him by his social relations. Or, again, your life may indeed be one of social conformity, of merely conventional morality. But such a life you, as individualist, have learned to despise,—I think justly. Your only recourse, then, is to assert your autonomy by choosing a cause, and by loyally living, and, when need be, dying for that cause. Then you will not only assert yourself by your choice of a cause, but express yourself articulately by your service. The only way to be practically autonomous is to be freely loyal.

Such considerations serve to indicate my answer to those individualists who insist upon moral independence. My young Russian and my friend, the teacher, were individualists of this type. My answer to them both, as you see, is that the only coherent moral independence which you can define is one that has to find its expression in a loyal life. There is endless room, as we shall hereafter see, for a rational autonomy in your choice of your cause.

But you may still insist that one other form of individualism remains open to you. You may say: "I seek spirituality, serenity, an inward peace, which the world cannot give or take away. Therefore my highest good lies not in loyalty, but in this interior perfection." But once more I answer you with the whole verdict of human experience regarding the true nature of spiritual self-possession. You seek serenity. Yes, but you do not want your serenity to mean mere apathy. You seek peace, but you do not want dreamless sleep, nor yet the repose of a swoon. The stones seem to remain serene when you by chance stumble over them; some tropical islanders slumber peacefully in their huts when there is no work pressing. But the types of serenity that are for you in question are not of such sort. You are an ethical individualist. Your repose must therefore be the only repose possible to a being with a conscious and a vital will of his own. It must be the repose of activity; the assurance of one who lives energetically, even because he lives in the spirit. But in what spirit shall you live? Are you not a man? Can you live with an active will of your own without living amongst your brethren? Seek, then, serenity, but let it be the serenity of the devotedly and socially active being. Otherwise your spiritual peace is a mere feeling of repose, and, as such, contents at its best but one side of your nature, namely, the merely sensuous side. The massive sensation that all things are somehow well is not the highest good of an active being. Even one of the most typical of mystics, Meister Eckhart, once stated his case, regarding a true spiritual life, thus: "That a man should have a life of rest and peace in God is good; that he should bear a painful life with patience is better; but that he should find his rest even in his painful life, that is best of all." Now, this last state, the finding of one's rest and spiritual fulfilment even in one's very life of toil itself,—this state is precisely the state of the loyal, in so far as their loyalty gets full control of their emotional nature. I grant you that not all the loyal are possessed of this serenity; but that is because of their defects of nature or of training. Their loyalty would be more effective, indeed, if it were colored throughout by the serenity that you pursue. But your own peace of spirit will be meaningless unless it is the peace of one who is willingly devoted to his cause. "The loving," says Bayard Taylor, in his lyric of Sebastopol, "the loving are the daring." And I say: The truly serene of spirit are to be found at their best amongst the loyal.

In view of such considerations, when I listen to our modern ethical individualists,—to our poets, dramatists, essayists who glorify personal initiative—to our Walt Whitman, to Ibsen, and, above all, when I listen to Nietzsche,—I confess that these men move me for a time, but that erelong I begin to listen with impatience. Of course, I then say, be indeed autonomous. Be an individual. But for Heaven's sake, set about the task. Do not forever whet the sword of your resolve. Begin the battle of real individuality. Why these endless preliminary gesticulations? "Leave off thy—grimaces," and begin. There is only one way to be an ethical individual. That is to choose your cause, and then to serve it, as the Samurai his feudal chief, as the ideal knight of romantic story his lady,—in the spirit of all the loyal.

Loyalty to Loyalty

The two foregoing lectures have been devoted to defending the thesis that loyalty is, for the loyal individual himself, a supreme good, whatever be, for the world in general, the worth of his cause. We are next to consider what are the causes which are worthy of loyalty.

I

But before I go on to this new stage of our discussion, I want, by way of summary of all that has preceded, to get before your minds as clear an image as I can of some representative instance of loyalty. The personal dignity and worth of a loyal character can best be appreciated by means of illustrations. And I confess that those illustrations of loyalty which my earlier lectures used must have aroused some associations which I do not want, as I go on to my further argument, to leave too prominent in your minds. I chose those instances because they were familiar. Perhaps they are too familiar. I have mentioned the patriot aflame with the war-spirit, the knight of romance, and the Japanese Samurai. But these examples may have too much emphasized the common but false impression that loyalty necessarily has to do with the martial virtues and with the martial vices. I have also used the instance of the loyal captain standing by his sinking ship. But this case suggests that the loyal have their duties assigned to them by some established and customary routine of the service to which they belong. And that, again, is an association that I do not want you to make too prominent. Loyalty is perfectly consistent with originality. The loyal man may often have to show his loyalty by some act which no mere routine predetermines. He may have to be as inventive of his duties as he is faithful to them.

Now, I myself have for years used in my own classes, as an illustration of the personal worth and beauty of loyalty, an incident of English history, which has often been cited as a precedent in discussions of the constitutional privileges of the House of Commons, but which, as I think, has not been sufficiently noticed by moralists. Let me set that incident now before your imagination. Thus, I say, do the loyal bear themselves: In January, 1642, just before the outbreak of hostilities between King Charles I and the Commons, the King resolved to arrest certain leaders of the opposition party in Parliament. He accordingly sent his herald to the House to demand the surrender of these members into his custody.

The Speaker of the House in reply solemnly appealed to the ancient privileges of the House, which gave to that body jurisdiction over its own members, and which forbade their arrest without its consent. The conflict between the privileges of the House and the royal prerogative was herewith definitely initiated. The King resolved by a show of force to assert at once his authority; and, on the day following that upon which the demand sent through his herald had been refused, he went in person, accompanied by soldiers, to the House. Then, having placed his guards at the doors, he entered, went up to the Speaker, and, naming the members whom he desired to arrest, demanded, "Mr. Speaker, do you espy these persons in the House?"

You will observe that the moment was an unique one in English history. Custom, precedent, convention, obviously were inadequate to define the Speaker's duty in this most critical instance. How, then, could he most admirably express himself? How best preserve his genuine personal dignity? What response would secure to the Speaker his own highest good? Think of the matter merely as one of the Speaker's individual worth and reputation. By what act could he do himself most honor?

In fact, as the well-known report, entered in the Journal of the House, states, the Speaker at once fell on his knee before the King and said: "Your Majesty, I am the Speaker of this House, and, being such, I have neither eyes to see nor tongue to speak save as this House shall command; and I humbly beg your Majesty's pardon if this is the only answer that I can give to your Majesty."

Now, I ask you not, at this point, to consider the Speaker's reply to the King as a deed having historical importance, or in fact as having value for anybody but himself. I want you to view the act merely as an instance of a supremely worthy personal attitude. The beautiful union of formal humility (when the Speaker fell on his knee before the King) with unconquerable self-assertion (when the reply rang with so clear a note of lawful defiance); the willing and complete identification of his whole self with his cause (when the Speaker declared that he had no eye or tongue except as his office gave them to him),—these are characteristics typical of a loyal attitude. The Speaker's words were at once ingenious and obvious. They were in line with the ancient custom of the realm. They were also creative of a new precedent. He had to be inventive to utter them; but once uttered, they seem almost commonplace in their truth. The King might be offended at the refusal; but he could not fail to note that, for the moment, he had met with a personal dignity greater than kingship,—the dignity that any loyal man, great or humble, possesses whenever he speaks and acts in the service of his cause.

Well—here is an image of loyalty. Thus, I say, whatever their cause, the loyal express themselves. When any one asks me what the worthiest personal bearing, the most dignified and internally complete expression of an individual is, I can therefore only reply: Such a bearing, such an expression of yourself as the Speaker adopted. Have, then, your cause, chosen by you just as the Speaker had chosen to accept his office from the House. Let this cause so possess you that, even in the most thrilling crisis of your practical service of that cause, you can say with the Speaker: "I am the servant of this cause, its reasonable, its willing, its devoted instrument, and, being such, I have neither eyes to see nor tongue to speak save as this cause shall command." Let this be your bearing, and this your deed. Then, indeed, you know what you live for. And you have won the attitude which constitutes genuine personal dignity. What an individual in his practical bearing can be, you now are. And herein, as I have said, lies for you a supreme personal good.

II

With this image of the loyal self before us, let us now return to the main thread of our discourse. We have deliberately declined, so far, to consider what the causes are to which men ought to be loyal. To turn to this task is the next step in our philosophy of loyalty.

Your first impression may well be that the task in question is endlessly complex. In our opening lecture we defined indeed some general characteristics which a cause must possess in order to be a fitting object of loyalty. A cause, we said, is a possible object of loyalty only in case it is such as to join many persons into the unity of a single life. Such a cause, we said, must therefore be at once personal, and, for one who defines personality from a purely human point of view, superpersonal. Our initial illustrations of possible causes were, first, a friendship which unites several friends into some unity of friendly life; secondly, a family, whose unity binds its members' lives together; and, thirdly, the state, in so far as it is no mere collection of separate citizens, but such an unity as that to which the devoted patriot is loyal. As we saw, such illustrations could be vastly extended. All stable social relations may give rise to causes that may call forth loyalty.

Now, it is obvious that nobody can be equally and directly loyal to all of the countless actual social causes that exist. It is obvious also that many causes which conform to our general definition of a possible cause may appear to any given person to be hateful and evil causes, to which he is justly opposed. A robber band, a family engaged in a murderous feud, a pirate crew, a savage tribe, a Highland robber clan of the old days —these might constitute causes to which somebody has been, or is, profoundly loyal. Men have loved such causes devotedly, have served them for a lifetime. Yet most of us would easily agree in thinking such causes unworthy of anybody's loyalty. Moreover, different loyalties may obviously stand in mutual conflict, whenever their causes are opposed. Family feuds are embittered by the very strength of the loyalty of both sides. My country, if I am the patriot inflamed by the war-spirit, seems an absolutely worthy cause; but my enemy's country usually seems hateful to me just because of my own loyalty; and therefore even my individual enemy may be hated because of the supposed baseness of his cause. War-songs call the individual enemy evil names just because he possesses the very personal qualities that, in our own loyal fellow-countrymen, we most admire. "No refuge could save the hireling and slave." Our enemy, as you see, is a slave, because he serves his cause so obediently. Yet just such service we call, in our own country's heroes, the worthiest devotion.

Meanwhile, in the foregoing account of loyalty as a spiritual good to the loyal man, we have insisted that true loyalty, being a willing devotion of the self to its cause, involves some element of autonomous choice. Tradition has usually held that a man ought to be loyal to just that cause which his social station determines for him. Common sense generally says, that if you were born in your country, and still live there, you ought to be loyal to that country, and to that country only, hating the enemies across the border whenever a declaration of war requires you to hate them. But we have declared that true loyalty includes some element of free choice. Hence our own account seems still further to have complicated the theory of loyalty. For in answering in our last lecture the ethical individualists who objected to loyalty, we have ourselves deliberately given to loyalty an individualistic coloring. And if our view be right, and if tradition be wrong, so much the more difficult appears to be the task of defining wherein consists that which makes a cause worthy of loyalty for a given man, since tradition alone is for us an insufficient guide.

To sum up, then, our apparent difficulties, they are these: Loyalty is a good for the loyal man; but it may be mischievous for those whom his cause assails. Conflicting loyalties may mean general social disturbances; and the fact that loyalty is good for the loyal does not of itself decide whose cause is right when various causes stand opposed to one another. And if, in accordance with our own argument in the foregoing lecture, we declare that the best form of loyalty, for the loyal individual, is the one that he freely chooses for himself, so much the greater seems to be the complication of the moral world, and so much the more numerous become the chances that the loyalties of various people will conflict with one another.

III

In order to overcome such difficulties, now that they have arisen in our way, and in order to discover a principle whereby one may be guided in choosing a right object for his loyalty, we must steadfastly bear in mind that, when we declared loyalty to be a supreme good for the loyal man himself, we were not speaking of a good that can come to a few men only—to heroes or to saints of an especially exalted mental type. As we expressly said, the mightiest and the humblest members of any social order can be morally equal in the exemplification of loyalty. Whenever I myself begin to look about my own community to single out those people whom I know to be, in the sense of our definition, especially loyal to their various causes, I always find, amongst the most exemplary cases of loyalty, a few indeed of the most prominent members of the community, whom your minds and mine must at once single out because their public services and their willing sacrifices have made their loyalty to their chosen causes a matter of common report and of easy observation. But my own mind also chooses some of the plainest and obscurest of the people whom I chance to know, the most straightforward and simple-minded of folk, whose loyalty is even all the more sure to me because I can certainly affirm that they, at least, cannot be making any mere display of loyalty in order that they should be seen of men. Nobody knows of their loyalty except those who are in more or less direct touch with them; and these usually appreciate this loyalty too little. You all of you similarly know plain and wholly obscure men and women, of whom the world has never heard, and is not worthy, but who have possessed and who have proved in the presence of you who have chanced to observe them, a loyalty to their chosen causes which was not indeed expressed in martial deeds, but which was quite as genuine a loyalty as that of a Samurai, or as that of Arnold von Winkelried when he rushed upon the Austrian spears. As for the ordinary expressions of loyalty, not at critical moments and in the heroic instants that come to the plainest lives, but in daily business, we are all aware how the letter carrier and the housemaid may live, and often do live, when they choose, as complete a daily life of steadfast loyalty as could any knight or king. Some of us certainly know precisely such truly great personal embodiments of loyalty in those who are, in the world's ill-judging eyes, the little ones of the community.

Now these facts, I insist, show that loyalty is in any case no aristocratic gift of the few. It is, indeed, too rare a possession today in our own American social order; but that defect is due to the state of our present moral education. We as a nation, I fear, have been forgetting loyalty. We have been neglecting to cultivate it in our social order. We have been making light of it. We have not been training ourselves for it. Hence we, indeed, often sadly miss it in our social environment. But all sound human beings are made for it and can learn to possess it and to profit by it. And it is an essentially accessible and practical virtue for everybody.

This being true, let us next note that all the complications which we just reported are obviously due, in the main, to the fact that, as loyal men at present are, their various causes, and so their various loyalties, are viewed by them as standing in mutual, sometimes in deadly conflict. In general, as is plain if somebody's loyalty to a given cause, as for instance to a family, or to a state, so expresses itself as to involve a feud with a neighbor's family, or a warlike assault upon a foreign state, the result is obviously an evil; and at least part of the reason why it is an evil is that, by reason of the feud or the war, a certain good, namely, the enemy's loyalty, together with the enemy's opportunity to be loyal, is assailed, is thwarted, is endangered, is, perhaps, altogether destroyed. If the loyalty of A is a good for him, and if the loyalty of B is a good for him, then a feud between A and B, founded upon a mutual conflict between the causes that they serve, obviously involves this evil, namely, that each of the combatants assails, and perhaps may altogether destroy, precisely what we have seen to be the best spiritual possession of the other, namely, his chance to have a cause and to be loyal to a cause. The militant loyalty, indeed, also assails, in such a case, the enemy's physical comfort and well-being, his property, his life; and herein, of course, militant loyalty does evil to the enemy. But if each man's having and serving a cause is his best good, the worst of the evils of a feud is the resulting attack, not upon the enemy's comfort or his health or his property or his life, but upon the most precious of his possessions, his loyalty itself.

If loyalty is a supreme good, the mutually destructive conflict of loyalties is in general a supreme evil. If loyalty is a good for all sorts and conditions of men, the war of man against man has been especially mischievous, not so much because it has hurt, maimed, impoverished, or slain men, as because it has so often robbed the defeated of their causes, of their opportunities to be loyal, and sometimes of their very spirit of loyalty.

If, then, we look over the field of human life to see where good and evil have most clustered, we see that the best in human life is its loyalty; while the worst is whatever has tended to make loyalty impossible, or to destroy it when present, or to rob it of its own while it still survives. And of all things that thus have warred with loyalty, the bitterest woe of humanity has been that so often it is the loyal themselves who have thus blindly and eagerly gone about to wound and to slay the loyalty of their brethren. The spirit of loyalty has been misused to make men commit sin against this very spirit, holy as it is. For such a sin is precisely what any wanton conflict of loyalties means. Where such a conflict occurs, the best, namely, loyalty, is used as an instrument in order to compass the worst, namely, the destruction of loyalty.

It is true, then, that some causes are good, while some are evil. But the test of good and evil in the causes to which men are loyal is now definable in terms which we can greatly simplify in view of the foregoing considerations.

If, namely, I find a cause, and this cause fascinates me, and I give myself over to its service, I in so far attain what, for me, if my loyalty is complete, is a supreme good. But my cause, by our own definition, is a social cause, which binds many into the unity of one service. My cause, therefore, gives me of necessity, fellow-servants, who with me share this loyalty, and to whom this loyalty, if complete, is also a supreme good. So far, then, in being loyal myself, I not only get but give good; for I help to sustain, in each of my fellow-servants, his own loyalty, and so I help him to secure his own supreme good. In so far, then, my loyalty to my cause is also a loyalty to my fellows' loyalty. But now suppose that my cause, like the family in a feud, or like the pirate ship, or like the aggressively warlike nation, lives by the destruction of the loyalty of other families, or of its own community, or of other communities. Then, indeed, I get a good for myself and for my fellow-servants by our common loyalty; but I war against this very spirit of loyalty as it appears in our opponent's loyalty to his own cause.

And so, a cause is good, not only for me, but for mankind, in so far as it is essentially a *loyalty to loyalty*, that is, is an aid and a furtherance of loyalty in my fellows. It is an evil cause in so far as, despite the loyalty that it arouses in me, it is destructive of loyalty in the world of my fellows. My cause is, indeed, always such as to involve some loyalty to loyalty, because, if I am loyal to any cause at all, I have fellow-servants whose loyalty mine supports. But in so far as my cause is a predatory cause, which lives by overthrowing the loyalties of others, it is an evil cause, because it involves disloyalty to the very cause of loyalty itself.

IV

In view of these considerations, we are now able still further to simplify our problem by laying stress upon one more of those very features which seemed, but a moment since, to complicate the matter so hopelessly. Loyalty, as we have defined it, is the willing devotion of a self to a cause. In answering the ethical individualists, we have insisted that all of the higher types of loyalty involve autonomous choice. The cause that is to appeal to me at all must indeed have some elemental fascination for me. It must stir me, arouse me, please me, and in the end possess me. Moreover, it must, indeed, be set before me by my social order as a possible, a practically significant, a living cause, which binds many selves in the unity of one life. But, nevertheless, if I am really awake to the significance of my own moral choices, I must be in the position of accepting this cause, as the Speaker of the House, in the incident that I have narrated, had freely accepted his Speakership. My cause cannot be merely forced upon me. It is I who make it my own. It is I who willingly say: "I have no eyes to see nor tongue to speak save as this cause shall command." However much the cause may seem to be assigned to me by my social station, I must cooperate in the choice of the cause, before the act of loyalty is complete.

Since this is the case, since my loyalty never is my mere fate, but is always also my choice, I can of course determine my loyalty, at least to some extent, by the consideration of the actual good and ill which my proposed cause does to mankind. And since I now have the main criterion of the good and ill of causes before me, I can define a principle of choice which may so guide me that my loyalty shall become a good, not merely to myself, but to mankind.

This principle is now obvious. I may state it thus: In so far as it lies in your power, so choose your cause and so serve it, that, by reason of your choice and of your service, there shall be more loyalty in the world rather than less. And, in fact, so choose and so serve your individual cause as to secure thereby the greatest possible increase of loyalty amongst men. More briefly: *In choosing and in serving the cause to which you are to be loyal, be, in any case, loyal to loyalty.*

This precept, I say, will express how one should guide his choice of a cause, in so far as he considers not merely his own supreme good, but that of mankind. That such autonomous choice is possible, tends, as we now see, not to complicate, but to simplify our moral situation. For if you regard men's loyalty as their fate, if you think that a man must be loyal simply to the cause which tradition sets before him, without any power to direct his own moral attention, then indeed the conflict of loyalties seems an insoluble problem; so that, if men find themselves loyally involved in feuds, there is no way out. But if, indeed, choice plays a part,—a genuine even if limited part, in directing the individual's choice of the cause to which he is to be loyal, then indeed this choice may be so directed that loyalty to the universal loyalty of all mankind shall be furthered by the actual choices which each enlightened loyal person makes when he selects his cause.

V

At the close of our first discussion we supposed the question to be asked, Where, in all our complex and distracted modern world, in which at present cause wars with cause, shall we find a cause that is certainly worthy of our loyalty? This question, at this very moment, has received in our discussion an answer which you may feel to be so far provisional,—perhaps unpractical,—but which you ought to regard as, at least in principle, somewhat simple and true to human nature. Loyalty is a good, a supreme good. If I myself could but find a worthy cause, and serve it as the Speaker served the House, having neither eyes to see nor tongue to speak save as that cause should command, then my highest human good, in so far as I am indeed an active being, would be mine. But this very good of loyalty is no peculiar privilege of mine; nor is it good only for me. It is a universally human good. For it is simply the finding of a harmony of the self and the world,—such a harmony as alone can content any human being.

In these lectures I do not found my argument upon some remote ideal. I found my case upon taking our poor passionate human nature just as we find it. This "eager anxious being" of ours, as Gray calls it, is a being that we can find only in social ties, and that we, nevertheless, can never fulfil without a vigorous self-assertion. We are by nature proud, untamed, restless, insatiable in our private self-will. We are also imitative, plastic, and in bitter need of ties. We profoundly want both to rule and to be ruled. We must be each of us at the centre of his own active world, and yet each of us longs to be in harmony with the very outermost heavens that encompass, with the lofty orderliness of their movements, all our restless doings. The stars fascinate us, and yet we also want to keep our own feet upon our solid human earth. Our fellows, meanwhile, overwhelm us with the might of their customs, and we in turn are inflamed with the naturally unquenchable longing that they should somehow listen to the cries of our every individual desire.

Now this divided being of ours demands reconciliation with itself; it is one long struggle for unity. Its inner and outer realms are naturally at war. Yet it wills both realms. It wants them to become one. Such unity, however, only loyalty furnishes to us,—loyalty, which finds the inner self intensified and exalted even by the very act of outward looking and of upward looking, of service and obedience,—loyalty, which knows its eyes and its tongue to be never so much and so proudly its own as when it earnestly insists that it can neither see nor speak except as the cause demands,—loyalty, which is most full of life at the instant when it is most ready to become weary, or even to perish in the act of devotion to its own. Such loyalty unites private passion and outward conformity in one life. This is the very essence of loyalty. Now loyalty has these characters in any man who is loyal. Its emotions vary, indeed, endlessly with the temperaments of its adherents; but to them all it brings the active peace of that rest in a painful life,—that rest such as we found the mystic, Meister Eckhart, fully ready to prize.

Loyalty, then, is a good for all men. And it is in any man just as much a true good as my loyalty could be in me. And so, then, if indeed I seek a cause, a worthy cause, what cause could be more worthy than the cause of loyalty to loyalty; that is, the cause of making loyalty prosper amongst men? If I could serve that cause in a sustained and effective life, if some practical work for the furtherance of universal human loyalty could become to me what the House was to the Speaker, then indeed my own life-task would be found; and I could then be assured at every instant of the worth of my cause by virtue of the very good that I personally found in its service.

Here would be for me not only a unity of inner and outer, but a unity with the unity of all human life. What I sought for myself I should then be explicitly seeking for my whole world. All men would be my fellow-servants of my cause. In principle I should be opposed to no man's loyalty. I should be opposed only to men's blindness in their loyalty, I should contend only against that tragic disloyalty to loyalty which the feuds of humanity now exemplify. I should preach to all others, I should strive to practise myself, that active mutual furtherance of universal loyalty which is what humanity obviously most needs, if indeed loyalty, just as the willing devotion of a self to a cause, is a supreme good.

And since all who are human are as capable of loyalty as they are of reason, since the plainest and the humblest can be as true-hearted as the great, I should nowhere miss the human material for my task. I should know, meanwhile, that if indeed loyalty, unlike the "mercy" of Portia's speech, is not always mightiest in the mightiest, it certainly, like mercy, becomes the throned monarch better than his crown. So that I should be sure of this good of loyalty as something worthy to be carried, so far as I could carry it, to everybody, lofty or humble.

Thus surely it would be humane and reasonable for me to define my cause to myself,—if only I could be assured that there is indeed some practical way of making loyalty to loyalty the actual cause of my life. Our question therefore becomes this: Is there a practical way of serving the universal human cause of loyalty to loyalty? And if there is such a way, what is it? Can we see how personally so to act that we bring loyalty on earth to a fuller fruition, to a wider range of efficacy, to a more effective sovereignty over the lives of men? If so, then indeed we can see how to work for the cause of the genuine kingdom of heaven.

VI

Yet I fear that as you have listened to this sketch of a possible and reasonable cause, such as could be a proper object of our loyalty, you will all the while have objected: This may be a definition of a possible cause, but it is an unpractical definition. For what is there that one can do to further the loyalty of mankind in general? Humanitarian efforts are an old story. They constantly are limited in their effectiveness both by the narrowness of our powers, and by the complexity of the human nature which we try to improve. And if any lesson of philanthropy is well known, it is this, that whoever tries simply to help mankind as a whole, loses his labor, so long as he does not first undertake to help those nearest to him. Loyalty to the cause of universal loyalty—how, then, shall it constitute any practical working scheme of life?

I answer at once that the individual man, with his limited powers, can indeed serve the cause of universal loyalty only by limiting his undertakings to some decidedly definite personal range. He must have his own special and personal cause. But this cause of his can indeed be chosen and determined so as to constitute a deliberate effort to further universal loyalty. When I begin to show you how this may be, I shall at once pass from what may have seemed to you a very unpractical scheme of life, to a realm of familiar and commonplace virtuous activities. The only worth of my general scheme will then lie in the fact that, in the light of this scheme, we can, as it were, see the commonplace virtues transfigured and glorified by their relation to the one highest cause of all. My thesis is *that all the commonplace virtues, in so far as they are indeed defensible and effective, are special forms of loyalty to loyalty,* and are to be justified, centralized, inspired, by the one supreme effort to do good, namely, the effort to make loyalty triumphant in the lives of all men.

The first consideration which I shall here insist upon is this: Loyalty, as we have all along seen, depends upon a very characteristic and subtle union of natural interest, and of free choice. Nobody who merely follows his natural impulses as they come is loyal. Yet nobody can be loyal without depending upon and using his natural impulses. If I am to be loyal, my cause must from moment to moment fascinate me, awaken my muscular vigor, stir me with some eagerness for work, even if this be painful work. I cannot be loyal to barren abstractions. I can only be loyal to what my life can interpret in bodily deeds. Loyalty has its elemental appeal to my whole organism. My cause must become one with my human life. Yet all this must occur not without my willing choice. I must control my devotion. It will possess me, but not without my voluntary complicity; for I shall accept the possession. It is, then, with the cause to which you personally are loyal, as it was with divine grace in an older theology. The cause must control you, as divine grace took saving control of the sinner; but only your own will can accept this control, and a grace that merely compels can never save.

Now that such a union of choice with natural interest is possible, is a fact of human nature, which every act of your own, in your daily calling, may be used to exemplify. You cannot do steady work without natural interest; but whoever is the mere prey of this passing interest does no steady work. Loyalty is a perfect synthesis of certain natural desires, of some range of social conformity, and of your own deliberate choice.

In order to be loyal, then, to loyalty, I must indeed first choose forms of loyal conduct which appeal to my own nature. This means that, upon one side of my life, I shall have to behave much as the most unenlightened of the loyal do. I shall serve causes such as my natural temperament and my social opportunities suggest to me. I shall choose friends whom I like. My family, my community, my country, will be served partly because I find it interesting to be loyal to them.

Nevertheless, upon another side, all these my more natural and, so to speak, accidental loyalties, will be controlled and unified by a deliberate use of the principle that, whatever my cause, it ought to be such as to further, so far as in me lies, the cause of universal loyalty. Hence I shall not permit my choice of my special causes to remain a mere chance. My causes must form a system. They must constitute in their entirety a single cause, my life of loyalty. When apparent conflicts arise amongst the causes in which I am interested, I shall deliberately undertake, by devices which we shall hereafter study in these lectures, to reduce the conflict to the greatest possible harmony. Thus, for instance, I may say, to one of the causes in which I am naturally bound up:—

> "I could not love thee, dear, so much,
> Loved I not honour more."

And in this familiar spirit my loyalty will aim to be, even within the limits of my own personal life, a united, harmonious devotion, not to various conflicting causes, but to one system of causes, and so to one cause.

Since this one cause is my choice, the cause of my life, my social station will indeed suggest it to me. My natural powers and preferences will make it fascinating to me, and yet I will never let mere social routine, or mere social tradition, or mere private caprice, impose it upon me. I will be individualistic in my loyalty, carefully insisting, however, that whatever else I am, I shall be in all my practical activity a loyal individual, and, so far as in me lies, one who chooses his personal causes for the sake of the spread of universal loyalty. Moreover, my loyalty will be a growing loyalty. Without giving up old loyalties I shall annex new ones. There will be evolution in my loyalty.

The choice of my cause will in consequence be such as to avoid unnecessary conflict with the causes of others. So far I shall indeed negatively show loyalty to loyalty. It shall not be my cause to destroy other men's loyalty. Yet since my cause, thus chosen and thus organized, still confines me to my narrow personal range, and since I can do so little directly for mankind, you may still ask whether, by such a control of my natural interests, I am indeed able to do much to serve the cause of universal loyalty.

Well, it is no part of the plan of this discourse to encourage illusions about the range of influence that any one poor mortal can exert. But that by the mere force of my practical and personal loyalty, if I am indeed loyal, I am doing something for the cause of universal loyalty, however narrow my range of deeds, this a very little experience of the lives of other people tends to teach me. For who, after all, most encourages and incites me to loyalty? I answer, any loyal human being, whatever his cause, so long as his cause does not arouse my hatred, and does not directly injure my chance to be loyal. My fellow's special and personal cause need not be directly mine. Indirectly he inspires me by the very contagion of his loyalty. He sets me the example. By his loyalty he shows me the worth of loyalty. Those humble and obscure folk of whom I have before spoken, how precious they are to us all as inspiring examples, because of their loyalty to their own.

From what men, then, have I gained the best aid in discovering how to be myself loyal? From the men whose personal cause is directly and consciously one with my own? That is indeed sometimes the case. But others, whose personal causes were apparently remote in very many ways from mine, have helped me to some of my truest glimpses of loyalty.

For instance: There was a friend of my own youth whom I have not seen for years, who once faced the choice between a scholarly career that he loved, on the one hand, and a call of honor, upon the other,— who could have lived out that career with worldly success if he had only been willing to conspire with his chief to deceive the public about a matter of fact, but who unhesitatingly was loyal to loyalty, who spoke the truth, who refused to conspire, and who, because his chief was a plausible and powerful man, thus deliberately wrecked his own worldly chances once for all, and retired into a misunderstood obscurity in order that his fellow-men might henceforth be helped to respect the truth better. Now, the worldly career which that friend thus sacrificed for the sake of his loyalty is far from mine; the causes that he has since loyally served have not of late brought him near to me in worldly doings. I am not sure that we should ever have kept our interests in close touch with one

another even if we had lived side by side. For he was and is a highly spe-
cialized type of man, austere, and a little disposed, like many scholars, to a
life apart. For the rest, I have never myself been put in such a place as his
was when he chose to make his sacrifice, and have never had his great
choice set before me. Nor has the world rewarded him at all fairly for his
fidelity. He is, then, as this world goes, not now near to me and not a
widely influential man. Yet I owe him a great debt. He showed me, by
the example of his free sacrifice, a good in loyalty which I might otherwise have been too blind to see. He is a man who does not love flattery.
It would be useless for me now to offer to him either words of praise or
words of comfort. He made his choice with a single heart and a clear
head, and he has always declined to be praised. But it will take a long
time, in some other world, should I meet him in such a realm, to tell him
how much I owe to his example, how much he inspired me, or how
many of his fellows he had indirectly helped to their own loyalty. For I
believe that a good many others besides myself indirectly owe far more
to him than he knows, or than they know. I believe that certain standards of loyalty and of scientific truthfulness in this country are today
higher than they were because of the self-surrendering act of that one
devoted scholar.

Loyalty, then, is contagious. It infects not only the fellow-servant of
your own special cause, but also all who know of this act. Loyalty is a
good that spreads. Live it and you thereby cultivate it in other men. Be
faithful, then, so one may say, to the loyal man; be faithful over your few
things, for the spirit of loyalty, secretly passing from you to many to
whom you are a stranger, may even thereby make you unconsciously
ruler over many things. Loyalty to loyalty is then no unpractical cause.
And you serve it not by becoming a mere citizen of the world, but by
serving your own personal cause. We set before you, then, no unpractical
rule when we repeat our moral formula in this form: Find your own
cause, your interesting, fascinating, personally engrossing cause; serve it
with all your might and soul and strength; but so choose your cause, and
so serve it, that thereby you show forth your loyalty to loyalty, so that
because of your choice and service of your cause, there is a maximum of
increase of loyalty amongst your fellow-men.

VII

Yet herewith we have only begun to indicate how the cause of loyalty
to loyalty may be made a cause that one can practically, efficaciously,

and constantly serve. Loyalty, namely, is not a matter merely of today or of yesterday. The loyal have existed since civilization began. And, even so, loyalty to loyalty is not a novel undertaking. It began to be effective from the time when first people could make and keep a temporary truce during a war, and when first strangers were regarded as protected by the gods, and when first the duties of hospitality were recognized. The way to be loyal to loyalty is therefore laid down in precisely the rational portion of the conventional morality which human experience has worked out.

Herewith we approach a thesis which is central in my whole philosophy of loyalty. I announced that thesis in other words in the opening lecture. My thesis is that *all those duties which we have learned to recognize as the fundamental duties of the civilized man, the duties that every man owes to every man, are to be rightly interpreted as special instances of loyalty to loyalty.* In other words, all the recognized virtues can be defined in terms of our concept of loyalty. And this is why I assert that, when rightly interpreted, loyalty is the whole duty of man.

For consider the best-known facts as to the indirect influence of certain forms of loyal conduct. When I speak the truth, my act is directly an act of loyalty to the personal tie which then and there binds me to the man to whom I consent to speak. My special cause is, in such a case, constituted by this tie. My fellow and I are linked in a certain unity,—the unity of some transaction which involves our speech one to another. To be ready to speak the truth to my fellow is to have, just then, no eye to see and no tongue to speak save as this willingly accepted tie demands. In so far, then, speaking the truth is a special instance of loyalty. But whoever speaks the truth, thereby does what he then can do to help everybody to speak the truth. For he acts so as to further the general confidence of man in man. How far such indirect influence may extend, no man can predict.

Precisely so, in the commercial world, honesty in business is a service, not merely and not mainly to the others who are parties to the single transaction in which at any one time this faithfulness is shown. The single act of business fidelity is an act of loyalty to that general confidence of man in man upon which the whole fabric of business rests. On the contrary, the unfaithful financier whose disloyalty is the final deed that lets loose the avalanche of a panic, has done far more harm to general public confidence than he could possibly do to those whom his act directly assails. Honesty, then, is owed not merely and not even mainly to those with whom we directly deal when we do honest acts; it is owed to mankind at large, and it benefits the community and the general cause of commercial loyalty.

Such a remark is in itself a commonplace; but it serves to make concrete my general thesis that every form of dutiful action is a case of loyalty to loyalty. For what holds thus of truthfulness and of commercial honesty holds, I assert, of every form of dutiful action. Each such form is a special means for being, by a concrete deed, loyal to loyalty.

We have sought for the worthy cause; and we have found it. This simplest possible of considerations serves to turn the chaotic mass of separate precepts of which our ordinary conventional moral code consists into a system unified by the one spirit of universal loyalty. By your individual deed you indeed cannot save the world, but you can at any moment do what in you lies to further the cause which both for you and for the human world constitutes the supreme good, namely, the cause of universal loyalty. Herein consists your entire duty.

Review in the light of this simple consideration, the usually recognized range of human duties. How easily they group themselves about the one principle: *Be loyal to loyalty*.

Have I, for instance, duties to myself? Yes, precisely in so far as I have the duty to be actively loyal at all. For loyalty needs not only a willing, but also an effective servant. My duty to myself is, then, the duty to provide my cause with one who is strong enough and skilful enough to be effective according to my own natural powers. The care of health, self-cultivation, self-control, spiritual power—these are all to be morally estimated with reference to the one principle that, since I have no eyes to see or tongue to speak save as the cause commands, I will be as worthy an instrument of the cause as can be made, by my own efforts, out of the poor material which my scrap of human nature provides. The highest personal cultivation for which I have time is thus required by our principle. But self-cultivation which is not related to loyalty is worthless.

Have I private and personal rights, which I ought to assert? Yes, precisely in so far as my private powers and possessions are held in trust for the cause, and are, upon occasion, to be defended for the sake of the cause. My rights are morally the outcome of my loyalty. It is my right to protect my service, to maintain my office, and to keep my own merely in order that I may use my own as the cause commands. But rights which are not determined by my loyalty are vain pretence.

As to my duties to my neighbors, these are defined by a well-known tradition in terms of two principles, justice and benevolence. These two principles are mere aspects of our one principle. Justice means, in general, fidelity to human ties in so far as they are ties. Justice thus concerns itself with what may be called the mere forms in which loyalty expresses itself. Justice, therefore, is simply one aspect of loyalty—the more formal and abstract side of loyal life. If you are just, you are decisive in your choice of your personal cause, you are faithful to the loyal decision once made, you keep your promise, you speak the truth, you respect the loyal ties of all other men, and you contend with other men only in so far as the defence of your own cause, in the interest of loyalty to the universal cause of loyalty, makes such contest against aggression unavoidable. All these types of activity, within the limits that loyalty determines, are demanded if you are to be loyal to loyalty. Our principle thus at once requires them, and enables us to define their range of application. But justice, without loyalty, is a vicious formalism.

Benevolence, on the other hand, is that aspect of loyalty which directly concerns itself with your influence upon the inner life of human beings who enjoy, who suffer, and whose private good is to be affected by your deeds. Since no personal good that your fellow can possess is superior to his own loyalty, your own loyalty to loyalty is itself a supremely benevolent type of activity. And since your fellow-man is an instrument for the furtherance of the cause of universal loyalty, his welfare also concerns you, in so far as, if you help him to a more efficient life, you make him better able to be loyal. Thus benevolence is an inevitable attendant of loyalty. And the spirit of loyalty to loyalty enables us to define wherein consists a wise benevolence. Benevolence without loyalty is a dangerous sentimentalism. Thus viewed, then, loyalty to universal loyalty is indeed the fulfilment of the whole law.

CONSCIENCE

One of the main purposes of these lectures is to simplify our conceptions of duty and of the good. When I am in a practical perplexity, such as often arises in daily life, that friend can best advise me who helps me to ignore useless complications, to see simply and directly, to look at the central facts of my situation. And even so, when a moralist attempts a rational theory of duty, he ought, like the practical adviser of a friend in perplexity, to do what he can to rid our moral situation of its confusing complications. In these lectures I am trying to accomplish this end by centralizing our duties about the one conception of loyalty.

I

Conventional morality, as it is usually taught to us, consists of a maze of precepts. Some of these precepts we have acquired through the influence of Christianity. Some of them are distinctly unchristian, or even antichristian. Whatever their origin, whether Christian or Greek or barbarian, they lie side by side in our minds; and sometimes they tend to come into conflict with one another. Be just; but also be kind. Be generous; but also be strict in demanding what is your due. Live for others; but be careful of your own dignity, and assert your rights. Love all mankind; but resent insults, and be ready to slay the enemies of your country. Take no thought for the morrow; but be careful to save and to insure. Cultivate yourself; but always sacrifice yourself. Forget yourself; but never be so thoughtless in conduct that others shall justly say, "You have forgotten yourself." Be moderate in all things; but know no moderation in your devotion to righteousness. Such are a few of the well-known paradoxes of our popular morality. And these paradoxes are, for the most part, no mere accidents. Nearly all of these apparently conflicting moral maxims express some significant truth. What we want is a method of finding our way through the maze, a principle that shall unify our moral life, and that shall enable us to solve its paradoxes.

Such a centralizing and unifying principle we tried to propose at the last lecture. Our topic in the foregoing discussion was the question: By what criterion may we know that a proposed cause is one which is worthy of our loyalty? We answered the question by asserting that there is in any case *one* cause which is worthy of every man's loyalty. And that is the cause of loyalty itself. Do what you can to make men loyal, and to keep them in a loyal attitude; this was the sense of the general precept that we derived from our study of the value of loyalty to those who are loyal. Whoever follows this precept inevitably defines for himself a cause, and becomes loyal to that cause. His sovereign and central moral maxim may otherwise be stated thus: *Be loyal to loyalty.*

Our reasons for asserting that this maxim is a sound guide to dutiful action were these: First, the primal fact that loyalty, in any man who possesses it, is his supreme good. Secondly, the further fact that such loyalty is not a good which only a few are able to get,—an aristocratic possession of a small company of saints; but it is, on the contrary, a good which is accessible to all sorts and conditions of men, so far as they have normal human interests and normal self-control. We saw that there is no sort of wholesome human life which does not furnish opportunities for loyalty. And whoever is loyal wins, whatever his social station, and precisely in so far as he is loyal, the same general form of spiritual fulfilment, namely, self-possession through self-surrender. The keeper of a lonely light-house and the leader of a busy social order, the housemaid and the king, have almost equal opportunities to devote the self to its own chosen cause, and to win the good of such devotion. In consequence of these two considerations, whoever undertakes to further the general cause of loyalty, is certainly aiming at the supreme good of mankind at large. His cause, therefore, is certainly a worthy cause.

Nor is the undertaking to further the general cause of loyalty itself an unpractical undertaking,—a vague philanthropy. On the contrary, of all the efforts that you can make on behalf of your fellow-men, the effort to make them loyal to causes of their own is probably the most generally and widely practicable. It is notoriously hard, by any direct philan-thropic effort, to give good fortune to any man, except to some few of those with whose fortunes you are most closely linked. Certain forms of suffering can be relieved by the hospitals, or by private skill and kindness. But when the sufferer is relieved, he stands once more merely on the threshold of life, and the question, What can you do to give him life itself? is not yet answered. If, hereupon, you try to make your fellow-man prosperous, by offering to him unearned good fortune, you may in fact merely teach him to be wasteful and indolent. If you seek to deal out happiness to him by devices of your own, you find that he generally pre-fers to look for happiness in his own way. If you attempt to give him contentment, you come into conflict with his insatiable natural desires.

But if you undertake to make him loyal, there is indeed much that you can do. For, as I pointed out at the close of the last lecture, all of what common sense rightly regards as your ordinary duties to mankind may be viewed, and ought to be viewed, as practically effective ways of help-ing on the cause of general loyalty. Thus, you can speak the truth to your fellow, and can thereby help him to a better confidence in mankind. This confidence in mankind will aid him in turn to speak the truth him-self. And in truth-speaking there will be for him much real peace, for truth-speaking is a form of loyalty and will aid him to be otherwise loyal to his own. Precisely so, there are as many other ways of helping him to be loyal as there are other such obvious and commonly recognized duties to be done in your ordinary and peaceful dealings with him.

Let me mention one further instance that was not used amongst our illustrations at the last meeting: The true value of courtesy in ordinary human intercourse lies in the fact that courtesy is one expression of loyalty to loyalty, and helps every one who either receives or witnesses courtesy to assume himself a loyal attitude towards all the causes that are represented by the peaceful and reasonable dealings of man with man. The forms of courtesy, in fact, are largely derived from what once were, or still are, more or less ceremonious expressions of loyal devotion. Courtesy, then, may be defined as an explicit assumption of a loyal bearing. To adopt such a bearing with a real sincerity of heart is to express, in your passing actions, loyalty to universal loyalty. To act thus towards your individual fellow-man is then and there to help all who know of your act to be loyal. Courtesy, then, is a duty owed not so much to the individual to whom you are courteous, as to humanity at large.

There are, then, many ways of aiding your fellow-man to be loyal. Now, as we also set forth at the last lecture, one of the most effective of these ways lies in being loyal yourself to some personally chosen and determinate social cause which constitutes your business. This special cause need not be one in which the particular fellow-man whom you are just now to help is, at the moment, directly interested. Your very loyalty to your own cause will tend to prove infectious. Whoever is loyal to his own therefore helps on the cause of universal loyalty by his every act of devotion, precisely in so far as he refrains from any hostile attack upon the loyalty of other people, and simply lets his example of loyalty work. Whoever makes the furtherance of universal loyalty his cause, lacks, therefore, neither practical means nor present opportunity for serving his cause.

To each man our principle therefore says: *Live in your own way a loyal life and one subject to the general principle of loyalty to loyalty.* Serve your own cause, but so choose it and so serve it that in consequence of your life loyalty amongst men shall prosper. Fortune may indeed make the range of your choice of your calling very narrow. Necessity may bind you to an irksome round of tasks. But sweeten these with whatever loyalty you can consistently get into your life. Let loyalty be your pearl of great price. Sell all the happiness that you possess or can get in disloyal or in non-loyal activities, and buy that pearl. When you once have found, or begun to find, your personal cause, be as steadily faithful to it as loyalty to loyalty henceforth permits. That is, if you find that a cause once chosen does indeed involve disloyalty to loyalty, as one might find who, having sworn fidelity to a leader, afterwards discovered his

leader to be a traitor to the cause of mankind, you may have altogether
to abandon the cause first chosen. But never abandon a cause except for
the sake of some higher or deeper loyalty such as actually requires the
change.

Meanwhile, the principle of loyalty to loyalty obviously requires you
to respect loyalty in all men, wherever you find it. If your fellow's cause
has, in a given case, assailed your own, and if, in the world as it is, conflict
is inevitable, you may then have to war with your fellow's cause, in order
to be loyal to your own. But even then, you may never assail whatever is
sincere and genuine about his spirit of loyalty. Even if your fellow's
cause involves disloyalty to mankind at large, you may not condemn the
loyalty of your fellow in so far as it is loyalty. You may condemn only his
blindly chosen cause. All the loyal are brethren. They are children of
one spirit. Loyalty to loyalty involves the active furtherance of this spirit
wherever it appears. Fair play in sport, chivalrous respect for the adversary in war, tolerance of the sincere beliefs of other men,—all these virtues are thus to be viewed as mere variations of loyalty to loyalty. Prevent the conflict of loyalties when you can, minimize such conflict where
it exists, and, by means of fair play and of the chivalrous attitude towards
the opponent, utilize even conflict, where it is inevitable, so as to further
the cause of loyalty to loyalty. Such maxims are obvious consequences
of our principle. Do we not gain, then, a great deal from our principle in
the way of unifying our moral code?

II

But next, as to those just-mentioned paradoxes of popular morality, do
we not gain from our principle a guide to help us through the maze? "Be
just; but also be kind." These two precepts, so far as they are sound,
merely emphasize, as we pointed out at the close of our last lecture, two
distinct but inseparable aspects of loyalty. My cause links my fellow and
myself by social ties which, in the light of our usual human interpretation
of life, appear to stand for super-personal interests,—for interests in property rights, in formal obligations, in promises, in various abstractly definable relations. If I am loyal, I respect these relations. And I do so since,
from the very definition of a cause to which one can be loyal, this cause
will become nothing unless these ties are preserved intact. But to respect
relations as such is to be what men call just. Meanwhile, our common
cause also personally interests both my fellow and myself. So far as we

both know the cause, we love it, and delight in it. Hence in being loyal to our cause, I am also being kind to my fellow. For hereby I further his delight in just so far as I help him to insight. But kindness which is not bound up with loyalty is as a sounding brass and as a tinkling cymbal, a mere sentimentalism. And abstract justice, apart from loyalty, is a cruel formalism. My fellow wants to be loyal. This is his deepest need. If I am loyal to that need, I therefore truly delight him. But kindness that is not bound up with loyalty may indeed amuse my fellow for a moment. Yet like "fancy," such kindness "dies in the cradle where it lies." Even so, if I am loyal, I am also just. But justice that is no aspect of loyalty has no reason for existence. The true relations of benevolence and justice can therefore be best defined in terms of our conception of loyalty. If any one says, "I will show thee my justice or my kindness without my loyalty," the loyal man may rightly respond, "I will show thee my kindness and my justice by my loyalty."

In a similar fashion, the moral problems regarding the right relations of strictness to generosity, of prudent foresight to present confidence, of self-surrender to self-assertion, of love to the righteous resistance of enemies,—all these moral problems, I say, are best to be solved in terms of the principle of loyalty to loyalty. As to the problem of the true concern and regard for the self, the loyal man cultivates himself, and is careful of his property rights, just in order to furnish to his cause an effective instrument; but he aims to forget precisely so much of himself as is, at any time, an obstruction to his loyalty; and he also aims to be careless of whatever about his private fortunes may be of no importance to his service of the cause. When he asserts himself, he does so because he has neither eyes to see nor tongue to speak save as his cause commands; and it is of precisely such self-sacrificing self-assertion that the foes of his cause would do well to beware. All the paradoxes about the care of self and the abandonment of self are thus soluble in terms of loyalty. Whoever knows and possesses the loyal attitude, *ipso facto* solves these paradoxes in each special case as it arises. And whoever comprehends the nature of loyalty to loyalty, as it is expressed in the form of fair play in sport, of chivalry in war, of tolerance in belief, and of the spirit that seeks to prevent the conflict of loyalties where such prevention is possible,—whoever, I say, thus comprehends what loyalty to loyalty means, holds the key to all the familiar mysteries about the right relation of the love of man to the strenuous virtues, and to the ethics of conflict.

III

As you see, it is my deliberate intention to maintain that the principle of loyalty to loyalty is a sufficient expression of what common sense calls "the dictates of conscience." When I state this thesis, it leads me, however, to a somewhat new question, which the title of this lecture is intended to emphasize.

Stated practically, this our next question takes the form of asking: Is the principle of loyalty to loyalty not only a means of solving certain perplexities, but an actually general, safe, and sufficient test of what is right and wrong in the doubtful moral situations which may arise in daily life? We have shown that the well-recognized duties and virtues, such as those which have to do with truth-speaking, with courtesy, with fair play in sport, and with chivalrous regard for enemies, can indeed be regarded, if we choose, as special forms of loyalty to loyalty. But it is indeed one thing (as you may now interpose) to interpret in terms of our principle, certain virtues or duties that we already recognize. It is another thing to use the concept of loyalty to loyalty as an universal means of finding out what it is right to do when one is otherwise in doubt. Is our principle always a serviceable practical guide? Or, to use the well-known term, does our principle adequately express what people usually mean by the "dictates of conscience"?

The word "conscience," which here becomes important for our philosophy of loyalty, is a term of many uses. The problem as to the true nature of the human conscience is a complicated and difficult one. I shall here deal with the matter only in so far as is necessary for our own distinctly practical purpose. In expounding my precept, *Be loyal to loyalty*, I have set forth what does indeed pretend to be a general guiding maxim for conduct. But most of us, when we say, "My conscience dictates this or this sort of conduct," are not disposed to think of conscience as definable in terms of any one maxim. Our conscience seems to us to represent, in our ordinary lives, a good many related but nevertheless distinct motives, such as prudence, charity, reasonableness, piety, and so on. Conscience also seems to us somewhat mysterious in many of its demands, so that we often say, "I do not precisely know why this or this is right; but I feel sure that it is right, for my conscience tells me so." Since, then, conscience seems so complex and sometimes so mysterious a power, you may naturally hesitate to accept the views of a moralist who attempts, as you may think, to simplify too much the requirements of conscience. You may still insist that the moral doctrine which I have so far set forth is in one respect like all other philosophies of conduct that fill the history of ethical thought; because, as you may insist, this theory is powerless to tell any one what to do when a really perplexing case of conscience arises.

The reproach that moral philosophers have fine-sounding principles to report, but can never tell us how these principles practically apply, except when the cases are such as common sense has already decided,— this is an old objection to philosophical ethics. I want to show you how I myself meet that objection, and in what way, and to what extent, as I think, the principle of loyalty to loyalty does express the true dictates of conscience, and does tell us what to do in doubtful cases.

What is conscience? You will all agree that the word names a mental possession of ours which enables us to pass some sort of judgment, correct or mistaken, upon moral questions as they arise. My conscience, then, belongs to my mental equipment, and tells me about right and wrong conduct. Moreover, my conscience approves or disapproves my conduct, excuses me or accuses me. About the general nature and office of the conscience we all of us, as I suppose, so far agree. Our differences regarding our conscience begin when questions arise of the following sort: Is our conscience inborn? Is it acquired by training? Are its dictates the same in all men? Is it God-given? Is it infallible? Is it a separate power of the mind? Or is it simply a name for a collection of habits of moral judgment which we have acquired through social training, through reasoning, and through personal experience of the consequences of conduct?

IV

In trying to meet these questions so far as they here concern us, it is important next to note a few fundamental features which characterize the personal life of all of us. The first of these features appears if one, instead of stopping with the question, "What is my conscience?" goes deeper still and asks the question, "Who and what am I?" This latter question also has indeed countless aspects, and a complete answer to it would constitute an entire system of metaphysics. But for our present purpose it is enough to note that I cannot answer the question, "Who am I?" except in terms of some sort of statement of the plans and purposes of my life. In responding to the question, "Who are you?" a man may first mention his name. But his name is a mere tag. He then often goes on to tell where he lives, and where he comes from. His home and his birthplace, however, are already what one may call purposeful aspects of his

personality. For dwelling-place, country, birthplace, and similar incidental facts about a man tend to throw light upon his personality mainly because they are of importance for a further knowledge of his social relations, and so of his social uses and activities.

But the answer to the question, "Who are you?" really begins in earnest when a man mentions his calling, and so actually sets out upon the
definition of his purposes and of the way in which these purposes get
expressed in his life. And when a man goes on to say, "I am the doer of
these and these deeds, the friend of these friends, the enemy of these opposing purposes, the member of this family, the one whose ideals are
such and such, and are so and so expressed in my life," the man expresses
to you at length whatever is most expressible and worth knowing in
answer to the question, "Who are you?"

To sum up, then, I should say that a person, an individual self, may be
defined as a human life lived according to a plan. If a man could live with
no plan at all, purposelessly and quite passively, he would in so far be an
organism, and also, if you choose, he would be a psychological specimen,
but he would be no personality. Wherever there is personality, there are
purposes worked out in life. If, as often happens, there are many purposes connected with the life of this human creature, many plans in this
life, but no discoverable unity and coherence of these plans, then in so
far there are many glimpses of selfhood, many fragmentary selves present in connection with the life of some human organism. But there is so
far no one self, no one person discoverable. You are one self just so far as
the life that goes on in connection with your organism has some one
purpose running through it. By the terms "this person" and "this self,"
then, we mean this human life in so far as it expresses some one purpose.
Yet, of course, this one purpose which is expressed in the life of a single
self need not be one which is defined by this self in abstract terms. On
the contrary, most of us are aware that our lives are unified, after a fashion, by the very effort that we more or less vaguely make to assert ourselves somehow as individuals in our world. Many of us have not yet
found out how it would be best to assert ourselves. But we are trying to
find out. This very effort to find out gives already a certain unity of
purpose to our lives.

But in so far as we have indeed found out some cause, far larger than
our individual selves, to which we are fully ready to be loyal, this very
cause serves to give the required unity to our lives, and so to determine
what manner of self each of us is, even though we chance to be unable to

define in abstract terms what is the precise nature of this very cause. Loyalty may be sometimes almost dumb; it is so in many of those obscure and humble models of loyalty of whom I have already spoken. They express their loyalty clearly enough in deeds. They often could not very well formulate it in words. They could not give an abstract account of their business. Yet their loyalty gives them a business. It unifies their activities. It makes of each of these loyal beings an individual self,—a life unified by a purpose. This purpose may in such cases come to consciousness merely as a willing hunger to serve the cause, a proud obedience to the ideal call. But in any case, wherever loyalty is, there is selfhood, personality, individual purpose embodied in a life.

And now, further, if the argument of our first and second lectures is right, wherever a human selfhood gets practically and consciously unified, there is some form of loyalty. For, except in terms of some sort of loyal purpose, as we saw, this mass of instincts, of passions, of social interests, and of private rebelliousness, whereof the nature of any one of us is originally compounded, can never get any effective unity whatever.

To sum up so far,—a self is a life in so far as it is unified by a single purpose. Our loyalties furnish such purposes, and hence make of us conscious and unified moral persons. Where loyalty has not yet come to any sort of definiteness, there is so far present only a kind of inarticulate striving to be an individual self. This very search for one's true self is already a sort of life-purpose, which, as far as it goes, individuates the life of the person in question, and gives him a task. But loyalty brings the individual to full moral self-consciousness. It is devoting the self to a cause that, after all, first makes it a rational and unified self, instead of what the life of too many a man remains,—namely, a cauldron of seething and bubbling efforts to be somebody, a cauldron which boils dry when life ends.

V

But what, you may now ask, has all this view of the self to do with conscience? I answer that the nature of conscience can be understood solely in terms of such a theory of the self as the one just sketched.

Suppose that I am, in the foregoing sense, a more or less completely unified and loyal self. Then there are two aspects of this selfhood which is mine. I live a life; and I have, as a loyal being, an ideal. The life itself is not the ideal. They are and always remain in some sense distinct. For no one act of my life, and no limited set of acts of mine, can ever completely embody my ideal. My ideal comes to me from my cause, as the ideal of the Speaker of the House of Commons, in the story that we have already used to illustrate loyalty, came to him from the House. My cause, however, is greater than my individual life. Hence it always sets before me an ideal which demands more of me than I have yet done,—more, too, than I can ever at any one instant accomplish. Even because of this vastness of my ideal, even because that to which I am loyal is so much greater than I ever become, even because of all this can my ideal unify my life, and make a rational self of me.

Hence, if I am indeed one self, my one ideal is always something that stands over against my actual life; and each act of this life has to be judged, estimated, determined, as to its moral value, in terms of the ideal. My cause, therefore, as it expresses itself to my own consciousness through my personal ideal,—my cause and my ideal taken together, and viewed as one, perform the precise function which tradition has attributed to conscience. My cause, then, for our philosophy of loyalty, *is* my conscience,—my cause as interpreted through my ideal of my personal life. When I look to my cause, it furnishes me with a conscience; for it sets before me a plan or ideal of life, and then constantly bids me contrast this plan, this ideal, with my transient and momentary impulses.

To illustrate: Were I a loyal judge on the bench, whose cause was my official function, then my judicial conscience would be simply my whole ideal as a judge, when this ideal was contrasted with any of my present and narrower views of the situation directly before me. If, at a given moment, I tended to lay unfair stress upon one side of a controversy that had been brought into my court, my ideal would say: But a judge is impartial. If I were disposed to decide with inadvised haste, the ideal would say: But a judge takes account of the whole law bearing on the case. If I were offered bribes, my judicial conscience would reject them as being once for all ideally intolerable. In order to have such a judicial conscience, I should, of course, have to be able to view my profession as the carrying out of some one purpose, and so as one cause. This purpose I should have learned, of course, from the traditions of the office. But I should have had willingly to adopt these traditions as my own, and to conceive my own life in terms of them, in order to have a judicial conscience of my own. Analogous comments could be made upon the conscience of an artist, of a statesman, of a friend, or of a devoted member of a family, of any one who has a conscience. To have a conscience, then, is to have a cause, to unify your life by means of an ideal determined by this cause, and to compare the ideal and the life.

If this analysis is right, your conscience is simply that ideal of life which constitutes your moral personality. In having your conscience you become aware of your plan of being yourself and nobody else. Your conscience presents to you this plan, however, in so far as the plan or ideal in question is distinct from the life in which you are trying to embody your plan. Your life as it is lived, your experiences, feelings, deeds,—these are the embodiment of your ideal plan, in so far as your ideal plan for your own individual life as this self, gets embodied at all.

But no one act of yours ever expresses your plan of life perfectly. Since you thus always have your cause beyond you, there is always more to do. So the plan or ideal of life comes to stand over against your actual life as a general authority by which each deed is to be tested, just as the judicial conscience of the judge on the bench tests each of his official acts by comparing it with his personal ideal of what a judge should be. My conscience, therefore, is the very ideal that makes me this rational self, the very cause that inspires and that unifies me. Viewed as something within myself, my conscience is the spirit of the self, first moving on the face of the waters of natural desire, and then gradually creating the heavens and the earth of this life of the individual man. This spirit informs all of my true self, yet is nowhere fully expressed in any deed. So that, in so far as we contrast the ideal with the single deed, we judge ourselves, condemn ourselves, or approve ourselves.

Our philosophy of loyalty thus furnishes us with a theory of a certain kind of consciousness which, in any case, precisely fulfils the functions of the traditional conscience. I need hardly say that the conscience which I have now described is not in its entirety at all innate. On the contrary, it is the flower rather than the root of the moral life. But unquestionably we should never get it unless we possessed an innate power to become reasonable, unless we were socially disposed beings, unless we were able so to develop our reason and our social powers as to see that the good of mankind is indeed also our own good, and, in brief, unless we inherited a genuine moral nature.

With this view of the nature of conscience, what can we say as to the infallibility of such a conscience? I answer: My conscience is precisely as fallible or as infallible as my choice of a cause is subject to error, or is of such nature as to lead me aright. Since loyalty, in so far as it is loyalty, is always a good, the conscience of any loyal self is never wholly a false guide. Since loyalty may be in many respects blind, one's conscience also may be in many respects misleading. On the other hand, your conscience, at any stage of its development, is unquestionably the best moral guide that you then have, simply because, so far as it is viewed as an authority outside of you, it is your ideal, your cause, set before you; while, in so far as it is within you, it is the spirit of your own self, the very ideal that makes you any rational moral person whatever. Apart from it you are a mere pretence of moral personality, a manifold fermentation of desires. And as you have only your own life to live, your conscience alone can teach you how to live that life. But your conscience will doubtless grow with you, just as your loyalty and your cause will grow. The best way to make both of them grow is to render up your life to their service and to their expression.

Conscience, as thus defined, is for each of us a personal affair. In so far as many of us are fellow-servants of the same cause, and, above all, in so far as all of us, if we are enlightened, are fellow-servants of the one cause of universal loyalty, we do indeed share in the same conscience. But in so far as no two of us can live the same life, or be the same individual human self, it follows that no two of us can possess identical consciences, and that no two of us should wish to do so. Your conscience is not mine; yet I share with you the same infinite realm of moral truth, and we are subject to the same requirement of loyalty to loyalty. This requirement must interpret itself to us all in endlessly varied ways. The loyal are not all monotonously doing the same thing. Yet they individually partake of the one endlessly varied and manifold spirit of loyalty.

As to whether conscience is in any sense divine, we shall learn something in our closing lecture upon the relations of Loyalty and Religion.

VI

So far as is needful for our present practical purpose, the theory of the conscience which our philosophy of loyalty requires is now before you. We needed this theory in order to prepare the way for answering the question: In how far does the law, *Be loyal to loyalty*, enable us to decide cases of moral doubt? In how far does this principle furnish a means of discovering these special precepts about single cases which common sense calls the "dictates of conscience"?

How do moral doubts arise in the mind of a loyal person? I answer: Moral doubts arise in the loyal mind when there is an apparent conflict between loyalties. As a fact, that cause, which in any sense unifies a life as complex as my human life is, must of course be no perfectly simple cause. By virtue of my nature and of my social training, I belong to a family, to a community, to a calling, to a state, to humanity. In order to be loyal to loyalty, and in order to be a person at all, I must indeed unify my loyalty. In the meantime, however, I must also choose special causes to serve; and if these causes are to interest me, if they are to engross and to possess me, they must be such as together appeal to many diverse sides of my nature; they must involve me in numerous and often conflicting social tasks; they can form one cause only in so far as they constitute an entire system of causes. My loyalty will be subject, therefore, to the ancient difficulty regarding the one and the many. Unless it is one in its ultimate aim, it will be no loyalty to universal loyalty; unless it is just to the varied instincts and to the manifold social interests of a being such as I am, it cannot engross me.

Despite this great difficulty, however, the loyal all about us show us that this union of one and many in life is, at least in great portions of long human careers, a possible thing. We never completely win the union; we never realize to the full the one loyal life; but in so far as we are loyal, we win enough of this unity of life to be able to understand the ideal, and to make it our own guide. Our question still remains, however, this: Since the only loyal life that we can undertake to live is so complex, since the one cause of universal loyalty can only be served, by each of us, in a personal life wherein we have to try to unify various special loyalties, and since, in many cases, these special loyalties seem to us to conflict with one another,—how shall we decide, as between two apparently conflicting loyalties, which one to follow? Does our principle tell us what to do when loyalties thus seem to us to be in conflict with one another?

It is, of course, not sufficient to answer here that loyalty to loyalty requires us to do whatever can be done to harmonize apparently conflicting loyalties, and to remove the conflict of loyalties from the world, and to utilize even conflict, where it is inevitable, so as to further general loyalty. That answer we have already considered in an earlier passage of this discussion. It is a sound answer; but it does not meet those cases where conflict is forced upon us, and where we ourselves must take sides, and must annul or destroy one of two conflicting loyalties. One or two illustrations of such a type will serve to show what sorts of moral doubts our own philosophy of loyalty has especially to consider.

At the outset of our Civil War, many men of the border states, and many who had already been in the service of the Union, but who were conscious of special personal duties to single states of the Union, found themselves in presence of a well-known conflict of loyalties. Consider the personal problem that the future General Lee had to solve. Could the precept, *Be loyal to loyalty, and to that end, choose your own personal cause and be loyal thereto,*—could this principle, you may say, have been of any service in deciding for Lee his personal problem at the critical moment?

Or again, to take a problem such as some of my own students have more than once urged, in various instances, as a test case for my theory of loyalty to decide: A young woman, after a thorough modern professional training, begins a career which promises not only worldly success, but general good to the community in which she works. She is heartily loyal to her profession. It is a beneficent profession. She will probably make her mark in that field if she chooses to go on. Meanwhile she is loyal to her own family. And into the home, which she has left for her work, disease, perhaps death, enters. Her younger brothers and sisters are now unexpectedly in need of such care as hers; or the young family of her elder brother or sister, through the death of their father or mother, has come to be without due parental care. As elder sister or as maiden aunt this young woman could henceforth devote herself to family tasks that would mean very much for the little ones in question. But this devotion would also mean years of complete absorption in these family tasks, and would also mean an entire abandonment of the profession so hopefully begun, and of all the good that she can now be fairly sure of doing if she continues in that field.

What are the dictates of conscience? How shall this young woman solve her problem? How shall she decide between these conflicting loyalties? To be loyal to the family, to the needs of brothers, sisters, nephews, nieces,—surely this is indeed devotion of a self to a cause. But to be loyal to her chosen profession, which, in this case, is no mere hope, but which is already an actual and successful task,—is not that also loyalty to a cause? And does the principle, *Be loyal to loyalty*, decide which of these two causes is the one for this young woman to serve?

These two cases of conscience may serve as example of the vast range of instances of a conflict of loyalties. And now you may ask: What will our principle do to decide such cases?

VII

I reply at once by emphasizing the fact that the precept, *Be loyal to loyalty*, implies two characteristics of loyal conduct which are, to my mind, inseparable. The first characteristic is Decisiveness on the part of the loyal moral agent. The second characteristic is Fidelity to loyal decisions once made, in so far as later insight does not clearly forbid the continuance of such fidelity. Let me indicate what I mean by these two characteristics.

Loyalty to loyalty is never a merely pious wish. It is personal devotion. This devotion shows itself by action, not by mere sentiments. Loyalty to loyalty hence requires the choice of some definite mode of action. And this mode of action involves, in critical cases, some new choice of a personal cause, through which the loyal agent undertakes to serve henceforth, as best he can, the general cause of the loyalty of mankind. Now, my special choice of my personal cause is always fallible. For I can never know with certainty but that, if I were wiser, I should better see my way to serving universal loyalty than I now see it. Thus, if I choose to be loyal to loyalty by becoming a loyal clerk or a watchman or a lighthouse keeper, I can never know but that, in some other calling, I might have done better. Now, it is no part of the precept, *Be loyal to loyalty*, to tell me, or to pretend to tell me, what my most effective vocation is. Doubts about that topic are in so far not moral doubts. They are mere expressions of my general ignorance of the world and of my powers. If I indeed happen to know that I have no power to make a good clerk or a good watchman, the precept about loyalty then tells me that it would be disloyal to waste my powers in an undertaking for which I am so unfit. If, of various possible ways of undertaking to be loyal to loyalty, my present insight already tells me that one will, in my case, certainly succeed best of all, then, indeed, the general principle of loyalty requires me to have neither eyes to see nor tongue to speak save as this best mode of service commands. But if, at the critical moment, I cannot predict which of two modes of serving the cause of loyalty to loyalty will lead to the more complete success in such service, the general principle certainly cannot tell me which of these two modes of service to choose.

And, nevertheless, the principle does not desert me, even at the moment of my greatest ignorance. It is still my guide. For it now becomes the principle, *Have a cause; choose your cause; be decisive.* In this form the principle is just as practical as it would be if my knowledge of the world and of my own powers were infallible. For it forbids cowardice; it forbids hesitancy beyond the point where further consideration can be reasonably expected, for the present, to throw new light on the situation. It forbids me to play Hamlet's part. It requires me, in a loyal spirit and in the light of all that I now know, to choose and to proceed to action, not as one who believes himself omniscient, but as one who knows that the only way to be loyal is to act loyally, however ignorantly one has to act.

Otherwise stated, the case is this. I hesitate at the critical moment between conflicting causes. For the sake of loyalty to loyalty, which one of two conflicting special causes shall I henceforth undertake to serve? This is my question. If I knew what is to be the outcome, I could at once easily choose. I am ignorant of the outcome. In so far I indeed cannot tell which to choose. But in one respect I am, nevertheless, already committed. I have already undertaken to be loyal to loyalty. In so far, then, I already have my cause. If so, however, I have neither eyes to see nor tongue to speak save as this my highest cause commands. Now, what does this my highest cause, loyalty to loyalty, command? It commands simply but imperatively that, since I must serve, and since, at this critical moment, my only service must take the form of a choice between loyalties, I shall choose, even in my ignorance, what form my service is henceforth to take. The point where I am to make this choice is determined by the obvious fact that, after a certain waiting to find out whatever I can find out, I always reach the moment when further indecision would of itself constitute a sort of decision,—a decision, namely, to do nothing, and so not to serve at all. Such a decision to do nothing, my loyalty to loyalty forbids; and therefore my principle clearly says to me after a fair consideration of the case: *Decide, knowingly if you can, ignorantly if you must, but in any case decide, and have no fear.*

The duty of decisiveness as to one's loyalty is thus founded upon considerations analogous to those which Professor James has emphasized, in speaking of certain problems about belief in his justly famous essay on the Will to Believe. *As soon as further indecision would itself practically amount to a decision to do nothing,*—and so would mean a failure to be loyal to loyalty,—*then at once decide.* This is the only right act. If you cannot decide knowingly, put your own personal will into the matter, and thereupon decide ignorantly. For ignorant service, which still knows itself as a willing attempt to serve the cause of universal loyalty, is better than a knowing refusal to undertake any service whatever. The duty to decide is, in such cases, just that upon which our principle insists.

Decision, however, is meaningless unless it is to be followed up by persistently active loyalty. Having surrendered the self to the chosen special cause, loyalty, precisely as loyalty to loyalty, forbids you to destroy the unity of your own purposes, and to set the model of disloyalty before your fellows, by turning back from the cause once chosen, unless indeed later growth in knowledge makes manifest that further service of that special cause would henceforth involve unquestionable disloyalty to universal loyalty. Fidelity to the cause once chosen is as obvious an aspect of a thorough devotion of the self to the cause of universal loyalty, as is decisiveness.

Only a growth in knowledge which makes it evident that the special cause once chosen is an unworthy cause, disloyal to universal loyalty,— only such a growth in knowledge can absolve from fidelity to the cause once chosen. In brief, the choice of a special personal cause is a sort of ethical marriage to this cause, with the exception that the duty to choose some personal cause is a duty for everybody, while marriage is not everybody's duty. The marriage to your cause is not to be dissolved unless it becomes unquestionably evident that the continuance of this marriage involves positive unfaithfulness to the cause of universal loyalty. But like any other marriage, the marriage of each self to its chosen personal cause is made in ignorance of the consequences. Decide, then, in the critical case, and, "forsaking all others, cleave to your own cause." Thus only can you be loyal to loyalty.

If you once view the matter in this way, you will not suppose that our principle would leave either the future General Lee or our supposed young professional woman without guidance. It would say: Look first at the whole situation. Consider it carefully. See, if possible, whether you can predict the consequences to the general loyalty which your act will involve. If, after such consideration, you still remain ignorant of decisive facts, then look to your highest loyalty; look steadfastly at the cause of universal loyalty itself. Remember how the loyal have always borne themselves. Then, with your eyes and your voice put as completely as may be at your service of that cause, arouse all the loyal interests of your own self, just as they now are, to their fullest vigor; and hereupon firmly and freely decide. Henceforth, with all your mind and soul and strength belong, fearlessly and faithfully, to the chosen personal cause until the issue is decided, or until you positively know that this cause can no longer be served without disloyalty. So act, and you are morally right.

Now, that is how Lee acted. And that, too, is how all the loyal of our own Northern armies acted. And today we know how there was indeed loyalty to loyalty upon both sides, and how all those thus loyal actually served the one cause of the now united nation. They loyally shed their blood, North and South, that we might be free from their burden of hatred and of horror. Precisely so should the young woman of our ideal instance choose. It is utterly vain for another to tell her which she ought to choose,—her profession or her family. But it would be equally vain, and an insult to loyalty, lightly to say to her: Do as you please. One can say to her: Either of these lives,—the life of the successful servant of a profession, or the life of the devoted sister or aunt,—either, if loyally lived, is indeed a whole life. Nobody ought to ask for a more blessed lot than is either of these lives,—however obscure the household drudgery of the one may be, however hard beset by cares the worldly success of the other may prove, or however toilsome either of them in prospect is, so long as either is faithfully lived out in full devotion. For nobody has anything better than loyalty, or can get anything better. But one of them alone can you live. No mortal knows which is the better for your world. With all your heart, in the name of universal loyalty, choose. And then be faithful to the choice. So shall it be morally well with you.

Now, if this view of the application of our precept is right, you see how our principle is just to that mysterious and personal aspect of conscience upon which common sense insists. Such a loyal choice as I have described demands, of course, one's will,—one's conscious decisiveness. It also calls out all of one's personal and more or less unconsciously present instincts, interests, affections, one's socially formed habits, and whatever else is woven into the unity of each individual self. Loyalty, as we have all along seen, is a willing devotion. Since it is willing, it involves conscious choice. Since it is devotion, it involves all the mystery of finding out that some cause awakens us, fascinates us, reverberates through our whole being, possesses us. It is a fact that critical decisions as to the direction of our loyalty can be determined by our own choice. It is also a fact that loyalty involves more than mere conscious choice. It involves that response of our entire nature, conscious and unconscious, which makes loyalty so precious. Now, this response of the whole nature of the self, when the result is a moral decision, is what common sense has in mind when it views our moral decisions as due to our conscience, but our conscience as a mysterious higher or deeper self.

As a fact, the conscience is the ideal of the self, coming to consciousness as a present command. It says, *Be loyal*. If one asks, *Loyal to what?*

the conscience, awakened by our whole personal response to the need of mankind replies, *Be loyal to loyalty*. If, hereupon, various loyalties seem to conflict, the conscience says: *Decide*. If one asks, *How decide?* conscience further urges, *Decide as I, your conscience, the ideal expression of your whole personal nature, conscious and unconscious, find best*. If one persists, *But you and I may be wrong*, the last word of conscience is, *We are fallible, but we can be decisive and faithful; and this is loyalty*.

SOME AMERICAN PROBLEMS IN THEIR RELATION TO LOYALTY

In the philosophy of loyalty, whose general statement has been contained in the foregoing lectures, I have made an effort to reconcile the conception of loyalty with that of a rational and moral individualism. To every ethical individualist I have said: In loyalty alone is the fulfilment of the reasonable purposes of your individualism. If you want true freedom, seek it in loyalty. If you want self-expression, spirituality, moral autonomy, loyalty alone can give you these goods. But equally I have insisted upon interpreting loyalty in terms that emphasize the significance of the individual choice of that personal cause to which one is to be loyal. This evening, as I approach the application of our philosophy of loyalty to some well-known American problems, it is important for us to bear in mind from the outset this synthesis of individualism and loyalty which constitutes our whole ethical doctrine.

I

The traditional view of loyalty has associated the term, in the minds of most of you, with moral situations in which some external social power predetermines for the individual, without his consent, all the causes to which he ought to be loyal. Loyalty so conceived appears to be opposed to individual liberty. But in our philosophy of loyalty there is only one cause which is rationally and absolutely determined for the individual as the right cause for him as for everybody,—this is the general cause defined by the phrase *loyalty to loyalty*. The way in which any one man is to show his loyalty to loyalty is, however, in our philosophy of loyalty, something which varies endlessly with the individual, and which can never be precisely defined except by and through his personal consent. I can be loyal to loyalty only in my own fashion, and by serving my own special personal system of causes. How wide a range of moral freedom of conscience this fact gives me, we began at the last time to see. In order to make that fact still clearer, let me sum up our moral code afresh, and in another order than the one used at the last time.

As our philosophy of loyalty states the case, the moral law is: (1) be loyal; (2) to that end have a special cause or a system of causes which shall constitute your personal object of loyalty, your business in life; (3) choose this cause, in the first place, for yourself, but decisively, and so far as the general principle of loyalty permits, remain faithful to this chosen cause, until the work that you can do for it is done; and (4) the general principle of loyalty to which all special choices of one's cause are subject, is the principle: Be loyal to loyalty, that is, do what you can to produce a maximum of the devoted service of causes, a maximum of fidelity, and of selves that choose and serve fitting objects of loyalty.

From the point of view of this statement of the moral law, we are all in the wrong in case we have no cause whatever to which we are loyal. If you are an individualist in the sense that you are loyal to nothing, you are certainly false to your duty. Furthermore, in order that you should be loyal at all, the cause to which you are loyal must involve the union of various persons by means of some social tie, which has in some respects an impersonal or superindividual character, as well as a distinct personal interest for each of the persons concerned.

On the other hand, my statement of the moral principle gives to us all an extremely limited right to judge what the causes are to which any one of our neighbors ought to devote himself. Having defined loyalty as I have done as a devotion to a cause, outside the private self, and yet chosen by this individual self as his cause; having pointed out the general nature which such a cause must possess in order to be worthy,—namely, having shown that it must involve the mentioned union of personal and impersonal interests; having, furthermore, asserted that all rightly chosen loyalty is guided by the intent not to enter into any unnecessary destruction of the loyalty of others, but is inspired by loyalty to loyalty, and so seeks, as best the loyal individual can, to further loyalty as a common good for all mankind,—having said so much, I must, from my point of view, leave to the individual the decision as to the choice of the cause or causes to which he is loyal, subject only to these mentioned conditions. I have very little right to judge, except by the most unmistakable expression of my fellow's purpose, whether he is actually loyal, in the sense of my definition, or not.

I may say of a given person that I do not understand to what cause he is loyal. But I can assert that he is disloyal only when I know what cause it is to which he has committed himself, and what it is that he has done to be false to his chosen fidelity. Or again, I can judge that he lacks loyalty if he makes it perfectly evident by his acts or by his own confessions that he has chosen no cause at all. If he is unquestionably loyal to something, to his country or to his profession or to his family, I may criticise his expression of loyalty, in so far as I clearly see that it involves him in unnecessary assault upon the loyalty of others, or upon their means to be loyal. Thus, all unnecessary personal aggression upon what we commonly call the rights of other individuals are excluded by my formula, simply because in case I deprive my fellow of his property, his life, or his physical integrity, I take away from him the only means whereby he can express in a practical way whatever loyalty he has. Hence such aggression, unless necessary, involves disloyalty to the general loyalty of mankind, is a crime against humanity at large, and is inconsistent with any form of loyalty. Such is the range of judgment that we have a right to use in our moral estimates of other people. The range thus indicated is, as I have insisted, large enough to enable us to define all rationally defensible special principles regarding right and wrong acts. Murder, lying, evil speaking, unkindness, are from this point of view simply forms of disloyalty.

But my right to judge the choices of my fellow is thus very sharply limited. I cannot say that he is disloyal because his personal cause is not my cause, or because I have no sympathy with the objects to which he devotes himself. I have no right to call him disloyal because I should find that if I were to do what he does, I should indeed be disloyal to causes that I accept. I may not judge a man to be without an object of loyalty merely because I do not understand what the object is with which he busies himself. I may regard his cause as too narrow, if I clearly see that he could do better service than he does to the cause of universal loyalty. But when I observe how much even the plainest and humblest of the loyal sometimes unconsciously do to help others to profit by the contagion of their own loyalty, by the example of their faithfulness, I must be cautious about judging another man's cause to be too narrow. You cannot easily set limits to the occupations that the sincere choice of somebody will make expressions of genuine loyalty. The loyal individual may live largely alone; or mainly in company. His life may be spent in the office or in the study or in the workshop or in the field; in arctic exploration, in philanthropy, in a laboratory. And yet the true form and spirit of loyalty, and of loyalty to loyalty, when once you get an actual understanding of the purposes of the self that is in question, is universal and unmistakable.

I hesitate, therefore, to decide for another person even such a question as the way in which his most natural and obvious opportunities for loyalty shall be used. It is true that nature furnishes to us all opportunities for loyalty which it seems absurd to neglect. Charity, as they say, begins at home. Still more obviously does loyalty naturally begin at home. People who wholly neglect their natural family ties often thereby make probable that they are disloyal people. Yet the well-known word about hating father and mother in the service of a universal cause paradoxically states a possibility to which the history of the early Christian martyrs more than once gave an actual embodiment. If the martyr might break loose from all family ties in his loyal service of his faith, one cannot attempt to determine for another person at just what point the neglect of a naturally present opportunity for loyalty becomes an inevitable incident of the choice of loyalty that one has made. Nature, after all, furnishes us merely our opportunities to be loyal. Some of these must be used. None of them may be so ignored that thereby we deliberately increase the disloyalty of mankind. But the individual retains the inalienable duty, which nobody, not even his most pious critical neighbor, can either perform or wholly judge for him,—the duty to decide wherein his own loyalty lies. Yet the duty to be loyal to loyalty is absolutely universal and rigid.

As we also saw at the last time, since fidelity and loyalty are indeed inseparable, the breaking of the once plighted faith is always a disloyal act, unless the discovery that the original undertaking involves one in disloyalty to the general cause of loyalty requires the change. Thus, indeed, the once awakened and so far loyal member of the robber band would be bound by his newly discovered loyalty to humanity in general, to break his oath to the band. But even in such a case, he would still owe to his comrades of the former service a kind of fidelity which he would not have owed had he never been a member of the band. His duty to his former comrades would change through his new insight. But he could never ignore his former loyalty, and would never be absolved from the peculiar obligation to his former comrades,—the obligation to help them all to a higher service of humanity than they had so far attained.

You see, from this point of view, how the requirements of the spirit of loyalty are in one sense perfectly stern and unyielding, while in another sense they are and must be capable of great freedom of interpretation. In judging myself, in deciding how I can best be loyal to loyalty, in deciding what special causes they are through which I am to express my loyalty, in judging whether my act is justified by my loyalty,—in all these respects I must be with myself, at least in principle, entirely rigid. As I grow in knowledge, I shall better learn how to be loyal. I shall learn to serve new causes, to recover from vain attempts at a service of which I was incapable, and in general to become a better servant of the cause. But at each point of my choice my obligation to be loyal, to have a cause, to have for the purposes of voluntary conduct no eyes and ears and voice save as this cause directs,—this obligation is absolute. I cannot excuse myself from it without being false to my own purpose. I may sleep or be slothful, but precisely in so far as such relaxation fits me for work. I may amuse myself, but because amusement is again a necessary preliminary to or accompaniment of loyal service. I may seek my private advantage, but only in so far as, since I am an instrument of my cause, it is indeed my duty, and is consistent with my loyalty, to furnish to the cause an effective instrument. But the general principle remains: Working or idle, asleep or awake, joyous or sorrowful, thoughtful or apparently careless, at critical moments, or when engaged in the most mechanical routine, in so far as my will can determine what I am, I must be whatever my loyalty requires me to be. And in so far my voluntary life is from my point of view a topic for judgments which are in principle perfectly determinate.

Profoundly different must be my judgment in case of my estimate of the loyalty of my fellow. The tasks of mankind are not only common but also individual. So long as you are sure of your own loyalty, and do not break your trust, I cannot judge that you are actually disloyal. I can only judge in some respects whether your loyalty is or is not enlightened, is or is not successful, is or is not in unnecessary conflict with the loyalty of others. I have to be extremely wary of deciding what the loyalty of others demands of them. But this I certainly know, that if a man has made no choice for himself of the cause that he serves, he is not yet come to his rational self, he has not yet found his business as a moral agent.

II

Such are our general results regarding the nature of loyalty as an ethical principle. This complete synthesis of loyalty with a rational individualism must be borne in mind as we attempt a certain practical application of these principles to the problem of our present American life. If there is any truth in the foregoing, then our concept especially helps us in trying to define what it is that we most need in the social life of a democracy, and what means we have of doing something to satisfy the moral needs of our American community, while leaving the liberties of the people intact.

Liberty without loyalty—of what worth, if the foregoing principles are sound, could such liberty be to any people? And yet, if you recall the protest of my young friend, the Russian immigrant's son, as cited to you in a former lecture, you will be reminded of the great task that now lies before our American people,—the task of teaching millions of foreign birth and descent to understand and to bear constantly in mind the value of loyalty, the task also of keeping our own loyalty intact in the presence of those enormous complications of social life which the vastness of our country, and the numbers of our foreign immigrants are constantly increasing. The problem here in question is not merely the problem of giving instruction in the duties of citizenship to those to whom our country is new, nor yet of awakening and preserving patriotism. It is the problem of keeping alive what we now know to be the central principle of the moral life in a population which is constantly being altered by new arrivals, and unsettled by great social changes.

If you recall what was said in our former lecture regarding modern individualism in general, you will also see that our American immigration problem is only one aspect of a world-wide need of moral enlightenment, —a need characteristic of our time. One is tempted to adapt Lincoln's great words, and to say that in all nations, but particularly in America, we need in this day to work together to the end that loyalty of the people, by the people, and for the people shall not perish from the earth.

It is not, indeed, that loyal people no longer are frequent amongst us. The faithful who live and die in loyalty so far as they know loyalty are indeed not yet uncommon. The loyalty of the common people is precisely the most precious moral treasure of our world. But the moral dangers of our American civilization are twofold. First, loyalty is not sufficiently prominent amongst our explicit social ideals in America. It is too much left to the true-hearted obscure people. It is not sufficiently emphasized. Our popular literature too often ignores it or misrepresents it. This is one danger, since it means that loyalty is too often discouraged and confused, instead of glorified and honored. In the long run, if not checked, this tendency must lead to a great decrease of loyalty. The second danger lies in the fact that when loyalty is indeed emphasized and glorified, it is then far too seldom conceived as rationally involving loyalty to universal loyalty. Hence we all think too often of loyalty as a warlike and intolerant virtue, and not as the spirit of universal peace. Enlightened loyalty, as we have now learned, means harm to no man's loyalty. It is at war only with disloyalty, and its warfare, unless necessity constrains, is only a spiritual warfare. It does not foster class hatreds; it knows of nothing reasonable about race prejudices, and it regards all races of men as one in their need of loyalty. It ignores mutual misunderstandings. It loves its own wherever upon earth its own, namely, loyalty itself, is to be found. Enlightened loyalty takes no delight in great armies or in great navies for their own sake. If it consents to them, it views them merely as transiently necessary calamities. It has no joy in national prowess, except in so far as that prowess means a furtherance of universal loyalty. And it regards the war-spirit, which in our first lecture we used as an example of loyalty,—it regards this spirit, I say, as at its best an outcome of necessity or else of unenlightened loyalty, and as at its worst one of the basest of disloyalties to universal loyalty.

Now, it is precisely this enlightened form of loyalty, this conception of loyalty to loyalty, which we most need to have taught to our American people,—taught openly, explicitly,—yet not taught, for the most part, by the now too familiar method of fascinating denunciations of the wicked, nor by the mere display of force, social or political, nor by the setting of class against class, nor yet by any glorification of mere power, nor by appeals merely to patriotic but confused fervor. We want loyalty to loyalty taught by helping many people to be loyal to their own special causes, and by showing them that loyalty is a precious common human good, and that it can never be a good to harm any man's loyalty except solely in necessary defence of our own loyalty.

III

From the point of view of the foregoing discussion, if you want to do the best you can to teach loyalty, not now to single individuals, but to great masses of people,—masses such as our whole nation,—you should do three things: (1) You should aid them to possess and to keep those physical and mental powers and possessions which are the necessary conditions for the exercise of loyalty. (2) You should provide them with manifold opportunities to be loyal, that is, with a maximum of significant, rational enterprises, such as can be loyally carried out; you should, if possible, secure for them a minimum of the conditions that lead to the conflicts of various forms of loyalty; and you should furnish them a variety of opportunities to get social experience of the value of loyalty. (3) You should explicitly show them that loyalty is the best of human goods, and that loyalty to loyalty is the crown and the real meaning of all loyalty.

Helping the people to the attainment and preservation of their powers obviously involves the sort of care of public health, the sort of general training of intelligence, the sort of protection and assistance, which our philanthropists and teachers and public-spirited people generally regard as important. There is no doubt that in our modern American life our social order does give to great numbers of people care and assistance and protection, such as earlier stages of civilization lacked. But the other side of the task of providing our people with the means of ethical advancement, the side that has to do with letting them know what loyalty is, and with giving them opportunities to be loyal, this side, I say, of what we ought to do to further the moral progress of our people, is at present very imperfectly accomplished.

With prosperity, as we may well admit, sympathy, benevolence, public spirit, even the more rational philanthropy which seeks not merely to relieve suffering, but to improve the effective powers of those whom we try to help,—all these things have become, in recent decades, more and more prominent on the better side of our civilization. And yet I insist, just as prosperity is not virtue, and just as power is not morality, so too even public charity, and even the disposition to train people, to make them more intelligent, to give them new power, all such dispositions are insufficient to insure the right moral training of our people, or the effective furtherance of ideal life amongst them.

What men need involves opportunity for loyalty, And such opportunity they get, especially through the suggestion of objects to which they can be loyal. If you want to train a man to a good life, you must indeed do what you can to give him health and power. And you do something for him when, by example and by precept, you encourage him to be sympathetic, public-spirited, amiable, or industrious. But benevolence, sympathy, what some people love to call altruism,—these are all mere fragments of goodness, mere aspects of the dutiful life. What is needed is loyalty. Meanwhile, since loyalty is so plastic a virtue, since the choice of the objects of loyalty must vary so widely from individual to individual, and since, above all, you can never force anybody to be loyal, but can only show him opportunities for loyalty, and teach him by example and precept what loyalty is, the great need of any higher civilization is a vast variety of opportunities for individual loyalty, and of suggestion regarding what forms of loyalty are possible.

Now, I need not for a moment ignore the fact that every higher civilization, and of course our own, presents to any intelligent person nummerous opportunities to be loyal. But what I must point out in our present American life is, that our opportunities for loyalty are not rightly brought to our consciousness by the conditions of our civilization, so that a great mass of our people are far too little reminded of what chances for loyalty they themselves have, or of what loyalty is. Meanwhile our national prosperity and our national greatness involve us all in many new temptations to disloyalty, and distract our minds too much from dwelling upon the loyal side of life; so that at the very moment when our philanthropy is growing, when our sympathies are constantly aroused through the press, the drama, and our sensitive social life generally, our training in loyalty is falling away. Our young people grow up with a great deal of their attention fixed upon personal success, and also with a great deal of training in sympathetic sentiments; but they get far too little knowledge, either practical or theoretical, of what loyalty means.

IV

The first natural opportunity for loyalty is furnished by family ties. We all know how some of the conditions of our civilization tend with great masses of our population to a new interpretation of family ties in which family loyalty often plays a much less part than it formerly did in family life. Since our modern family is less patriarchal than it used to be, our children, trained in an individualistic spirit, frequently make little of certain duties to their parents which the ancient family regarded as imperative and exalted as ideal. Many of us deliberately prefer the loss of certain results of the patriarchal family tie, and are glad that in the modern American family the parental decisions regarding the marriage choices of children are so much less decisive than they used to be. Many insist that other weakenings of the family tie, such as divorce legislation and the practice of divorce have involved, are in the direction of a reasonable recognition of individual interests.

I will not try to discuss these matters at length. But this I can say without hesitation: The family ties, so far as they are natural, are opportunities for loyalty; so far as they are deliberately chosen or recognized, are instances of the choice of a loyalty. From our point of view, therefore, they must be judged as all other opportunities and forms of loyalty are judged. That such opportunities and forms alter their character as civilization changes is inevitable, and need be no matter for superstitious cares regarding whatever was arbitrary in traditional views of family authority. But, after all, fidelity and family devotion are amongst the most precious opportunities and instances of loyalty. Faithlessness can never become a virtue, however your traditions about the forms of faithfulness may vary in their external details. Whoever deliberately breaks the tie to which he is devoted loses the opportunity and the position of the loyal self, and in so far loses the best sort of thing that there is in the moral world. No fondness for individualism will ever do away with this fact. We want more individuals and more rational individualism; but the only possible ethical use of an individual is to be loyal. He has no other destiny.

When a man feels his present ties to be arbitrary or to be a mechanical bondage, he sometimes says that it is irrational to be a mere spoke in a wheel. Now, a loyal self is always more than a spoke in a wheel. But still, at the worst, it is better to be a spoke in the wheel than a spoke out of the wheel. And you never make ethical individuals, or enlarge their opportunities, merely by breaking ties. Hence, so far as a change in family tradition actually involves a loss of opportunities and forms of loyalty, which tradition used to emphasize, our new social order has lost a good thing. Do we see at present just what is taking its place? If the patriarchal family must pass away or be profoundly altered, surely we should not gain thereby unless there were to result a new family type, as rich in appeal to our human affections and our domestic instincts as the old forms ever were.

But in our present American life the family tie has been weakened, and yet no substitute has been found. We have so far lost certain opportunities for loyalty.

Now, how shall we hope to win back these opportunities? I answer: We can win back something of what we have lost if only we in this country can get before ourselves and our public a new, a transformed conception of what loyalty is. The loyalties of the past have lost their meaning for many people, simply because people have confounded loyalty with mere bondage to tradition, or with mere surrender of individual rights and preferences. Such people have forgotten that what has made loyalty a good has never been the convention which undertook to enforce it, but has always been the spiritual dignity which lies in being loyal.

As to individual rights and preferences, nobody can ever attain either the one or the other, in full measure, apart from loyalty to the closest and the most lasting ties which the life of the individual in question is capable of accepting with hearty willingness. Ties once loyally accepted may be broken in case, but only in case, the further keeping of those ties intact involves disloyalty to the universal cause of loyalty. When such reason for breaking ties exists, to break them becomes a duty; and then, indeed, a merely conventional persistence in what has become a false position, is itself a disloyal deed. But ties may never be broken except for the sake of other and still stronger ties. No one may rationally say: "Loyalty can no longer bind me, because, from my deepest soul, I feel that I want my individual freedom." For any such outcry comes from an ignorance of what one's deepest soul really wants.

Disloyalty is moral suicide. Many a poor human creature outlives all that, in the present life, can constitute his true self,—outlives as a mere psychological specimen any human expression of his moral personality, and does so because he has failed to observe that his loyalty, so far and so long as it has been his own, has been the very heart of this moral personality. When loyalty has once been fully aroused, and has then not merely blundered but died, there may, indeed, remain much fluttering eagerness of life; as if a stranded ship's torn canvas were still flapping in the wind. But there cannot remain freedom of personal existence. For the moral personality that once was loyal, and that then blindly sought freedom, is, to human vision, dead. What is, in such a case, left of the so-called life is merely an obituary. Curious people of prominence have sometimes expressed a wish to read their own obituaries. But it is hardly worth while to live them.

People sometimes fail to observe this fact, partly because they conceive loyalty as something which convention forces upon the individual, and partly because they also conceive loyalty, where it exists, as merely a relation of one individual to other individuals. Both views, as we now know, are wrong. No convention can predetermine my personal loyalty without my free consent. But then, if I loyally consent, I mean to be faithful; I give myself; I am henceforth the self thus given over to the cause; and therefore essential unfaithfulness is, for me, moral suicide. Meanwhile, however, no mere individual can ever be my whole object of loyalty; for to another individual human being I can only say, "So far as in me lies I will be loyal to *our* tie, to *our* cause, to *our union.*" For this reason the loyal are never the mere slaves of convention; and, on the other hand, they can never say one to another, "Since we have now grown more or less tired of one another, our loyalty ceases." To tire of the cause to which my whole self is once for all committed, is indeed to tire of being my moral self. I cannot win my freedom in that way. And no individual, as individual, ever has been, or ever can be, my whole cause. My cause has always been a tie, an union of various individuals in one.

Now, can our American people learn this lesson in so far as this lesson is illustrated by family ties? Can they come to see that loyalty does not mean the bondage of one individual to another, but does mean the exaltation of individuals to the rank of true personalities by virtue of their free acceptance of enduring causes, and by virtue of their lifelong service of their common personal ties? If this lesson can be learned by those serious-minded people who have been misled, in recent times, by a false form of individualism, then we shall indeed not get rid of our moral problems, but we shall vastly simplify our moral situation. And a rational individualism will still remain our possession. How to treat the disloyal remains indeed a serious practical problem. But we shall never learn to deal with that problem if we suppose that the one cure for disloyalty, or the one revenge which we can take upon the disloyal, lies in a new act of disloyalty, that is, in the mere assertion of our individual freedom. Train our people to know the essential preciousness of loyalty. In that way only can you hope to restore to the family, not, indeed, all of its older conventional forms, but its true dignity. The problem, then, of the salvation of the family life of our nation resolves itself into the general problem of how to train our people at large into loyalty to loyalty.

V

The second great opportunity for loyalty is furnished, to the great mass of our people, by their relations to our various political powers and institutions, and to our larger social organizations generally. And here we meet, in the America of today, with many signs that our political and social life form at present a poor school in the arts of loyalty to loyalty.

Loyalty, indeed, as I have repeatedly said, we still have present all about us. The precious plain and obscure people, who are loyal to whatever they understand to be worthy causes, and, on the other hand, those prominent and voluntary public servants, who in so many cases are our leaders in good works,—these we have so far still with us. And new forms of loyalty constantly appear in our social life. Reform movements, trades-unions, religious sects, partisan organizations, both good and evil, arouse in various ways the loyalty of great numbers of people. Yet these special loyalties do not get rightly organized in such form as to further loyalty to loyalty. Narrow loyalties, side by side with irrational forms of individualism and with a cynical contempt for all loyalty,—these are what we too often see in the life of our country. For where the special loyalties are, amongst our people, most developed, they far too often take the form of a loyalty to mutually hostile partisan organizations, or to sects, or to social classes, at the expense of loyalty to the community or to the whole country. The labor unions demand and cultivate the loyalty of their members; but they do so with a far too frequent emphasis upon the thesis that in order to be loyal to his own social class, or, in particular, to his union, the laborer must disregard certain duties to the community at large, and to the nation,—duties which loyalty to loyalty seems obviously to require. And party loyalty comes to be misused by corrupt politicians to the harm of the state. Therefore loyalty to special organizations such as labor-unions comes to be misdirected by such leaders as are disloyal, until the welfare of the whole social order is endangered.

The result is that the very spirit of loyalty itself has come to be regarded with suspicion by many of our social critics, and by many such partisans of ethical individualism as those whose various views we studied in our second lecture. Yet surely if such ethical individualists, objecting to the mischiefs wrought by the corrupt politicians, or by the more unwise leaders of organized labor, imagine that loyalty is responsible for these evils, such critics have only to turn to the recent history of corporate misdeeds and of the unwise mismanagement of corporations in this country, in order to be reminded that what we want, at present, from some of the managers of great corporate interests is more loyalty, and less of the individualism of those who seek power. And I myself should say that precisely the same sort of loyalty is what we want both from the leaders and from the followers of organized labor. There is here one law for all.

Meanwhile, in case of the ill-advised labor agitations, and of the corrupt party management, the cure, if it ever comes, surely will include cultivating amongst our people the spirit of loyalty to loyalty. Loyalty in itself is never an evil. The arbitrary interference with other men's loyalties, the disloyalty to the universal cause of loyalty, is what does the mischief here in question. The more the laborer is loyal to his union, if only he learns to conceive this loyalty as an instance of loyalty to loyalty, the more likely is his union to become, in the end, an instrument for social harmony, and not, as is now too often the case, an influence for oppression and for social disorganization. The loyalty which the trades unions demand of their members is at present too often viewed as a mere class loyalty, and also as opposed to the individual freedom of choice on the part of those laborers who do not belong to a given union, or even to those who are in the union, but whose right choice and interests are sometimes hindered by their own union itself. But our people must learn that loyalty does not mean hostility to another man's loyalty. Loyalty is for all men, kings and laborers alike; and whenever we learn to recognize that fact, loyalty will no longer mean fraternal strife, and will no longer excuse treason to the country for the sake of fidelity to corrupt leaders or to mischievous agitations.

VI

But you may hereupon ask how the masses of our people are to learn such a lesson of loyalty to loyalty. I admit that the problem of teaching our people what the larger loyalty means is at present peculiarly difficult. And it is rendered all the more difficult by the fact that, for us Americans, loyalty to our nation, as a whole, is a sentiment that we find to be at present by no means as prominent in the minds of our people as such sentiments have been in the past in other nations. Let me explain what I mean by this assertion.

The history of our sentiment towards our national government is somewhat different from the history of the sentiment of patriotism in other countries. We have never had a king as the symbol of our national dignity and unity. We have, on the other hand, never had to war against a privileged class. Our constitutional problem which led to the Civil War was a different problem from that which the French Revolution, or the English political wars of the seventeenth century, have exemplified. At one time loyalty to the nation stood, in the minds of many of our people, in strong contrast to their loyalty to their state, or to their section of the country. This contrast led in many cases to a bitter conflict between the two sorts of loyal interests. At last such conflicts had to be decided by war. The result of the war was such that, from one point of view, the national government and the authority of the nation, as a whole, have won a position that is at present politically unquestionable. The supremacy of the national government in its own sphere is well recognized. Within its legal limits, its power is popularly regarded as irresistible. The appearance of its soldiers at any moment of popular tumult is well known to be the most effective expression of public authority which we have at our disposal, even although the body of soldiers which may be accessible for such a show of force happens to be a very small body. Viewed, then, as a legal authority and as a physical force, our national government occupies at present a peculiarly secure position. And so, the President of the United States is, at any moment, more powerful than almost any living monarch. All this, viewed as the outcome of our long constitutional struggle, would seem of itself to suggest that the American people have become essentially loyal to our national government.

But, nevertheless, is this quite true? I think that almost any thoughtful American has to admit that in time of peace we do not regard our national government with any such intense sentiments of loyalty as would seem from report to be the living, the vital, the constant possession of Japanese patriots when they consider their traditional devotion to the nation and to their emperor. For them their country is part of a religion. In their consciousness it is said especially to be the land sacred to the memory of their dead. The living, as they say, are but of to-day. The dead they have always with them in memory, even if not in the determinate form of any fixed belief with regard to the precise nature of the life beyond the grave. It is said that the Japanese are very free as to the formulation of all their religious opinions. But in any case their religion includes a reverence for the historic past, a devotion to the dead whose memory makes their country sacred, and a present loyalty which is consciously determined by these religious motives.

Now, the most patriotic American can hardly pretend that he consciously views his country, taken as a whole, in any such religious way. The country is to us an unquestionable political authority. Were it in danger, we should rally to its defence. We have a good many formal phrases of reverence for its history and for its dignity,—phrases which had a much more concrete meaning for our predecessors, when the country was smaller, or when the country was in greater danger from its foes. But, at present, is not our national loyalty somewhat in the background of our practical consciousness? Are we really at present a highly patriotic people? Certainly, the observer of a presidential canvass can hardly think of that canvass as a religious function, or believe that a profound reverence for the sacred memory of the fathers is at present a very prominent factor in determining our choice of the party for which we shall vote at the polls.

And if you say that political dissensions are always of such a nature as to hide for the moment patriotism behind a mist of present perplexities, you may well be asked in reply whether anywhere else, outside of political dissensions, we have in our national life functions, ceremonies, expressions of practical devotion to our nation as an ideal, which serve to keep our loyalty to our country sufficiently alive, and sufficiently a factor in our lives. When can the ordinary American citizen say in time of peace that he performs notable acts of devotion to his country, such that he could describe those acts in the terms that the Speaker of the House of Commons used, in the story that I reported to you in my former lecture? In other words, how often, in your own present life, or in the lives of your fellow-citizens, as now you know them, is it the case that you do something critical, significant, involving personal risk or sacrifice to yourself, and something which is meanwhile so inspired by your love of your nation as a whole that you can say that just then you have neither eyes to see nor tongue to speak save as the country itself, in your opinion, requires you to see and to speak?

Now, all this state of things is opposed to our easily forming a conception of what loyalty to loyalty demands of us in our social and political relations. But the faults in question are not peculiar to our American people. They seem to my mind to be merely symptomatic of something which naturally belongs to the general type of civilization upon which, in our national history, we are entering. The philosopher Hegel, in one of his works on the philosophy of history, depicts a type of civilization, which, in his mind, was especially associated with the decline and fall of the Roman Empire, as well as with the political absolutism of the seventeenth and of the early eighteenth centuries in modern Europe. This type itself was conceived by him as a general one, such that it might be realized in very various ages and civilizations. Hegel called this type of social consciousness the type of the social mind, or of the "Spirit," that had become, as he said, "estranged from itself." Let me explain what Hegel meant by this phrase.

A social consciousness can be of the provincial type; that is, of the type which belongs to small commonwealths or to provinces, such as our own thirteen colonies once were. Or, on the other hand, the social life can be that of the great nation, which is so vast that the individuals concerned no longer recognize their social unity in ways which seem to them homelike. In the province the social mind is naturally aware of itself as at home with its own. In the Roman Empire, or in the state of Louis XIV, nobody is at home. The government in such vast social orders represents the law, a dictation that the individual finds relatively strange to himself. Or, again, the power of the state, even when it is attractive to the individual, still seems to him like a great nature force, rather than like his own loyal self, writ large. The world of the "self-estranged social mind" of Hegel's definition we might, to use a current phraseology, characterize as the world of the imperialistic sort of national consciousness, or simply as the world of imperialism. In such a world, as Hegel skilfully points out, the individual comes to regard himself as in relation to the social powers, which, in the first place, he cannot understand. The fact that, as in our present civilization, he is formally a free citizen, does not remove his character of self-estrangement from the social world in which he moves. Furthermore, since such a society is so vast as to be no longer easily intelligible, not only its political, but also its other social powers, appear to the individual in a similarly estranged and arbitrary fashion. In Hegel's account stress is laid upon the inevitable conflicts between wealth and governmental authority, between corporate and political dignities,—conflicts which characterize the imperial stage of civilization in question. In the world of the "self-estranged social mind," loyalty passes into the background, or tends to disappear altogether. The individual seeks his own. He submits to major force. Perhaps he finds such submission welcome, if it secures him safety in the acquisition of private gain, or of stately social position. But welcome or unwelcome, the authority to which he submits, be it the authority of the government or the authority which wealth and the great aggregations of capital imply, is for him just the fact, not a matter for loyalty.

Such a formula as the one which Hegel suggests is always inadequate to the wealth of life. But we are able to understand our national position better when we see that our nation has entered in these days into the realm of the "self-estranged spirit," into the social realm where the distant and irresistible national government, however welcome its authority may be, is at best rather a guarantee of safety, an object for political contest, and a force with which everybody must reckon, than the opportunity for such loyalty, as our distinctly provincial fathers used to feel and express in their early utterances of the national spirit. In the same way in this world of the self-estranged spirit, the other forces of society

arouse our curiosity, interest us intensely, must be reckoned with, and
may be used more or less wisely to our advantage. But they are the great
industrial forces, the aggregations of capital, the combinations of enormous physical power, employed for various social ends. These vast social
forces are like the forces of nature. They excite our loyalty as little as do
the trade-winds or the blizzard. They leave our patriotic sentiments
cold. The smoke of our civilization hides the very heavens that used to
be so near, and the stars to which we were once loyal. The consequences
of such social conditions are in part inevitable. I am not planning any
social reform which would wholly do away with these conditions of the
world of the self-estranged spirit. But these conditions of our national
social order do not make loyalty to loyalty a less significant need. They
only deprive us of certain formerly accessible opportunities for such
loyalty. They lead us to take refuge in our unpatriotic sects, partisan organizations, and unions. But they make it necessary that we should try
to see how, under conditions as they are, we can best foster loyalty in its
higher forms, not by destroying the sects or the unions, but by inspiring
them with a new loyalty to loyalty.

As the nation has in so many respects become estranged from our more
intimate consciousness, we have lost a portion of what, in the days before
the war, used to absorb the loyalty of a large proportion of our countrymen. I speak here of loyalty to the separate states and to the various
provinces of our country. Such provincial loyalty still exists, but it has
no longer the power that it possessed when it was able to bring on civil
war, and very nearly to destroy the national unity. Instead of dangerous
sectionalism, we now have the other dangerous tendency towards a war
of classes, which the labor unions and many other symptoms of social
discontent emphasize. We have that corrupt political life which partisan
mismanagement exemplifies. And we have that total indifference to all
forms of loyalty which our seekers after individual power sometimes
exhibit, and which occasionally appears as so serious an evil in the conduct of the business of certain great corporations.

All these, I insist, are in our present American life symptoms of the
state of the self-estranged spirit. The decline of family loyalty, of which
I spoke a while since, may be regarded as another symptom of the same
general tendency. Loyalty itself, under such conditions, remains too
often unconscious of its true office. Instead of developing into the true
loyalty to loyalty, it fails to recognize its own in the vast world of national affairs. It is dazzled by the show of power. It limits its devotion to the

service of the political party, or of the labor-union, or of some other sec-
tarian social organization. In private life, as we have seen, it too often
loses control of the family. In public life it appears either as the service of
a faction, or as a vague fondness for the remote ideals.

VII

And nevertheless, as I insist, loyalty to loyalty is not a vague ideal.
The spirit of loyalty is practical, is simple, is teachable, and is for all
normal men. And in order to train loyalty to loyalty in a great mass of
the people, what is most of all needed is *to help them to be less estranged
than they are from their own social order.*

To sum up, then, this too lengthy review, the problem of the training
of our American people as a whole to a larger and richer social loyalty is
*the problem of educating the self-estranged spirit of our nation to know
itself better.* And now that we have the problem before us, what solution
can we offer?

The question of what methods a training for loyalty should follow, is
the special problem of our next lecture. But there is indeed one proposal,
looking towards a better training of our nation to loyalty, which I have
here to make as I close this statement of our national needs. The proposal
is this. We need and we are beginning to get, in this country, a new and
wiser provincialism. I mean by such provincialism no mere renewal of the
old sectionalism. I mean the sort of provincialism which makes people
want to idealize, to adorn, to ennoble, to educate, their own province; to
hold sacred its traditions, to honor its worthy dead, to support and to
multiply its public possessions. I mean the spirit which shows itself in the
multiplying of public libraries, in the laying out of public parks, in the
work of local historical associations, in the enterprises of village improvement societies,—yes, even in the genealogical societies, and in the provincial clubs. I mean also the present form of that spirit which has originated,
endowed, and fostered the colleges and universities of our Western
towns, cities, and states, and which is so well shown throughout our
country in our American pride in local institutions of learning. Of course,
we have always had something of this provincialism. It is assuming new
forms amongst us. I want to emphasize how much good it can do in
training us to higher forms of loyalty.

That such provincialism is a good national trait to possess, the examples
of Germany and of Great Britain, in their decidedly contrasting but

equally important ways, can show us. The English village, the English country life, the Scotsman's love for his own native province,—these are central features in determining the sort of loyalty upon which the British Empire as a whole has depended. Germany, like ourselves, has suffered much from sectionalism. But even to-day the German national consciousness presupposes and depends upon a highly developed provincial life and loyalty. One of the historical weaknesses of France has been such a centralization of power and of social influence about Paris as has held in check the full development of the dignity of provincial consciousness in that country. Now, in our country we do not want any mutual hatred of sections. But we do want a hearty growth of provincial ideals. And we want this growth just for the sake of the growth of a more general and effective patriotism. We want to train national loyalty through provincial loyalty. We want the ideals of the various provinces of our country to be enriched and made definite, and then to be strongly represented in the government of the nation. For, I insist, it is not the sect, it is not the labor-union, it is not the political partisan organization, but it is the widely developed provincial loyalty which is the best mediator between the narrower interests of the individual and the larger patriotism of our nation. Further centralization of power in the national government, without a constantly enriched and diversified provincial consciousness, can only increase the estrangement of our national spirit from its own life. On the other hand, history shows that if you want a great people to be strong, you must depend upon provincial loyalties to mediate between the people and their nation.

The present tendency to the centralization of power in our national government seems to me, then, a distinct danger. It is a substitution of power for loyalty. *To the increase of a wise provincialism in our country, I myself look for the best general social means of training our people in loyalty to loyalty.*

THE HOPE OF THE GREAT COMMUNITY

These words are written at a moment when the issues of the great war are still undecided. They are founded upon no foresight of the course which the world's political and military fortunes are to follow. They therefore refer wholly to ideals, to duties, to hopes, and to the interests of humanity.

There are moments when the lover of mankind, in these days, seems to catch a glimpse of a wonderful dawn light. If this dawn soon gives place to the coming day, an era of inspiring promise for the best hopes of all human ages will begin. If the clouds persistently gather again, as at some moments they do; if the night returns, as, for all that the present writer can know, it may return,—then the world must wait again for centuries, and must wait in sorrow, for that which the wise and the faithful of many generations have longingly expected.

"More than they that watch for the morning," the true lovers of mankind now watch to see whether the seeming promise of the dawn is to be, in any genuine sense, fulfilled. More than the spoilers of mankind ever before scoffed at the hope of humanity, powerful enemies of the good now confidently look for the triumph of Satan. The outcome of the present struggle between good and ill remains still a mystery.

All that one can hope to do at such a moment, is to try to clarify his ideas about what ought to be—wholly powerless as the lover of the ideal is to determine, through any skilfully devised engines of destruction, or through any efficiency of the general staff of any national army, what shall be. All that one can now utter must be called at best "A Song before Sunrise." We do not know whether the sun for which the genuine lovers of mankind and of the ideal long, will ever rise in any future which we human beings can foresee for our own race.

Every idealist believes himself to have rational grounds for the faith that somewhere, and in some world, and at some time, the ideal will triumph, so that a survey, a divine synopsis of all time, somehow reveals the lesson of all sorrow, the meaning of all tragedy, the triumph of the spirit. But it is not ours to say, in the world in which we at present have to live from one day to another, and to follow the fortunes of man from one newspaper to another,—when and how the true revelation of the world's meaning is faced and found. We often do our best when we fix our mind on the thought which Kant expressed in the words: "If justice meets utter wreck, then there is no worth whatever in the continued existence of human life in this world." That word, at least, relieves us from the requirement of trying to prove that justice in mortal affairs will escape total wreck.

Perhaps the time will come when, indeed, there will be no further worth in the continued existence of men on this planet. If the purposes and deeds which some of the powerful enemies of mankind now boastfully attempt to make successful ever become permanently triumphant, then in truth there will be no further worth in the continued existence of human beings. As a matter of fact, this planet has seen its "Age of Reptiles." The sabre-toothed tiger has also had its day. Perhaps the ideals of those who defend and praise the destruction of mothers and of their babes on the "Lusitania" represent the sort of humanity that is henceforth, for an indefinite time, to win possession of the powers which are to control the fortunes of human civilization. About such matters a genuine idealist has no philosophical right, just as he has no scientific right, to make any particular prediction. His business is with the justice whose nature is such that if here on earth it is permanently wrecked, then the life of man becomes utterly worthless. There are to-day boastful powers, as hopeful of their own success as Milton's fallen angels were when

> . . . Satan exalted sat,
> By merit raised to that bad eminence,

on his throne before them, and made preparations for a sort of submarine campaign against the salvation of man. The lover of ideals has no more right to make predictions about the hopes of these boastful powers, than Milton's good angels would have had to make predictions about the results of Satan's subsequent search for this little earth, and about what his visits to the Garden of Eden would accomplish.

In Milton's tale these visits accomplished the Fall of Man. The good and the bad angels have been struggling for the final possession of man ever since. The struggle continues to-day. And there can be no doubt that the evil powers are prodigiously efficient, and that the servants of ill are devotedly loyal to their diabolical cause. As for humanity, man, like the sabre-toothed tiger, may ere long have had his day and may have ceased to be. The lover of ideals can make no predictions as to such results. He can only "watch for the morning" until, for him and for some of his human fellows, the darkness has indeed settled down. It remains, however, still worth while to tell what hopes one's "Song before Sunrise" would express if one were permitted not merely to watch and sometimes to hope for the morning, but to tell what the sun would show us if it had already risen for humanity, or will show us whenever for humanity it does rise, if indeed on this planet it ever is to rise.

I

In order rightly to estimate the ideal issues which are at stake in the present crisis of humanity, it is first necessary to make clear a matter concerning which there is a good deal of confusion in recent discussion. Some of this confusion is benevolent and well-meaning; some of it is due to wilful disregard of certain ethical issues which ought to be as obvious as they are deep. The matter to which I refer can best be brought nearer to clearness by contrasting two views of the world's present moral situation which frequently appear in recent expressions concerning the morals of the war. According to one of these views, the present war is essentially a conflict between nations and between national ideals. The essence of this doctrine is, that just as the conflicting powers are nations, so the main moral concern ought to be expressed in hopes that this or that nation will obtain a deserved success.

Opposed to this view is a second and very different view of the moral situation of the world and of the meaning of the war. According to this view, the present war is a conflict more conscious, more explicit, and for that very reason more dangerous than any we have ever had before, a conflict between the community of mankind and the particular interests of individual nations. Consequently, no nation engaged in this war is, or can be, right in its cause, except in so far as it is explicitly aiming towards the triumph of the community of mankind. As a fact, the various warring nations are at present acting with a decidedly various degree of clearness about their relation to the unified interests of humanity; that is, to what I call the cause of the community of mankind. Hence the various nations differ in the degree to which, at any stage of the conflict, their cause is just. In certain respects and with regard to certain of their enterprises, they may be, and are, explicitly aware that they intend to serve the community of mankind; while in other respects, or in regard to other matters, they may act with a more or less explicitly deliberate hostility to the cause of the community of mankind. Their moral position may, therefore, vary accordingly. But owing to the vastness and to the definiteness of many of the special international passions and issues concerned in the present conflict, the outcome of the war promises to be either a victory or a defeat, not for any one of the warring nations nearly so much as for humanity in its wholeness, and hence for what I shall venture also to call the church universal. It is important, therefore, to indicate as clearly as possible what in this discussion I mean by the community of mankind, and what by the church universal.

Ancient Israel somewhat early reached a religious ideal which is expressed in the doctrine of some of its Prophets, that the redeemed and transformed Jerusalem of the future was to be the centre of a redeemed humanity, the spiritual ruler of a kingdom which should have no end. In reaching this ideal, the religion of the Prophets did not look forward merely to a political conquest of the rest of the world by the future people of Israel. The ideal of the transformed humanity of the future had, indeed, in case of the religion of the Prophets, its political metaphors and inevitably its political coloring. The subsequent results when the ideal religion of the Prophets degenerated into the formalities of later Judaism, were in many ways disastrous both for the morals and for the religion of Judaism. But the ideal city of Zion, the centre of a new heaven and earth, passed over as an ideal into the possession of the early Christian church. The Apostle Paul gave to its inner life the character which he called "charity," and which he expounded to the Corinthians in one of the greatest documents of Christian literature.

The often misunderstood heart and essence of the Pauline vision of charity is that it is a virtue belonging to a community, a community which Paul conceives as finding its future home in a heaven where the Divine Spirit both informs it and fulfils its life and its desire. Charity does not mean mere love of individuals for individuals; since if, according to Paul, I gave all my goods to feed the poor, and my body to be burned, I might still be without charity, and then be as a sounding brass or as a tinkling cymbal. Charity, for Paul, is not a merely mystical power to prophesy, nor does it consist in any other form of merely individual efficiency or proficiency. It is a virtue which Paul recommends to his Corinthians as to an united community who, in the bonds of the spirit, are one body despite the multitude of the members. Charity never faileth, and outlasts all earthly vicissitudes in its own heavenly world, because there we know even as we are known, and our mutual relations are those of a perfected spiritual community.

Paul viewed the salvation of humanity as consisting in the triumph of the Christian church. This triumph was for him something miraculous, catastrophic, and future; and his expectations regarding the triumph and end of humanity were obviously quite mythical. But this triumph of humanity, this hope of all the faithful, this salvation of a community through an universally significant human transformation, without which no salvation of an individual man would be possible, this idea, in terms of which the Apostle Paul universalized the ideal Jerusalem of the early Prophets, this became the most essential and characteristic idea of the Christian church.

The historical church has never been true to it and has seldom understood it. Most Christians suppose that the salvation of men is an affair involving the distinct, and in many ways the isolated, spiritual fortunes of individual men. Such Christians, however, have not understood what the vision of the New Jerusalem was in which the seer of the Apocalypse gloried. What the tree of life bears for the healing of the nations, such Christians have never rightly comprehended. What the farewell address of the Logos of the Fourth Gospel meant, when the departing Lord prayed to the Father, "That those whom Thou hast given me may be One as We are One," such individualistic Christianity (which has been only too popular in the various Protestant sects) has neglected, if not forgotten. But however ill-comprehended, the "sign" in which and by which Christianity conquered the world was the sign of an ideal community of all the faithful, which was to become the community of all mankind, and which was to become some day the possessor of all the earth, the exponent of true charity, at once the spirit and the ruler of the humanity of the future.

Such is a bare suggestion of that ideal of the community of mankind which it was the historical mission of Christianity to introduce into the world, to keep alive through centuries of human crimes, oppressions, rebellions, and hatreds, and to hold before the world for the healing of the nations. The present situation of humanity depends upon the fact that for good reasons, which have to do not merely with the sentimental and romantic aspirations of humanity, but also with the most serious business in which men are engaged, the idea of the community of mankind has become more concrete, more closely related to the affairs of daily life, has become more practicable than ever before. At this very moment the material aspect of civilization favors, as never before, the natural conditions upon which the community of mankind, if it were reasonably successful, would depend for its prosperity. The growth of the natural sciences as well as of the technical industries of mankind also makes possible and comprehensive forms and grades of cooperation which men have never before known. Some motives which tend to render the genuine Pauline charity, the genuine love of the unity of the great community to which all civilized men may, when enlightened, consciously belong,—such motives, I say, have been furthered by the arts, the industries, the sciences, and the social developments of the nineteenth and twentieth centuries, as thousands of years of previous human activity have never furthered them. The brilliant coloring, the luxuriant images with which the fancy of the seer of the Apocalypse adorned his New Jerusalem, readily suggest themselves to the imagination of the lover of human kind, who dwells on some of the more benign aspects of our recent civilization, and who considers how far-reaching the abundant powers of human life are tending to become under the influence of those humane arts and sciences which of late have so successfully combated disease, and have brought together nations and races of men who once could not in the least feel their brotherhood, or mutually understand the tongues which they spoke.

These benevolent and benign influences do not, indeed, of themselves constitute the true Pauline charity; but within the last two centuries we have for the first time seen glimpses of how, under perfectly human conditions, they could become a basis for a charity which might transform our society in many of its most significant features into a social order worthy both of a new heaven and of a new earth. In brief, the last two centuries have given us a right to hope for the unity of mankind, a right of which we had only mythical glimpses and mystical visions before. This right we gained through the recent development both of our natural sciences and of our modern humanities. The idea of the human community has tended of late to win a certain clearness which it never could possess until now.

Paul could believe in his vision of the redeemed humanity of the future, because he had his own perfectly concrete and human, if to him unsatisfactory, experiences of the apparently miraculous life which was present in his enthusiastic little churches. When he talked of the redeemed humanity in heaven, and had his vision of the charity that never faileth, he could say to his brethren: "Thus the Spirit manifests itself amongst you." When, in an unquestionably more fantastic manner and language, the author of the Fourth Gospel made the speaker of the farewell addresses characterize the present life and the future life of his little company of disciples, whom "having loved them, he loved them to the end," the writer of this Gospel could use his concrete, although historically idealized, portrait of the last meeting between the Lord and his disciples as the basis and background of this vision of the salvation of mankind.

In our day this vision of the salvation of mankind, while indeed far enough away from us to cause constant and grave concern, and to demand endless labor, has been for a long time becoming clearer than ever, while both science and industry have tended to bring men together in new fashions of cooperation, in new opportunities and exercises that involve an expressed charity in its true form, as a devotion not merely to individuals but to the united life of the community. The belief that mankind can be and in the end shall be one, has thus for a long time had an increased concreteness, definiteness, practical applicability, and despite all the vast evils of our modern social order, a genuine hopefulness. What has to be borne in mind is, that in former centuries, and above all in ancient times, the community of mankind was hindered from becoming an object either of experience or of reasonable hope by the confusions of men's tongues, by the mutual hostilities of nations, of religions, and of sects, and by the absence of means whereby men might learn to work together. Since the beginning of the modern world, not only have the sciences and the arts helped us to work together in a material way and to understand one another regarding our various ideas, but very many of our modern intellectual and practical modes of progress have possessed a significance not only material, but deeply spiritual and, what is more to the point in our present discussion, wisely international. The modern world has become in many ways more and more an international world. And this, I insist, has been true not merely as to its technical and material ties, but as to its spiritual union.

It has been this vision upon which a recent international crime has so violently intruded. The hope of the community lies in trying to keep before us a vision of what the community of mankind may yet become despite this tragic calamity.

II

In speaking at such a moment of the community of mankind viewed simply as an ideal of the future, there are two matters which, as I believe, we ought to bear in mind. First, its members will not be merely individual human beings, nor yet mere collections or masses of human beings, however vast, but communities of some sort, communities such as, at any stage of civilization in which the great community is to be raised to some higher level of organization, already exist. Ethical individualism has been, in the past, one great foe of the great community. Ethical individualism, whether it takes the form of democracy or of the irresponsible search on the part of individuals for private happiness or for any other merely individual good, will never save mankind. Equally useless, however, for the attainment of humanity's great end would be any form of mere ethical collectivism, that is, any view which regarded the good of mankind as something which masses or crowds or disorganized collections of men should win.

For this reason Bentham's utilitarianism, in the form which he gave to it, and which the English political Liberals of the middle of the nineteenth century emphasized, does not express what the community of mankind needs for its existence and for its general welfare. That is why mere philanthropy, merely seeking for the greatest happiness for the greatest number, merely endeavoring to alleviate the pains of individual men or of collections of men, will never bring about the end for which mankind has always been seeking, and for the sake of which our individual life is worth living. That, too, is the reason why at the present time many humane people, despite their former horror of war, in view of its sorrows and of the misery which it causes, find to their surprise that, as Mr. Robert Herrick has said in a recent number of "The New Republic," war seems to them now no longer as great an evil as it used to seem; for in each of the warring peoples the war has brought about a new consciousness of unity, a new willingness to surrender private good to the welfare of the community, a new sense of the sacredness of duty, a new readiness to sacrifice.

Such converts to the doctrine that war is good ascribe their sudden conversion to the wonder and reverence which have been aroused in them by the sight of France regenerated through the very dangers which the invader has brought with him, awakened to a new sense that the value of life lies not in what individuals get out of it, but in what the exertions and the perils of war call out and illustrate, namely, the supreme and super-individual value of loyalty. Loyalty, the devotion of the self to the interests of the community, is indeed the form which the highest life of humanity must take, whether in a political unity, such as in a nation, or in the church universal, such as Paul foresaw. Without loyalty, there is no salvation. Therefore loyalty can never completely express itself in the search for individual happiness, whether the happiness that is in question be that of the individual who teaches, or that of the mere collections of masses of individuals for whom some philanthropist seeks happiness.

Therefore it is indeed true that, if the only alternative for mankind were either to continue the arts of war or to lose its vision of high attainment in the form of a mere search for happiness, then it would be better that war should rage, with all its horrors, so long as humanity lasts, rather than that what Emerson called "hearts in sloth and ease" should live in an endlessly dissatisfied search for pleasures which deceive and which fade in the enjoyment, and for a happiness which no human individual can possibly attain, unless indeed he is viewed as a member of the community.

The detached individual is an essentially lost being. That ethical truth lies at the basis of the Pauline doctrine of original sin. It lies also at the basis of the pessimism with which the ancient southern Buddhism of the original founder of that faith, Gotama Buddha, viewed the life of man. The essence of the life of the detached individual is, as Gotama Buddha said, an unquenchable desire for bliss, a desire which "hastens to enjoyment, and in enjoyment pines to feel desire." Train such a detached individual by some form of highly civilized cultivation, and you merely show him what Paul called "the law." The law thus shown he hereupon finds to be in opposition to his self-will. Sin, as the Pauline phrase has it, "revives."

The individual, brought by his very cultivation to a clearer consciousness of the conflict between his self-will and the social laws which tradition inflicts upon him, finds a war going on in his own members. His life hereupon becomes only a sort of destruction of what is dearest to him. For as a social being, he has to recognize both the might of his social order and the dignity of its demands. But as a detached individual, he naturally hates restraint; that is, as Paul says, he hates the law. However correct his outward conduct may be, he inwardly says: "Oh, wretched man that I am, who shall deliver me from the body of this death?"

Such is the picture of the essentially disastrous life of the detached individual which you find in the much misunderstood, and in our day comparatively unpopular seventh chapter of the Epistle to the Romans. In the following chapter, Paul characterizes the only mode of salvation which can be offered with any hope to such a detached individual. Gotama Buddha sought the salvation of the detached individual through an act of resignation whereby all desires are finally abandoned. Paul describes what is essentially salvation through loyalty, salvation through the willing service of a community, the salvation of those whom he characterizes by the words: "They are in Christ Jesus, and walk not after the flesh, but after the spirit." But for Paul the being whom he called Christ Jesus was in essence the spirit of the universal community.

The lesson with regard to which both Buddhism and Christianity agree, is the lesson that for the detached individual there is no salvation. Since, therefore, you can never make the detached individual securely and steadily happy, it is useless to try to save him, or any mere crowd or collection of detached individuals, by mere philanthropy. Since the detached individual is essentially a lost being, you cannot save masses of lost individuals through the triumph of mere democracy. Masses of lost individuals do not become genuine freemen merely because they all have votes. The suffrage can show the way of salvation only to those who are already loyal, who already, according to their lights, live in the spirit, and are directed not by a mere disposition to give good things to everybody, or to give all their goods to feed the poor, or to give their body to be burned, but by a genuinely Pauline charity.

Since, then, it is only the consciously united community—that which is in essence a Pauline church—which can offer salvation to distracted humanity and can calm the otherwise insatiable greed and longing of the natural individual man, the salvation of the world will be found, if at all, through uniting the already existing communities of mankind into higher communities, and not through merely freeing the peoples from their oppressors, or through giving them a more popular government, unless popular government always takes the form of government by the united community, through the united community, and for the united community.

Therefore, while the great community of the future will unquestionably be international by virtue of the ties which will bind its various nationalities together, it will find no place for that sort of internationalism which despises the individual variety of nations, and which tries to substitute for the vices of those who at present seek merely to conquer mankind, the equally worthless desire of those who hope to see us in future as "men without a country." Whatever that form of loyalty which is now patriotism expresses, must be in spirit preserved by the great community of the future. That unity within the national growth which the observers of the war watch with such fascination, when they see how each people is better knit and more serious, more conscious of the sacredness of its national life than it was before the great peril, that unity will not, and must not, be lost when the new international life comes into existence. There can be no true international life unless the nations remain to possess it. There can never be a spiritual body unless that body, like the ideal Pauline church, has its many members. The citizens of the world of the future will not lose their distinct countries. What will pass away will be that insistent mutual hostility which gives to the nations of to-day, even in times of peace, so many of the hateful and distracting characters of a detached individual man. In case of human individuals, the sort of individualism which is opposed to the spirit of loyalty, is what I have already called the individualism of the detached individual, the individualism of the man who belongs to no community which he loves and to which he can devote himself with all his heart, and his soul, and his mind, and his strength. In so far as liberty and democracy, and independence of soul, mean that sort of individualism, they never have saved men and never can save men. For mere detachment, mere self-will, can never be satisfied with itself, can never win its goal. What saves us on any level of human social life is union. And when Webster said, in his familiar reply to Hayne, that what alone could save this country must be described as "Liberty and Union, now and forever, one and inseparable!"—Webster expressed in fine phrase, and with special reference to this country, the true doctrine of the church universal.

Liberty alone never saves us. Democracy alone never saves us. Our political freedom is but vanity unless it is a means through which we come to realize and practise charity, in the Pauline sense of that word. Hence the community of mankind will be international in the sense that it will ignore no rational and genuinely self-conscious nation. It will find the way to respect the liberty of the individual nations without destroying their genuine spiritual freedom. Its liberty and union, when attained, will be "now and forever, one and inseparable."

III

I have now mentioned one character which, as I believe, must belong to the international community of the future. Hereupon I must turn to a second character, which seems to me of equal importance with the first, although reformers and the creators of Utopias have almost uniformly neglected, or misunderstood this second character.

The distinct national unities must remain intact, each with its own internal motives for loyalty and with its modes of expression whereby the loyalty of its individual citizens will be won and sustained in the community of mankind, which the ideal future must contain if humanity is to be really saved. In the far-off future, as in the past, humanity will include amongst its number nations whose citizens belong not merely to various national types but to distinct races. No dream of universal conquest, if it were carried out, could ever lead to anything but to a more or less universal community of hate, to a social world essentially distracted, much as the world of the Gentiles, depicted by Paul at the outset of the Epistle to the Romans, was distracted. In and for such a community, no man, still less a nation, could deeply feel or long retain any genuine loyalty. Neither the pan-Germanists nor the pan-Slavists, neither the partisans of the white race nor those who hope for the supremacy of the yellow race, have any true conception of what the community of mankind is intended to be or of what the spirit of loyalty demands that it shall be. Both the nations and the races are needed for the future of mankind. The problem of humanity is to see that their liberty and their union shall remain "forever one and inseparable."

But what the lovers of national rivalries, who look forward to an endless strife of peoples, as well as the makers of the Utopias of universal peace, have equally failed to see is that amongst the many social functions of a nation or, for that matter, of any human community, the political functions of such a community, at any rate, as they have been conceived and carried out up to the present time, are ethically amongst the least important.

Greece never attained political unity. To-day it rules the world, as Germany will never rule it, though its inventions and its efficiency should continue and grow for a thousand years. Greece rules a spiritual world, and rules it spiritually. No modern nation that has won political power has ever expressed its best contribution to humanity through this political power, or has ever made a contribution to the community of mankind which is nearly equal to the contribution made by Greece, and made by a nation which proved wholly incapable of political unity. The greatest rival which Greece has ever possessed as a contributor to the cause of the community of mankind is the nation Israel—by which I mean, not the Israel whose history was rewritten from the point of view of later Judaism and was so misrepresented in what we call the Old Testament. The Israel of which I speak is the Israel of the great formative period of the prophetic religion, the Israel whose religious beginnings are sketched for us in that brief and impressive fragment of poetry called the Song of Deborah—the Israel whose maturer consciousness found its voice in Amos and Isaiah, and in the records of the prophetic literature. Even after its formative period was past, and after Judaism had nearly quenched the spiritual fire which had burned in the religion of the Prophets, Israel still gave us the Psalms, still expressed, in the great speeches which an unknown master put into the mouth of Job, ideas and problems which are with us to-day, and which will record some of the great problems of human destiny for all coming ages of mankind, just as the great Greek tragedians of the formative period of the Hellenic mind have spoken for all time. But Israel, like Greece, never won, and from the nature of the case could not win, a lasting political unity.

When we remember how all the highest products of the German mind have so far been the products of times when the national unity in a political sense was not yet attained, while the mightiest accomplishment of Prussian domination has thus far been that, like the base Indian of Othello's last words, this Prussian domination, in dealing with the magnificent ideal legacy of the Germanic mind, has simply "thrown a pearl away, richer than all his tribe"; and when we remember how an analogous rule holds in case of several other European nations, we are reminded that, on the whole, there seems to be some opposition between the political power of a nation and its power to contribute to the ideal goods of the community of mankind.

The political contributions of nations either to the unity or to the life of the great community are by no means their only or, on the whole, their principal contributions. For that very reason it is not wise to hope that when the Holy City of the community of mankind descends from heaven to earth, it will come in political form. According to a well-known tradition, the Master said: "My kingdom is not of this world, else would my servants fight." I do not think that this reported word of the Master represents what the ideal course of human progress ought to be. The ideal community of mankind, whenever it really descends from heaven to earth, will indeed appear in a definitely worldly fashion. If the ideal is approximately realized, the kingdom will be in this world, yet its servants will not fight, simply because they will be loyally engrossed in much better business than fighting. That upon which I here insist is, that in learning such business they will not principally be guided by political arts and motives.

IV

But if the great community is not to win its loyal consciousness through inventing new political forms and through depending upon political institutions for its principal advances, must it then be confined to "the empire of the air"? Must it always be dependent upon its poets and its prophets? or upon their brethren, the great scientific discoverers, the genuinely inventive leaders of thought? Must its kingdom be a wholly ideal kingdom? Must its fortunes be those which, in a somewhat disheartening sequence of faiths and of practices, have so far constituted the history of religion?

I do not believe this. I believe that the future will invent, and will in due time begin very actively and productively to practise, forms of international activity which will be at once ideal in their significance and business-like in their methods, so that we shall no longer be dependent upon the extremely rare and precious beings called prophets or poets, to show us the way towards the united life of the great community. I have recently ventured to point out certain ways in which international business is already approaching a stage wherein, if the spoilers do not indeed too seriously wreck or too deeply impair our progress, we may actively begin to further international unity, without in the least interfering with the free internal development of the social orders of individual nations. It is not at all necessary to look towards the triumph of Socialism or of any other equally revolutionary social tendency, whether political or non-political, in order to foresee possible modes of international unification, which, if they were once tried, if a fair beginning of some such international activity were made, would almost certainly prove to be self-sustaining as well as conducive to a mutual understanding amongst the nations.

There is, for instance, a type of business which has been invented only within a little more than a century. In origin it is due to no poet and to no prophet. It has already transformed the civilization of the principal nations of Europe. The transformation in question is nowhere, except by accident, very closely bound up with political changes. The social transformations which it has already wrought within the communities of single nations, are not due to the spread of socialistic doctrines or to any notable political tensions or strifes within the communities which have thus been influenced.

The form of business which I have in mind is the form known as insurance. Within the life of a single civilized people, it is capable of accomplishing an immense variety of types of social service. The internal organization of Germany itself has been prodigiously furthered, the social unity and the impressive efficiency of the German people have been in recent decades very vastly furthered by the use which Bismarck and those who followed him were led to make of various forms of "state insurance" and of "social insurance," largely as means of meeting the demands which the socialistic movement was already making upon the state in general. What has been proved is that the type of business called insurance is so plastic and has such vast direct as well as indirect effects, that, within a single nation, if the purpose is to give a community such unity and such organization as naturally hold the attention and win the practical loyalty of the members of the community, the insurance type of organization is the best type invented for the purpose in question. This is no place to speak of the details of recent social insurance which Germany has so largely and so successfully used. It is enough to say that the business of insurance depends upon devices which are, so to speak, essentially unifying, essentially reconciling, essentially such as to exemplify a type of social community to which in a recent book of my own I have ventured to give a name, not, as I hope, too technical.

An insuring financial organization, whether it be an ordinary corporation or, as in Germany's case, a state or a government, has what I may call a mediating, a reconciling, a unifying function. If you regard the insurer as an individual man—and such in special cases he may be,—he mediates between the interests of two persons whose concerns, apart from the work of the insurer, are subject to an often painful conflict. These two persons may be called "the adventurer" and "the beneficiary." The adventurer is somebody who takes a risk, a practically significant risk. Like all risks, this one does not affect the fortunes of the adventurer alone. For the adventurer has, or at some time in the future will have, heirs or successors, or a family or other co-adventurers, who may, or who under certain conditions will benefit by the adventurer's undertakings if they succeed, but who will otherwise get quite the reverse of benefit out of the adventurer's failure. Thus the interests of the adventurer and of his possible beneficiaries, who may or will win if he wins, or who may or will lose if he loses, stand in a relation involving a certain rivalry, a tension, a source of possible conflict of the most varied kind. In other words, the adventurer and the possible beneficiary constitute what, in my "War and Insurance," I have called "a dangerous pair" of human beings. That is, their conflicting interests may lead to misunderstandings, to mutual wrongs, and to personal and social unrest of the most varied sorts.

Into this "dangerous pair" the insurer, in case his insurance enterprise is well founded and successful, introduces a reconciling element. It is the nature of his business to guarantee the beneficiary against the losses with which in the course of his fortunes the adventurer may meet. In consequence the dangerous pair becomes a genuine community, whose type is triadic and whose form is that of all the communities which I call "communities of interpretation." These are groups whose members comprise within themselves either individuals or communities. But in each of these communities, one of the members has the essentially spiritual function or task of representing or interpreting the plans, or purposes, or ideas, of one of his two fellows to the other of these two in such wise that the member of the community whom I call the "interpreter" works to the end that these three shall cooperate as if they were one, shall be so linked that they shall become members one of another, and that the community of the whole shall prosper and be preserved.

In "War and Insurance" I have defended the thesis that, if the principle of insurance were introduced into international affairs, even in a very small degree, it would involve, first the creation of an entirely new sort of international body—namely, an "international board of trustees." The functions of this board would not be those of a court of arbitration. They would not be diplomatic functions. The board would have no political powers or duties whatever. Hence its functions would constitute an entire novelty in human history. How such a board would be possible, how its funds might be protected from predatory assaults and kept free from the danger of being risked in international quarrels, my book has in a general way explained.

Since any reader of this book who may have time in the distractions of the present conflict to give it even the least careful attention, very naturally asks at once what common interests of the nations there are to insure, it is possibly worth while to say that in an article in *The New York Times* for July 25, 1915, I have pointed out certain international interests which, in fact, are greatly intensified by some of the conditions of the present conflict, and which are so definitely related to existing forms of the insurance business, that were a few nations at the close of the present war to appoint an international board of trustees to take practical charge of just these perfectly definable interests, and to treat them so as to meet the conditions which the nations concerned could readily agree upon without departing from fields of insurance that already exist and that have already acquired international importance, then a beginning in international insurance could actually be made at once upon the conclusion of the present war.

Were such an international board of trustees once appointed, were some such essentially simple and familiar type of insurance enterprise once undertaken, under perfectly reasonable and businesslike conditions, a beginning would be made in a process that would, from the very first, tend to make the unity of the various nations of mankind something practical and obvious, as well as certain to possess, as time went on, more and more significance for all concerned in such a process. For, as a fact, there are certain forms of insurance which, as I have just said, are already international in their scope. At the close of the present war, some of these forms of insurance will be in need of new international devices to render them useful and prosperous under the new financial conditions that will inevitably succeed the conflict.

Nobody has as yet attempted to devise an international board of trustees fitted to take charge of such international social interests. But in the article to which I have referred, I have endeavored not merely to show how the still very distant ideal of an international insurance against risks directly connected with war would be valuable if we could secure such a form of international insurance, but also to show that a special type of international insurance would be perfectly practicable and business-like at the close of the present war, if a few nations were to agree upon a plan for appointing an international board of trustees and for intrusting to it the new enterprise. This new enterprise would involve no essentially new type of insurance. It would be based upon international needs which are already recognized, which have already created certain very successful corporations, which actually do an international business. To make these already existing types of insurance international in my present sense, only the explicit recognition of a suitable international organ is necessary.

This new international organ would not be political in its nature, would not attempt to do the work of "a league of peace," while of course it would have no sort of opposition to the formation of any league of peace which proves in the future to be practicable. The new type of international organ would be founded upon no international treaty such as would need or invite arbitration. The nations that entered into the new enterprise would merely intrust certain funds to the new international board of trustees, and would remain perfectly free to retire from all relations to the enterprise at any moment, by the device which any ordinary holder of an insurance policy can use at present, namely, by surrendering the policy to the board of trustees.

The effects of the new enterprise would be in the main indirect. That is, the new enterprise would meet an actual need, and if it were reasonably devised, would meet that need at once, and would in so far do good. But if successful, it would lead to new enterprises of the type. The principle of insurance would, however, be definitely introduced into international affairs. Once introduced, and once made in the least effective, that principle might, I believe, safely be left to vindicate itself and its power to bring to consciousness the great community of the future. The realm of peace may, indeed, be far enough away from our distracted human nature. But the way towards peace, the way towards the winning of self-consciousness for the great community, the way towards a genuine and practically effective cooperation of the nations, at once in the spirit of sound and business-like devotion, and in its primitive true Pauline charity,—that way already lies open.

War and Insurance (1914)

ADDRESS ON WAR AND INSURANCE

Great tragedies are great opportunities. The new griefs which to-day beset the civilized nations call for new reflections and for new inventions. Our past methods of furthering the cause of peace on earth have disappointed many hopes that, in their day, seemed both fascinating and reasonable. We must not expect, at any time in the near future, to make an entire end of war, but we need to understand better than we now do the depth, the gravity, and the true nature of the motives which have thus far made war-like tendencies so persistent in the life of mankind. We also need to discover, if we can, methods not yet tried, whereby the wars of the nations may be gradually rendered less destructive, and less willful.

This essay is to be devoted to both the tasks thus indicated. The main part of this paper will give an account of some of the familiar, but too little heeded, and too ill defined reasons why wars are, despite our civilization, so fatally recurrent incidents of our international life. This first part of our paper must be somewhat lengthily stated; for, as the old Buddhist scripture says:

> "Long is the night to him who is awake; long is a mile
> to him who is tired; long is life to the foolish who do not
> know the true law."[1]

And our poor human nature is still on the level on which we are often wakeful in the night and often have yet to seek after the knowledge of the true law which may some day bring us nearer to the life of peace.

This earlier and also lengthier part of our paper will gradually lead us, however, to the definition of some principles bearing on a fragment of

1. Max Müller, "Sacred Books of the East," Vol. X, p. 20.

the true law both of war and of peace. And so far this paper will be a contribution to what has been called, by the Dutch Ethnologist Steinmetz, the "Philosophy of War." But, at the very close of our discussion, we shall be led to an application of these principles which I believe to be in certain respects new. We shall then, in the second and much shorter part of our discussion, propose a method of practically furthering the gradual growth and reënforcement of the cause of peace on earth. This method has not yet been tried. I believe that the principles upon which it is founded are, in certain concrete instances, as familiar to the modern civilized man as are his most characteristic forms of prudence, of thrift, and of coöperation. But the application of these principles to the philosophy of war remains still inadequate; and, at the present moment, this field for further efforts to form plans that look towards peace is still open. This paper will thus close with a brief indication of the nature of one such plan.

I

THE UTOPIA OF UNIVERSAL PEACE

To propose any way for furthering the cause of universal peace is to arouse the objection that all such proposals, if definite in their formulation, and universal in their intention, have thus far always proved utopian. As has often been asserted, man appears in history as essentially a fighting animal. When he becomes civilized, he changes, indeed, the fashion of his fighting, and, in the course of time, gradually improves both the morals and the methods of his warfare. Cruelty, pillage, and extermination become less prominent amongst the aims which absorb the warrior's mind. Wars are waged for purposes which become more ideal as time goes on. Humanity of mood directs, in a measure, the plans of rival nations. The modern national spirit itself sometimes appears to be a sort of preparation for some larger enthusiasm which, as we often hope, may, in a far-off future age, make the community of mankind its main object of fraternal devotion, and the whole earth its country.

But, on the other hand, as the nations grow in power and in self-consciousness, some of the disastrous but profoundly human motives which most tend to make men fight with their neighbors, not only survive in the midst of the highest cultivation which we have yet reached, but are even intensified by the very intelligence, by the loyalty, and by the resoluteness, which lie at the basis of what our civilization most needs and prizes. Nobody can rightly consider the problem of war who regards the war spirit as a mere relic of barbarism, or as due solely to the evil side of our nature. The mystery of war and of its fascination can be fathomed only in case we first observe that although, of old, wars were often due in a large part to the passions and ambitions of rulers and of the ruling classes of the warring peoples, modern wars, however much princes may take part in their beginnings, are, on the whole, waged by peoples, and are in part the expressions of the recently acquired power of an intelligent democracy. Ancient wars were frequently the result of ignorance, and of blind popular passion, of superstition, or of the greed of individuals. Modern wars are in many cases deliberately and thoughtfully planned by patriots who love their country's honor, who are clearly conscious of well-formulated ideals which they think righteous, and who fight in the name of the freedom of the people, and in the service of what they suppose to be the highest human culture. World-wide sympathies do not prevent warlike passions from seeming to many who cultivate them not only necessary, but morally indispensable; not only honorable, but holy; not only fascinating, but rational.

Let us remember then that, whatever the mere form of any national government may be, it is at present the democracy itself, or at all events, the prevailing popular will, however it is expressed, which, in the more warlike modern nations, actually prepares for war, which dreams of it in advance, which tries cheerfully to bear the burdens of its expenses, which glories in its risks and in its victories, and which frequently and consciously justifies it as the highest, as the completest, and so as the most ethical expression of national loyalty. Let us remember too that modern democracy, or whatever else expresses the will of a people, does this not because it lacks a sympathetic interest in the concerns and in the sentiments of the men of other nations, but because our modern form of human solidarity is such that international hate travels as far, as fast, and as persuasively as does love. The civilized world thrills with sympathy for the calamities of obscure or of distant men; but it also thrills with a common admiration for high spirit, and for warlike enthusiasm. Sympathy implies a disposition to imitate, and so, just because of our present degree of solidarity, we tend to imitate whatever is impressively vigorous about the will and the power of interesting men and nations. Such imitation is, in many cases, an imitation of the war spirit.

Only in case we keep in mind both the vast masses of popular interest and the very high grade of intelligence which are now devoted, in many great nations, to the cultivation of warlike motives, and to the preparation for war, can we see how far away is the utopia of universal peace.

As a fact, the advance of civilization not only brings with it motives which tend to check and to control the barbarous aspects of war, but also motives, some of them new, which tend to make war appear, to many individuals and nations, more ideal, more righteous, more significant, than ever. The modern world, wherein every great human experience of passion, of sorrow, and of love arouses a warm response in the most distant parts of the inhabited earth,—this same world echoes the warlike passions as readily as it does the humane ones, longs to imitate the powerful peoples as well as to relieve the sufferers from an earthquake, and is stirred by its far-reaching rivalries as much as by its other expressions of solidarity. Its social problems are common to all the civilized lands; but so too are the dispositions to encourage and to feel the contrasts of races, and the rivalries of commerce and of cultivation. The democracies are vast; but so too are the conflicting interests for which these democracies are ready to fight. Science brings all men near to each other; but science also originates new industrial arts, and these arts can be used for war as well as for peace. Civilization makes men more thoughtful about both social and moral issues. But such thoughtfulness, if once inspired by patriotism, and by international jealousies, can both counsel and wage war deliberately, and with a self-righteous assurance such as our elementally passionate or simply superstitious ancestors never knew.

So, of themselves, neither cultivation, nor thoughtfulness, nor humane breadth of sympathies, nor the discoveries of science, nor the aspirations of the democracy, have been able to make wars cease on the earth. Modern wars may, as we now know, become more widespread, more democratic in spirit, more ideally self-righteous, than ever they were before.

Whoever undertakes, then, to plan any method of decreasing the evils of war, must take account of these facts and must consider how deeply rooted in civilized man the tendency towards war still remains. One may well begin such an enterprise by asking whether it is not indeed altogether hopeless. In view of the facts thus summarily sketched, is not this great disease of mankind, the love of war, beyond cure, and perhaps beyond any lasting relief?

And yet: The spectator who to-day witnesses the tragedy entitled "Man," watches a scene wherein both the events and the characters arouse, side by side with many old emotions and reflections, certain wholly new movings of pity, of fear, and of wonder. Can one remain a merely passive spectator? Must one not seek, at least in imagination, some more active means whereby he may transform his pity into charity, his fear into an inspiring hope, his wonder into some sort of interpretation of the meaning of what he witnesses? In such an effort lies the task of this essay.

II

THE NEIGHBOR: LOVE AND HATE

The facts just cited, the prominence of warlike motives in modern men, the stubborn survival in culture of the tendencies which express themselves in armaments, in the jealousies of nations, and in actual wars,— all these things call for further characterization in terms of a principle which shall be sufficiently general in its scope, and sufficiently important in its practical applications, to serve as a guide in our search for a way of giving to humanity a measure of relief from its most dangerous social burdens. The higher religions have long sought for an expression of such a principle. Two of them in particular, namely Buddhism and Christianity, have found and used a formula which is, in fact, extremely general in its statement, and very highly practical in its demands, as well as in some of its applications. In its Christian expression this formula is as familiar as is its failure to guide men, and lies at the basis of the counsel which Christian teachers of the most various creeds daily give to each of the faithful regarding his relation to his fellow man. Just because of this familiarity of the best known forms of the Christian formula, we may be aided to make the principle in question momentarily vivid in our minds, if we here refer to one of the simplest and most popular of the scriptures of the original Southern Buddhism, the work from which I have already quoted the passage about those who find the night long. The name of this book is the Dhammapada. Let me cite from this scripture a mere fragment of a single text. At a moment when the world is at war, this ancient Buddhist word may awaken, by the very contrast between its spirit and that of the passing mood of modern European patriots, a comment which will help us to see where our real problem lies:—

" 'He abused me, he beat me, he defeated me, he robbed me';—in those who do not harbor such thoughts hatred will cease.

"For hatred does not cease by hatred at any time: hatred ceases by love, this is an old rule."

Such, then, is the formulation of the greatest of human practical problems by the Dhammapada; such is the solution of this problem which that ancient Buddhist scripture proposed, several hundred years before Christ. You have but to think of the best known words of the parables and of the Sermon on the Mount in order to recall other and now distinctively Christian forms of this same rule for ending wars and for saving mankind. "Little children, love one another:" these words, in another part of the New Testament, restate this view of the escape from all the horrors which war entails. In an equally simple, and, as I may at once add, in an equally imperfect shape, Tolstoi's version of the Christian spirit not long since filled with a sad longing the very European world whose destinies have, since then, been so dominated by preparation for war, and by acts of war.

Considered by itself, and apart from all theological formulations, this lore which is common to Buddhism and to Christianity may be summed up in the assertion that the moral destiny of man depends upon a certain pair of relations,—the relation of love towards his neighbor,—and the relation of hate. In so far as man is dominated by the hate-relation, this doctrine tells us that he is lost. In so far as the love-relation becomes his guide, he is, according to the same teaching, saved; for then he enters the realm of inner as well as of outer peace, and his life wins its only true sense, its only possible fulfillment. There is, then, so this view of life teaches, a good relation of man to his neighbor; it is the relation of lover to beloved. There is a relation to his neighbor which is not only dangerous, but deadly to man; and that is the relation of an enemy to the neighbor whom he hates. The whole problem of life lies here. Let men become lovers, and then whatever men's mere fortunes may be, all is well. Let them remain enemies, and then not only wars are waged, but also the shadow of death is upon the whole inner and outer life of man. The dead lie waiting burial. The mourners wail and cannot be comforted. Such, I say, is the substance of that view of our problem which Christianity and Southern Buddhism share in common.

Now this doctrine of life is so ancient, and is, in mere words, so widely accepted, that just because we are deadened by the mere repetition of such words, we have difficulty in making very vivid to our minds how far this common Buddhist and Christian lore is from telling us the whole truth about the way whereby the winning of peace and the fruitful union of human souls is to be sought, if ever such peace and union is to take place in the world of daily life at all.

In order to illustrate this contrast between real life and this ideal of life, let us simply fancy that some supernatural stranger, having an angel's tongue, and bearing a flag of truce, appears to-day upon a battlefield in Belgium or in Servia, and, having first somehow miraculously caused the conflict to cease for a time, announces to all present, so that they hear him, the news of how he has in his possession the formula for ending all wars, including the present strife on this field. Let him then read, over the heaps of the wounded and of the dead as they lie there the words I have just read from the Dhammapada:—

> "Hatred does not cease by hatred; hatred ceases by love;
> this is an old rule."

As soon as this angel of peace has finished his message and has departed, the warriors, so far as they are not yet helpless, will of course return to the tasks wherein they find their honor and their duty, as well as their own fierce joy and pain, their own bitter weariness, and their own passionate obedience and devotion. As they do so, will they not feel, along with us the spectators, that the words of this angel visitant, spoken during the brief truce, are not only impotent, but irrelevant?

In fact, these words do not even touch, by themselves, upon the real practical problem of this battlefield and of all battlefields.

This problem obviously is: *how* shall the hate-relation come to be forgotten, and how shall the love-relation come to be the dominant motive of a human life such as is ours? When not only our worst motives, but also our patriotism, our love of all that we hold dearest, our honor,— when all these counsel us, if we be men, to treat as enemies those who are the foes of this honor, we see that we are in the presence not only of passion, but of fate; and that this passive form of the law of love can successfully address its words only to those who, like the Buddhist monks, or like the Christian saints of the desert, have first abandoned, as Schopenhauer said, the will to live, have parted company with whatever makes a man's character vigorously active and unsparingly and constructively creative; have also parted company with whatever makes us ready to be like those angels who excel in strength. Hate, after all, is but one aspect of war. War's other aspect, what one may call its spiritual aspect, is the loyalty to which it gives active employment, the fearless faith in life which it converts into works, the endurance which it transforms into creative deeds. In this other aspect of war lies its appeal to what is best in man.

The real problems of war cannot be solved, then, merely in terms of this contrast between the love-relation and the hate-relation, and in terms of the mere condemnation of the hate-relation. For there are human relations which call out our most active loyalty, our most constructive devotion, our highest energy, and which cannot be defined merely in terms of the contrast between loving and hating a man's individual neighbor. Such are the human relations which are exemplified when many men are together devoted to one common although by chance unwarlike task, such as the task of an art, or of a science, or of some church wherein there is present a genuine communion of the faithful. Such tasks may indeed be called tasks of love, but they are not tasks of the merely self-forgetting and passive love which the Dhammapada contrasts with hate. They are the tasks of a sort of Pauline charity whose object is not merely the individual neighbor, but a whole community of many men viewed as a super-personal, and yet also as somehow a personal being. The one who loves in this spirit loves a spiritual body wherein individual men exist as members, and wherein he also is a member. He seeks not his own, but he loves, as Paul said, "Not after the flesh but after the spirit." He loves as Paul also said that Christ loved the church. Therefore he is above both the hates and the loves which contrast and which contend on the battlefield. When a company of artists or of scientific men work together upon the common tasks of their calling, they are not merely, as "little children," loving one another, nor yet are they hating, each his neighbor. Their human relations are those of the loyalty of individuals to the communities wherein the true tasks of life are found. The relation which is here present is expressed in the devotion of the individual's life to the spirit of some community, wherein he lives and moves and has his being.

Now such human relations, namely those which bind a patriot to his country, a warrior to his service, an artist to the community of all who love art, a scientific man to the community of all who study nature, these are indeed, as we have said, the highest human relations. These express the best in man. I have already said that the motives underlying these human relations often lead to the worst of warlike hatreds. This is as sad a fact as it is prominent in human history. But we have gained something for the understanding of our problem if we have first seen that this problem involves not merely the contrast between love and hate, but the contrast between those relations which an individual man bears to his individual neighbor, and the relation which a patriot bears to his country, or the individually faithful saint to the visible or invisible church to which, as he believes, all the faithful belong.

It is therefore not by mere love of one's neighbor that hatred can be made to cease. And in fact historical Christianity has never been merely a religion of such passive love. The Pauline charity involves a relation of the individual to the whole mystical body of the faithful. This relation is viewed by Paul as so important that he tells us how, without this charity, without this relation of the believer to the whole spiritual body of the faithful, *no* form of the love of an individual man for his neighbor, *no* giving of one's body to be burned, would really profit either a man or his neighbor in any respect. The Pauline charity involves a relation whose type profoundly differs from the type which the author of the Dhammapada has in mind. Paul does not say: "Think of that neighbor yonder, and love him; and then the hate-thoughts and the wars will cease." Paul says, in substance, "Be loyal to the spiritual body whereof you are a member. Gird on the whole armor of loyalty. Practice, meanwhile, not mere self-sacrifice, but positive virtues which, in form at least, are essentially although not merely militant. And then you will rise above petty hate as much as above merely private and individual love. You will perhaps wage war, but not because you are greedy; rather because you love the union, the community of all the loyal, the spiritual body of those who are one in faith and in service. Then you will be a man with a country; and for your country you will be ready, on occasion, both to fight and to die."

If our angel visitor on the battlefield proclaimed the words of Paul rather than those of the Dhammapada, he would express what I believe to be the really higher spirit of historical Christianity. And the warriors, before they returned to their awful tasks, would feel that, while he had not indeed justified the slaughter of men as anything that is in itself a good, he had given them some glimpse of the reason why the warlike spirit has its spiritual meaning, as well as its tragic horror of great darkness. He would have hinted that, if ever relief is to come to humanity's great woe of combat, it will come not merely through a cessation of hate and a prevalence of love for individual men, but through the growth of some higher type of loyalty, which shall absorb the men of the future so that the service of the community of all mankind will at last become their great obsession, while this world-patriotism, when it comes, will remain still as active, and on occasion as militant and as businesslike in its plans and in its devotion as is now the love of warring patriots for their mutually hostile countries.

In facing the problem as to how this possible future world-patriotism, how this distant but eagerly desired result can ever come to be, I will not say reached, but gradually approached, we have gained, I believe, something, however little, by seeing that we have not here chiefly to do with two contrasting relations of pairs of individual men, namely the love-relation, and the hate-relation. Our fiction of the angel visitant on the Belgian or Servian battlefield helps to remind us wherein consists the contrast between his advice, as we first stated it, and the sort of counsel which we ourselves in the present discussion are seeking. He says, to every warrior: "Love your neighbor, even if he has thus far been your enemy. Since you cannot love him and also willfully kill him, you have only to follow, all of you at once, my word, and then not only this, but all battles will automatically cease. You will all return to your homes. Then peace will come on earth."

But, as we have seen, the instinctive sentiment which the warriors, after their momentary truce, and even while the thunders of the captains and the shouting begin again, will feel (whether they have wit and patience to articulate their reply or not),—this sentiment may well take the form of saying : "I am not merely related to my neighbor here, who seeks my life as I seek his, and who is a hateful man hunter as I also am. My highest and deepest relations are to my country and to its allies and foes, to our common service, to my honor, and (if you will) to our forefathers and to our posterity, yes to the whole world of man."

And so, for the warriors, and for us who now study the philosophy of war, the genuine problem relates not so much to the contrast between the love-relation and the hate-relation, as to the contrast between our relations to our individual neighbors, and our relations to our honor, or to our duty, or to our country, or to mankind, or to whatever community you may choose to consider.

Here, at length, we enter the region where the issues of war and peace must be faced and thought out, if anywhere we are to find a reasonable guide towards a solution. My greatest question is not: "Do I love my neighbor or do I hate him?" but "Have I, or have I not the right, the worthy, the saving relation to my community, to my family, to my country, to mankind?" If we want to learn to answer this question, we next need to consider some very plain and familiar, but neglected, facts about the nature of communities, and about the social relations of men.

III

THE DANGEROUS SOCIAL RELATIONS AND COMMUNITIES

Kant, in one of his more practical and popular works, has used a well-known expression, which has often been cited, but which has little been heeded. This expression bears upon the natural relation of the individual man to his individual neighbor. Hobbes, in the seventeenth century, had said, "By nature every man is at war with his neighbor. Only some special social device can make him behave as if he were a peaceful creature." Rousseau, in Kant's own time, had asserted that by nature men love to be in harmony with one another, so that only the artificial customs of society are the source of the mutual hatreds and rivalries which lead to war. Kant, in the remark to which I now refer, goes deeper than both of these conflicting theses. Kant says, in substance: "By nature man both hates and loves his neighbor." And Kant goes on to point out that, in real life, each of these tendencies, the loving tendency as well as the hating tendency, actually both nourishes and inflames the other.

For man, as a social animal, cannot do without his neighbor. In solitude he pines or starves. It is not good for man to be alone. Yet, if you give a man a companion, it is equally natural that the two should, erelong, quarrel!

Their quarrel need not be due to the fact that they are naturally malicious. But, perhaps by mere accident, they soon get in each other's way. Then they easily begin to quarrel, and their quarrel tends to inflame its own motives. Hence Kant's formula for the natural relations of a pair of human beings is that the natural man can "Neither suffer his fellow nor do without him." Deprive a man of his mate, and he finds the world intolerably lonesome. Give him a companion, and the two irritate each other. For, if only by mere accident, they erelong become rivals in some quest; or perhaps they interrupt each other in a conversation and then each, if sufficiently eager, begins to say (out of pure love both for his fellow and for the sound of his own voice): "Do not interrupt me. Listen to me." Herewith begins a possible quarrel. Such a quarrel, if two nations were concerned, might lead to war.

This last example of social friction is not Kant's example, but it well illustrates why what one may call the *dyadic, the dual, the bilateral relations of man and man, of each man to his neighbor, are relations fraught with social danger. A pair of men is what I may call an essentially dangerous community.*

A man may, at any time, love his neighbor. They may both feel kindly towards each other. It may be that neither is malicious, that neither is, as people say, a totally selfish creature. All that is needed, however, to make serious friction possible between the two men is that each shall be active, and watchful, and that he shall have some sort of "business and desire, such as they are." It is tolerably certain that, if this condition is fulfilled, the business and desire of the two men shall be, in whatever way you please, *different*, and in some way *contrasting*. Even if they love each other, they will then be disposed not to do precisely the same thing at the same time. Or if, as in a conversation between two people, each of them does desire to say, at any moment, the very same thing which the other desires to say, this same act will have different relations to the conversation according to the intents which each of them has as he speaks to the other.

Now, in any such case, the perfectly natural, and in fact inevitable contrast, between the acts, or between the results of action, on the part of the two neighbors who love each other, will of itself tend to create friction.

A certain social tension is therefore a perfectly natural accompaniment of any concrete social relation between two people. However friendly they are, at the outset of a social task, to disagree in some respect is the normal result of any social intercourse between two neighbors. If two men are neighbors, each of them inevitably tends, in some respect, to get in the other's way.

Let the two eager speakers, who long to talk together, but who automatically tend to interrupt each other, just because each loves to have the other as his listener, let them serve as a perfectly elementary example of a tendency which you find assuming all grades of importance, from the most trivial to a furious quarrel which may lead to a death grip of two fighters, or to a war between two nations.

There is, therefore, a law of the social intercourse between the members of a pair of individual men, or (for that matter) of the social intercourse between the members of a pair of individual groups or nations of men,—a law for which I have long used the name: *The law not only*

*of the danger, but also of the original sin, of the dual, or dyadic social
relations of men.* The law is this: When two men, or two consolidated
groups of men, are set at some such social task as observing each other, or
playing a game together, or debating a question, or buying and selling, or
borrowing and lending, or hunting for food, or even when they explicitly undertake the task of helping each other, then, at any one stage of this
dual or bilateral activity, one of the two will indeed be either loving the
other, or else not loving him. And when a new and interesting relation to
a neighbor first comes in sight, love is quite as natural as is antipathy.

But as the two individuals pass from one stage to another of the activity
in question, the natural contrast between the two men or groups tends to
lead to some mutual interruption, of jostling, or to some other vexatious
contrast of behavior. Each therefore tends, in some fashion, to surprise
the other painfully, to snub his activities, and so to get in the other's way.
We naturally do such things not because we are by nature either mainly
selfish or primarily malicious or even greedy. We do all this merely because, if taken in pairs, we are in each pair, two different and contrasting
people or groups. Our whole self-consciousness, in fact, depends upon
noting how different from our neighbors each of us is. But contrasts that
strongly interest us can easily become unpleasant. Therefore mutual love
and agreement between the members of a pair of human beings is an easily
interrupted relation. Our differences can readily come at any moment to
seem mutual challenges. If love between a pair of friends survives such
endless trials, it does so through patience, or through the aid of other relations which are naturally more stable, or because love takes on the form
of true loyalty. *But loyalty, which is the love of a self for an united community, always involves relations which concern more than two people.*

Taken by itself, the mutual love of a mere pair of people tends, like
physical energy, to run downhill; to be baffled by personal contrasts, to
be thwarted by mutual interruptions, to give place to a consciousness of
painful differences, to be worn out by time. As Griselda says to her cruel
lord:—

> "But sooth is said; algate I find it true,
> For in effect it proved is on me,
> Love is not old as when that it is new."

This assertion constitutes the first half of the law of the original sin of the
dyadic human relations. Love, when it is a merely dyadic relation be-

tween a pair of lovers, is essentially unstable and inconstant. For the two tend in the long run to interrupt, to bore, or collide each with the other.

The second half of our law is easily stated. When mutual friction once arises between a pair of lovers or of rivals or of individuals otherwise interestingly related, whether they be men or groups of men, *the friction tends to increase,* unless some other relation intervenes, or unless more than a pair of members belong to the community wherein mutual love ought to be sustained, or mutual jealousy averted.

> "Never any more
> While I live,
> Need I hope to see his face
> As before.
>
> Once his love grown chill,
> Mine may strive—
> Bitterly we reembrace,
> Single still."

So laments the lonely wife in Browning's "Men and Women". The situation is human. It daily occurs, and is even commonplace. It illustrates the natural fortune of a pair either of lovers or of human beings otherwise related, who remain merely a pair. When, through any accident, mutual antipathy chances to arise in such a pair, then each of the members of the now distracted community of two irritates the other to new antipathies. Thus in such cases love grows old while hate renews its impish youth.

The only possible renewal of the youth of such an old love depends upon establishing new and creative social ties between the two who once loved, or else upon enlarging and enriching the community, so that it is no longer merely a community of two.

But at this moment we are reminded of a new consideration. As a fact, the natural unit of human society, in all its stages of evolution, is the family. But the normal family is not a pair, but is at least a triad, a group of three persons: Father, Mother, Child. What one might call the molecule of the most lasting and simply instinctive human social groups is, so to speak, an union wherein at least three individual persons, three social atoms, or, in higher stages, three social groups, participate. In such a community love can indeed readily assume its more stable forms, and can turn into a more ideal loyalty. In a mere pair of persons, love, while frequently both present and intense, is essentially unstable; while hate, when once it appears, tends to grow with what it feeds on, namely with the natural contrasts between individuals, and because of their mutual inter-ruptions, and by virtue of the constantly growing consciousness where-with each of the antipathetic persons observes how the other regards him. But in the family triad, the winning and common care for the child may charm away many of the most besetting influences that tend to wreck home unity.

Let us sum up the results thus far reached: The advice which the Dhammapada gives us, about love and hate, ignores an essential fact, namely, the fact of the dangerousness of the dyadic human relations; and forgets this reason why antipathy is so readily growing a weed in our social relations. We hate not merely because we remember injuries. Many of our sources of antipathy seem to be, in the single case, much more petty than is a desire for revenge; but are actually deeper in their meaning than is such a desire. Very often we tend to hate simply because there are so many of us, and because we are so different one from the other; and so because, when we are taken in pairs, we thus appear in each pair as interrupters and intruders, each member of the pair annoying his fellow even while trying to express whatever love he chances to possess for the other, and each emphasizing his own hatred when he feels it, by dwelling on these dual or bilateral contrasts.

Such is thus far our result, here then is the fundamental principle of the philosophy of war. The deepest reason why war is so persistent is that *the nations, thus far in history, are related chiefly in pairs,*—pairs of com-mercial rivals, pairs of borrowers and lenders, pairs of stronger and weak-er nations, pairs of superiors and inferiors, pairs of plunderers who do not understand each the other,—pairs of plotters, each of whom suspects his opponent.

And the deepest reason why what is best in individual men does not destroy but often inflames the warlike spirit, lies in the fact that the best in individual men depends upon their loyalty to their own groups, upon their patriotism, and also upon their interest in groups which are not mere pairs. In such interests in groups which are larger and richer than pairs, consists men's very desire for human solidarity. For human unions can become stable and fruitful only through the establishment of re-lations which are very different from the dangerous dyadic relations of lovers, of rivals, and of warriors.

The sound advice to men is then not completely expressed by the word: "Little children, love one another"; but rather by the Pauline advice to love some united community which has the characters ascribed by Paul to the church. *War itself persists because the nations still cultivate dyadic relations too exclusively.*

We have thus seen wherein lies the basis of the problem of war. War is simply one case whereby to illustrate how dangerous the dyadic relations are in the social world; and how dangerous a community is one which has the form of a pair either of individual men or individual nations.

In the social world which consists of pairs, love indeed finds many temporary dwelling places; but it also finds no continuing city, and so has to seek in utopia for a city out of sight; while hate is indeed not universal, and not all powerful, but is grounded in the natural diversities and in the mutual observations of men, and is therefore always ready to be aroused in those who had been, until it appeared, friends and brothers; while if once aroused, hate tends to grow more intense and distracting as it observes its own life. In those communities which are mere pairs, time is the consumer of love but the nourisher of hate. Love between the members of a mere pair tends to wax old as does a garment; while hate, when once it comes, flourishes in a malicious youth, witch-like and death-dealing.

IV

THE COMMUNITY OF INTERPRETATION

The outlook for humanity would indeed be dark, if our social relations were limited to mere pairs of individuals or of nations or of other groups of men, whether petty or vast. But, as a fact, this is not the case.

We have already seen that there is at least one human community which has characters and relations such as no mere pair of human beings can possibly possess. This is the community consisting of father, mother, and child. This natural and instinctively originated community is never perfect, and is never entirely stable. And hate can find a place in it as well as love. But we also know that this natural community possesses, even in the life of barbarous and uncultivated man, a normal stability, and a normal fruitfulness, as a basis of family peace and loyalty, which lies at the root of many very vast social organizations. Out of an aggregation and perfectly natural interconnection of such triadic family groups, or of what you may call triadic social molecules, a patriarchal social order can be built such as several very great and stable Oriental civilizations have richly illustrated. Time and fecundity favor the family. Its form tends to abide. It favors a type of love which forms a model for all the loyal.

It behooves us then next to consider whether there are other groups of human beings, other communities, perhaps artificial, but essentially sound and progressive, which have characters such as the triadic union of father, mother, and child illustrates. And herewith our quest enters upon a new stage. Pairs are dangerous communities. Are there triadic communities which are less dangerous? Are there many instances of such triads? Can we name such?

As a fact, all of us depend for the opportunity to do our daily business upon the existence, upon the stability, and upon the fruitfulness of such relatively peaceful and loyal triadic social groups. Let us name a few of them; for in this field concrete examples are especially instructive. Let us talk then no more of pairs of lovers or of rivals. Let us consider some communities which are essentially groups of three individuals, or of three groups of men.

Suppose that somebody,—let us call him A,—desires to do business with another man, whom we will call C. So far, some relation involving the pair consisting of A and C is sought. But perhaps A and C are dwellers in different cities, or in different countries. Perhaps they are not on speaking terms. Perhaps they speak different languages. Perhaps each is too busy about his own affairs to dream of interrupting the other. In such cases the dual relation whereby A might do business with C, cannot readily be established. What shall A do?

A form of business which daily grows, in the modern world, more and more important, hereupon suggests itself to our minds. Suppose that A finds some third man,—let us call him B,—who undertakes *to represent A's plans to C, to interpret, to explain, to urge them in C's presence; to act, in a word, as the agent of A in the proposed dealing with C.* Let the business hereupon be carried out according to this method. That is, let A find the agent B. Let this agent, let B do the proposed work.

Hereupon there will be formed a community consisting essentially of three persons, A, B, C, who occupy different places in this community. Their relations will be not merely dual or dyadic, but treble or triadic. And each will have, in the resulting triadic transaction, an unique place. Each can be named by this, his special function in this triadic community.

This community will consist of what is usually called a *principal*, of an *agent*, and of a *client*, or other such man, *to whom the agent represents the principal.* The relations of these three persons are such as need to be expressed in triadic terms. This community cannot be reduced to a mere collection of pairs. If you try to understand its structure, you will find that you have to think in terms and in relations with which the study of mere pairs of persons cannot make you familiar.

And now, this community is such that its relations have a most instructive practical value. To observe what this value is, you have first to observe that this community is naturally a peace-loving community. Every business involving a stable type of *agency* depends upon mutual respect and confidence. And you then have also to remember that in our modern world *we daily come to be more and more dependent upon finding and using agents.* New forms of agency, new classes of agents, accompany every advance of civilization. And you have still further to remember that agents *tend on the whole to further international as well as personal peace and good will.*

The type of community here in question needs in view of its vast power, effectiveness, and fruitfulness, a name of its own. Let me suggest a name. I need a very general name, for this type of community in question is also exemplified by triads of men, or groups of men, whose relations you would hardly think of defining by means of the term agent. Common to all the communities of this type is their tendency to further peace, good will, and loyalty, and to have an unifying influence both upon individuals and upon nations.

I venture to call a community such as that consisting of principal, agent, and client exemplifies, a *Community of Interpretation*. It is a community having a very wonderful adaptation to the most various social tasks. It is the best type of community that we know, just because of its general tendency, illustrated in widely various special examples, towards stability, unity, and practical effectiveness. Our most productive as well as our most ideal sorts of business daily require us either to become members of some sort of community of interpretation, or, when we are already members, to act loyally in accordance with the place that we occupy in such a community. Such communities are not merely convenient. They are indispensable to civilized life. They are not merely so frequent as to be commonplace, but they are socially so potent as to seem, in some of their exemplifications, almost superhuman in the skill and in the humane sort of social unity which they create and sustain. Having begun with the extremely well-known instance of the community consisting of a principal, an agent, and a man, sometimes called a client, to whom the agent represents the principal, we may at once characterize in very general terms the mere form which any community of interpretation possesses.

A community of interpretation consists of three persons, or groups of persons, who are its members. We may call these members A, B, and C. We may first think of them as individual men. We shall find, however, that in general, each of the members of a community of interpretation not only may also be a group of men; but that this individual group in such a community may be much more numerous than is any now existing nation. Our present interest lies in the form of the community of interpretation, in its relations to the warlike, to the peaceful, and to the loyal tendencies and dispositions of men. We wish to show that, on the whole, a community of interpretation, not only is, in itself, a peaceful group of men, but also may be, and frequently is, a very highly active and strenuous and creative community; and that its life essentially tends to enrich both the power and the unity of mankind. A community of interpretation is a sort of artificially created but marvelously fruitful family. Of social molecules, each of which consists of three atoms, or individuals united in a community of interpretation, the most potent and peaceful and reasonable social orders in the modern world consist.

We also wish to show that, *if the world's peace is to be furthered, such progress must take the form of creating and sustaining certain definable communities of interpretation.* We shall be able to show that this our main thesis, in this paper, is at once a philosophical principle, and a perfectly practical and businesslike proposal, whose truth and value the market place exemplifies as well as does any rightly constituted theory of society. By this thesis our philosophy of war will be at a stroke converted into a philosophy of peace, and that without our confining ourselves to any merely utopian dreams or plans. We shall show, not indeed how universal peace is at once to be attained, but how the human world is now actually on the way towards a possible, even if very distant, universal peace; and we shall also show that this way lies along the very lines of progress which the form and the functions of any community of interpretation exemplify.[1]

---

1. The idea, although not the name of the "Community of Interpretation," is derived by me from certain essays of the late logician, Mr. Charles Peirce. The philosophical bearing of this idea, and its relations to very deep and far-reaching philosophical issues, have been discussed in Vol. II of my recent work entitled the "Problem of Christianity" (New York, 1913). The present application of Peirce's theory of interpretation to the philosophy of war and peace is, so far as I know, new.

A, B, and C, the members of any community of interpretation, work together upon a task which is at once theoretical and practical,—at once businesslike and ideal,—a task which may be as unemotional and impersonally stern in its requirements as is any serious business of men, but which may also require all the passionate devotion, and all the eager loyalty, which any man can give. This task, in its simplest expression, is this. A and C, to use again the phrase of Hamlet, have their own individual "business and desire, such as they are." The remaining member of the community, whom I now call B, has, as his peculiar business in this community, the task of addressing C, and of explaining or interpreting to C what A's desire or business is, to the end that C may be brought into some definite sort of cooperation with A.

This cooperation, if it occurs at all, will bring A and C into some kind of social unity, such as will make them act as if they were, in a certain respect, *one man*. To bring about this sort of solidarity, and this cooperation of C with A, is the interpreter's main aim and interest, so far as he is indeed the interpreter of this community. He desires, just as any reasonable agent desires, not to do A's will alone, nor C's will alone, *but at once to create and to make conscious, and to carry out, their united will, in so far as they both are to become and remain members of that community in which he does the work of the interpreter.*

Since B has this united will of A and C as his aim and inspiration, he must be what I call loyal. That is, he must be the willing, and, for the purposes of this special task of interpretation, the thoroughgoing servant of the cause of uniting the will of C, to whom he represents the ideas of A, with the plans of A, whom he interprets. B, the interpreter, is therefore the most important member of the community in question. For he both defines and expresses its united purpose. He brings C into touch with A. He holds them together. His essential aim as interpreter is that not his own private will, but the will of the whole community, should be done, and that A and C should act as one man, while, in bringing A and C together, he usually discovers or in some measure creates their common will. Hence B is above all the most obviously and explicitly loyal member of the community. On the other hand,—"in his will," when he finds and expresses it, "is the peace" both of A and of C. His success lies in this peace. His "business and desire," if he is indeed a successful interpreter, create, sustain, and constantly increase their harmony. "To this end he comes" into this community. He incarnates and furthers and enlightens its aims, precisely in so far as he worthily fulfills his business as interpreter.

In the single case, as in the market place or in the office, the business or the idea which B interprets to C, and the common will of the community of interpretation which B discovers, expresses, or carries out, may relate to matters of a commonplace, or even of a sordid character; but on the whole there is no ideal activity of man which is too lofty to be expressed or furthered through a community of interpretation. For all rational plans involve the cooperation of pairs of men,—the union and the unity and harmony of the wills of those who are to cooperate. But, for the very reasons heretofore pointed out, such union and such unity cannot be stable, secure, and enlightened, unless to the pair of men who are to co-operate there is added the third man whose business and desire it is to bring and to keep these two in touch each with the other. Such a mediator is precisely an interpreter of one of the two men to the other. The interpreter has then the function *to transform the essentially dangerous pair into the consciously and consistently harmonious triad.*

Because the interpreter B at once discovers or creates and expresses the one meaning and will of A and C, I have called him "The Spirit of the Community."

V

Special Communities of Interpretation

Let me next return from the generalization which the mention of the ideal business of an agent has suggested to us, to further special examples of communities of interpretation. Let me call your attention to three such communities. They are both practical and ideal in their nature. They are both businesslike and redeeming in their influence.

The civilized world has long depended, for some of its most characteristic and precious life, upon one of these communities.

The two other communities are modern. Until very recently the world knew only the most rudimentary beginnings of them. But they have already transformed, in certain profoundly significant respects, the modern world. They dominate our social order more and more; and they will continue to do so, transforming it at a rate which promises for a long time to increase.

The three communities of interpretation which are now in my mind are these:—

1. The judicial community
2. The banker's community
3. The community of insurance

All of these three communities are coordinated with the agent's community, and cooperate with various forms of the latter, so that you may say: Our present civilization depends, for all its most peaceful, worldly, and practical activities, upon these four distinct sorts of communities of interpretation. If you removed all four from our social order, then this our human world, precisely upon its most practical and constructive side, would degenerate into a vast aggregate of the dangerous communities which are pairs. The family triads aforesaid would indeed remain as the principal basis for the loyal life of mankind; while a few other less visible and less obviously practical types of triads would characterize so much of our civilization as still would be left to us.

Let us look a little closer at the communities of interpretation now before us. The agent's community we have already characterized.

The judicial community consists of a pair of contending individuals or social groups, while the third member of the group is a judge, or umpire, or arbiter, or mediator, whose office consists in interpreting to a defendant the will, the case, and the legal or social rights of a complainant or plaintiff.

The judicial community is the most ancient and familiar of the communities of interpretation. Upon the dignity and authority of judges and umpires the social world depends for the control and transformation of certain well-known consequences of the original sin of the dyadic relations. From social conditions, which, if uncontrolled, directly lead to elemental warfare, the judicial community actively leads the way to other social conditions which constitute peace. The peace thus won is not in general the peace which the Dhammapada advises us to seek by substituting love for hate. But it is the peace which incites men to new cooperations as soon as the contention is thus judicially settled. Hence the judicial community is indispensable to civilization.

The banker's community consists of a borrower, of a lender, and of a third person whose life and interest it is, in general, to make the relation of the borrower and the lender a relation that is profitable to both of them. This third person is that active interpreter of credits, that expert as to the safety of loans, who is known as a banker. The lender deposits with the banker. The banker accommodates the borrower. Or, if the borrower and the lender are that very dangerous pair consisting of persons known as a promoter and an investor, the banker may then appear as a broker, whose business it is to bring and to keep investors in profitable and fruitful touch with those who undertake or promote novel enterprises, for which they need capital.

Apart from the banker or broker, acting as interpreter, the pair consisting of a borrower and a lender is a peculiarly dangerous pair. The advice of the Dhammapada, the "old rule" that hatred ceases by love, becomes not merely ineffective but bitterly and tragically humorous, when applied to the natural relations which tend to arise within this pair consisting of borrower and lender. The ancient and medieval social world knew of borrowing and lending mainly as calamitous social relations, which seemed fatally to lead to avarice, to fraud, and to the bondage of those debtors whom want or overconfidence had thrown into the hands of their creditors.

One of the most dramatic of all social transformations has been that which has been due to the appearance, in the modern world, of the banker's community of interpretation. Out of an aggregation of the social molecules which are, in one way or another, banker's communities, the whole vast and productive system of modern credit has grown. The result is that, as a noted publicist some years ago said to me: "Ours is the age, and ours is the civilization of the broker." You easily see what this publicist meant. You all know how, despite all the unhappy social accidents that interrupt the workings of the modern system, and that mar both its morals and its success, the modern credit system is, on the whole, both a result of loyalty and a trainer of loyalty.

For, necessary to the great banker's enduring success is his steadfast loyalty to his function as interpreter and so as the "spirit of his community." Just as he may otherwise fail, so he may defraud. But, on the whole, banking has made not only for thrift, for cooperation, for the constant increase of investment, for confidence, and so for the unity of mankind, but it has also made for loyalty; and has in fact both taught loyalty to the business world and exemplified loyalty, as only the work of a community of interpretation can do. The banker's community, then, is the social molecule of a vast organism, whose life is, on the whole, a life of peaceful construction, and in that sense a life of a true love of mankind. If war ever ceases, if peace ever comes, the banker's community will have had an important share in the process.

It remains next to speak of the community of insurance. Everybody knows in general of its vast and transforming influence, and of its recently acquired social importance. Few notice the reason why it has become so important. Our previous study of the general characters of the community of interpretation can be easily applied to the community of insurance.

Men take risks. They are often obliged to do so. Sometimes they take them merely because they love risks. But when a man takes a risk and loses, there is in general somebody else who has to bear the consequences of this loss. It may be his creditor, his assign, his heir, or his next friend, upon whom the loss falls; but, since nobody liveth unto himself, and nobody dieth unto himself, the man who takes a risk is seldom the only man who pays for the loss. Now let us call the man who takes the risk A. Then let the man who has to bear the loss if A loses, but who of course might correspondingly win if A won, be named C, and let us call him A's *possible beneficiary*, who of course may be, if A loses, quite the opposite of a receiver of benefits.

Now the relation of A to C, the relation of the man who takes the risk, to the man who may win if A wins, but who will lose if A loses, is a dyadic relation. Like the other human social relations of pairs, it is dangerous. It daily embitters the relations of debtors and creditors. It daily makes some people penniless, and inspires others with hate. Its very danger makes it morbidly fascinating to those who have once learned to gamble. It fills the social order with fears and suspicions. It wrecks souls. And you cannot escape from the poison of this dangerous relation by merely loving the man whose risks lead to losses which you have to bear. Love seldom cures any such fool of his folly, and the one who loves him suffers the more because of the love.

Now the community of insurance comes to exist when somebody, let us call him B, undertakes to bring the man who takes the risk into a true and active union of interest with his possible beneficiary. The members of the community of insurance are the *adventurer* A, that is the man who takes the risk, the *beneficiary* C, and the *insurer*, who is the spirit of the community, and who is commonly incarnate in some corporate community.

The insurer B estimates or interprets the *insurable value* of the risk which A takes. For a consideration corresponding to this insurable value, B undertakes to make C not only A's possible beneficiary, but A's actual and reasonably secure beneficiary. That is, *B insures the beneficiary C against any loss due to the risk which A takes.*

For reasons which can only be stated in terms of the theory of probability this result can be reached only in case many risks are estimated, and insured by the same insurer B. Hence the insurer's community tends, far more than even the banker's community, to demand some larger union of the social molecules whereof the single community of interpretation consists. In consequence insurance very largely takes the form of mutual insurance. It brings men together in vaster and in more highly organized and articulated groups than the banker's world knows. It leads to constantly new social expressions. It contributes to peace, to loyalty, to social unity, to active charity, as no other community of interpretation has ever done. It tends, in the long run, to carry us beyond the era of the agent and of the broker into the coming social order of the insurer. We cannot predict all that it will yet accomplish; but we can already see that *of all the business relations and of all the practical communities yet devised, the insurance relations and the insurance communities most tend to bring peace on earth, and to aid us towards the community of mankind.*

VI

MUTUAL INTERNATIONAL INSURANCE

In the search for influences that might further the cause of international peace, well-known efforts have already been made to devise practical and international uses of the judicial community, of the banker's community, and of the agent's community. Each of these efforts has so far proved both conditionally useful and frequently disappointing. *No adequate effort has yet been made to further the cause of peace through the deliberate application of the form of the insurer's community to international business. Now this is what I propose as my present contribution to these dark problems.*

The foregoing study of the triadic communities of interpretation, and of the dangerous character of those communities which are pairs, has been needed to enable us to show why this newest of the great communities of interpretation has so rapidly acquired its vast influence over the social destinies of men and why we need to put it to new uses.

Our whole discussion up to this point has prepared the way, therefore, for our final thesis, which is this:—

There is a still untried method of gradually leading towards international peace, and of rendering wars progressively less destructive and less willful. This is the method to which I call your attention. It is in general the method of undertaking mutual international insurance against some of the common calamities to which all mankind, or certain large portions of mankind, are subject. Stated in terms of our theory of the communities of interpretation, this method may assume the form of a maxim, or if you like, of a proposed constitution or international agreement upon which a new community of insurance may be founded, as follows:—

Apply to international relations, gradually and progressively, that principle of insurance which has been found so unexpectedly fruitful and peaceful and powerful and unifying in the life and in the social relations of individual men.

Begin to make visible the community of mankind, not merely, as at present, in the form of alliances which are ambiguous, and at times irritating, and of arbitration treaties which are likely to be broken at some passionate moment when they are most needed, but in the form of a sufficiently large board of financially expert trustees, whose membership is international, whose services are duly compensated from the funds of the trust, and whose conduct is guided by plainly stated rules which have the substantially unanimous consent of all the nations concerned in the plan of mutual insurance which is in question. Let these rules be changeable only by the substantially unanimous consent of the members of the already existing community of insurance, or in such wise as not to abridge rights which the already existent body of rules have created.

Let the funds of the mutual insurance organization in question be put, in form, into the charge of some well-known and, so to speak, essentially neutral power, such as Sweden, or Switzerland. Let this fund be protected from merely predatory assaults by the fact that under the rules, it would, from the first, be invested by the board of international trustees, that is by the incorporated insurance community, in decidedly various investments, and in various parts of the world, so that it could not be found or used by any one power unless this power had first violently conquered all of the nations that had contributed to the trust, and that had, under the rules thereby acquired, a definite interest in its distribution.

Let rules be formulated, as such became needful, to regulate the conditions under which one of the partners in the plan of mutual insurance could surrender, with or without notice, its already acquired rights under the insurance agreement.

Let the international insurance community in question have no direct political powers or duties whatever. Let it be purely a financial and fiduciary body, with a minimum of inevitable judicial functions.

Let its fidelity to its trust and to its rules be guaranteed simply by the size of its controlling board, by the personal character, the experience, and the mode of selection of the members of this board, and by the entire publicity of all its proceedings and official acts.

Let it have no powers as an arbitrator in case of international disputes, but *entire autonomy, under general rules, regarding those judicial decisions which it would inevitably have, from time to time, to render, when disputes arose as to what rights the individual members of this international union for mutual insurance had acquired or forfeited by their own acts as sovereign powers.*

Let it lay down no arbitrary rules for international morality; let it not undertake to codify international law; let it hold aloof from all politically colored international disputes.

On the other hand, let there be simply no appeal from its deliberate and judicial decisions as to the financial and fiduciary matters which were left to its decision and discretion by the international agreement for mutual insurance.

Let any and all the sovereign states of the world, great or small, at war or not at war, whether accused or not of present or past barbarism by their neighbors, be at any time at liberty under general and financially precise rules, to enter the international insurance community as new members, to contribute to its fund, and to receive in turn an amount of insurance against a definite sort of national calamities—an amount which, as in case of ordinary mutual insurance companies, should be duly proportioned to the deposit made.[1]

---

1. Let it freely co-operate, when it chose and in so far as its functions permitted, with the plans, the influences, and the undertakings of the Hague tribunal. But, since its own business is thus financial and fiduciary, let it not itself be subject to the Hague tribunal and let it carefully avoid, so far as possible, the actual taking part in arbitration or "judicial settlement of international disputes."

Finally, so far as this first outline sketch of our plan is concerned, let a provision be made for emergencies as follows: A nation, insured under the agreement, might undergo revolutions, or might be conquered in war, or might be divided into several states, or might be lost in some new federation of various states. This transformed sovereign state might already have acquired, before its disappearance, larger or smaller rights to an insurance payment, under conditions which might have come to be actually realized. In this case, *the trustees of the mutual international insurance organization would have sole power to decide what state or states, if any, had inherited the insurance payment or payments due to the state which had thus passed away from the now visibly represented family of nations.* If, however, the trustees of the fund decided, formally and judicially, and of course after due investigation, and quite publicly: "No now existing state has justly inherited the insurance rights which belonged to the formerly existing state. The dead state is now unrecognizable among the living states"—then *the insurance rights of the dead state would simply lapse;* and its insured funds would return to the general fund, to be used by the remaining members of the community of mutual insurance under the general rules. *Thus a motive would be furnished whereby both internal revolutions and external conquests would be made less attractive to disturbers of the social or of the international peace of mankind.*

Furthermore, if, at the end of a war, the vanquished power had some right under the mutual insurance agreement to certain funds, and if the victor hereupon insisted upon forcing the vanquished to surrender, as a spoil of war, its rights under the contract of mutual insurance or the funds due to it under these rights, *then a treaty thus to surrender the property rights or the money due to the vanquished under the insurance agreement, would automatically make void the whole insurance contract which the vanquished had made.* From the moment the vanquished had been forced to surrender its funds, now due, or its rights acquired under the insurance contract, from that moment the insurance trustees would *simply pay nothing of the funds in question either to the vanquished power or to any other single power. The whole fund in question would simply return to the common fund,* and be used for the common benefit of all the nations that participated.

So much for a first sketch of the proposed agreement of mutual insurance. You will ask: *Against what evils should this mutual international insurance company, when once organized, attempt to insure its clients?*

In answer, first, think of the long possible list of evils from which directly or indirectly all the nations suffer, and with which, in the first place, war itself has perhaps little,—perhaps nothing to do. Such evils are widely distributed, have an incidence which affects now this people and then that people, are capable of a careful statistical study, and are therefore in principle insurable. Individual nations cannot in general insure their subjects against them. *A community of nations could insure an individual nation against them,* and could pay over a guaranteed sum to the insured and suffering nation.

A brief and inadequate list of such calamities is as follows:—

1. Destructive earthquakes and volcanic eruptions.

2. Certain of the migratory pestilences, and in particular, certain of the tropical diseases.

3. Some of the destructive storms of the type which follow, in general, known tracks but strike special localities by chance (such for instance as the West India hurricanes, and the China Sea typhoons).

4. Recurrent famines and great crop failures.

5. Marine disasters. (For the ocean exacts a statistically definable toll from the commerce of the whole world.)

Herewith varying a little the type of cases, we may further mention:—

6. *The destruction in war time of the private property belonging to the subjects of unquestionably neutral states.* (This is a first mention of the "war risks" which our insurance company might learn, in its gradual growth, more and more to insure.)

Now suppose a community of mutual international insurance once instituted upon such general lines. To the foregoing list of internationally insurable losses, a great number of others can and would soon be added. What would be the general result?

The mutual insurance community would be sure to do what other mutual companies have done.

1. It would proceed *carefully to investigate such losses both from a statistical point of view and with regard to their causes.*

2. *It would attempt to reduce the number and magnitude of these causes.* To this end it would use all possible moral influences consistent with its functions as a trustee. Being no political state, and having no protection except the fact that its funds were *nearly inaccessible to any predatory power,* it could use none indeed but moral influences. But on the other hand, being no Hague tribunal, although often cooperating with that tribunal, it would not be likely to irritate its clients by unwel-

come judicial decisions about already bitterly controversial matters. It would need to ask for no new arbitration treaties. It would leave to the Hague tribunal the work of formulating international law. Its own function would be the higher one of cultivating international cooperation through mutual insurance against common evils and thereby teaching by example the meaning and the attractiveness of the loyalty of each individual nation to the community of all nations. Mutual insurance would make this community visible.

3. But these, its non-controversial and purely moral influences, would still be influences whose source would be the first *spirit of the community* of all mankind which would ever yet have won permanent and visible presence on earth. In its efforts not only to alleviate but to prevent pestilence and famine, the board of trustees, representing all the nations in the community of insurance, would *inspire all the nations actually to work together*, at once in a charitable and in a businesslike way, as they have never worked before. *As the spirit of this triadic community, the insurance organization would both exemplify and teach loyalty. Now the nations, living, thus far, in dangerous pairs, and in groups of pairs, have never yet had any chance of acquiring international loyalty.*

We have then a vast experience of business-like activities behind us when we assert that this triadic community, once founded, would ceaselessly tend to increase, to discover new powers, and to exercise new and peaceful influences.

But you will ask: Could it go farther? *Could it insure its members against any of the evils of actual war?* And if it did so, would that still more directly tend towards the diminishing of wars?

I answer that, if large enough, *this community of mutual international insurance could insure its members progressively against more and more of the evils and destructive calamities due to war*, by the simple addition of one very important rule to the rules so far laid down: If a nation had a war with another, the insurance trustees would never directly inquire as to the moral justification of this war, but would ask: *Who committed the first act of war? No nation would receive insurance compensation for any expenses due to a war in which it committed the first act of war.* This rule would, in each case, require judicial interpretation. But this again would be no arbitration of a Hague tribunal, but purely a financier's decision as to whether or no an insurance policy was at least temporarily or in a single case vitiated by an act of a nature known beforehand.

For the rest, in so far as our insurance company undertook to pay any war expenses, it would get a businesslike interest in averting the causes of war which would express the will of all the insuring nations, and which would possess a fecundity, an ingenuity, and a wisdom of which we shall know nothing until we get such a community of interpretation formed *to teach the nations, by the potent devices of mutual insurance, the art of loyalty to the community of mankind.*

But you will say, such a community would need to begin with very vast financial resources. How shall the nations, now absorbed in greed and in rivalries, the dangerous pairs, be induced to invest their funds in so prodigious and humane an undertaking?

To this question the present moment furnishes the fitting answer. Herein lies the very core of the present practical proposal. For, when the present war is ended, one side will be the victor. That side will include *more than one nation.* The victors will jointly or severally demand an indemnity or several indemnities from the vanquished, and might raise some new quarrel over the division of the spoils. Well,—*let the victors make their demand together. Let them demand one indemnity from all the vanquished. When it is paid, let the victors at once begin and actively establish the first mutual international insurance company against national calamities, including wars. Let them devote this whole indemnity to forming the initial fund of this company.* Let them deposit the fund with the trustees, and under the formal care of Switzerland or of Sweden. Then let them draw up their rules, and thenceforth *invite all sovereign states, great or small, including the vanquished states,* to insure by payments and enjoy all the advantages of the insurance. *This act of thus using the war indemnity will be much less wasteful than to waste it in preparations for future war.* The vanquished will not hope to make it an object of future plunder. *It will henceforth be the fund of the community of all mankind.* And this community of *all mankind will begin to take on visible form, presence, and power to save.*

Lincoln on a famous occasion used a triadic phrase. He spoke of "government of the people, by the people, and for the people."

My thesis is *that whenever insurance of the nations, by the nations, and for the nations begins, it will thenceforth never vanish from the earth, but will begin to make visible to us the holy city of the community of all mankind.* To such a vision perhaps we have a right, even while the slain lie awaiting burial. Let us dwell upon this vision, at once ideal and practical. Let us say of this vision, of this holy city,—"Even so, come quickly. For then, none of these dead will have died wholly in vain."

THE POSSIBILITY OF INTERNATIONAL INSURANCE

Near the beginning of the present war I wrote a little book entitled "War and Insurance," in which I stated and defended the thesis that the cause of the world's peace would be aided if in future the principle of insurance were gradually and progressively introduced into international business.

Insurance has already proved to be, in the modern life of individual nations, a cause of no little growth in social organization, in human solidarity, in reasonableness, and in peace. The best workings of the insurance principle have been, on the whole, its indirect workings. It has not only taught men, in manifold ways, both the best means and the wisdom of "bearing one another's burdens"; but it has also established many indirect, and for that very reason all the more potent, types of social linkage, which the individual policy-holder or underwriter very seldom clearly and consciously estimates at their true value.

These indirect and less frequently noticed types of linkage have already transformed our civilization, so that ours is already an age and a civilization of insurance. Thus the greatest service of insurance has been done, so to speak, beneath the surface of our social life; and the most significant changes of our modern world through the indirect influence of insurance have grown up as if in the dark, becoming manifest only after they have been long developing their effectiveness. This fact furnishes a reason for looking forward most hopefully to great and good indirect results when once insurance assumes a definite international form.

Thus, for instance, one of the most significant indirect results of the development of fire insurance in the social life of our own nation has been the fact that fire insurance has made possible, and has systematized, a method of business whereby great numbers of people who would otherwise have no way of acquiring homes of their own, are now able, through thrift and patience, to become in time the owners of dwelling houses.

The method of business in question consists simply in this, that the home-seeker at the outset induces some one to advance the money whereby the house can be built, while the man for whom the new house is built makes the one who has advanced this money not only his mortgagee, but also the holder of an insurance policy whereby the advance made on the new house is rendered secure. Without fire insurance this security, in great numbers of cases, could not be furnished.

In analogous ways, fidelity insurance, working in more or less indirect fashion, enables countless young men to begin life in positions of trust, and thus to find their places as people worthy of confidence in a world where they might otherwise be doomed to live only as temporary employes.

Life insurance may be used by the otherwise needy man to capitalize his own future, and thus to win his way through a period of struggle. And in all such cases social linkages are formed which depend upon the use of insurance and which tend to bind men in far-reaching unions such as without insurance would be impossible. Such social linkages are peace breeding, and are profoundly civilizing.

It is therefore not merely the "mutual" aspect of insurance wherein its most beneficent influence is manifested. Its greatest social power depends upon the fact that a man does not in general purchase an insurance policy merely for the transient creature of to-day called "himself." A man purchases insurance for his "beneficiary." His beneficiaries may include people or corporations of whose very existence he, the individual, is little aware. But his linkages with such beneficiaries may join him to the whole social order.

It is because the men of to-day are thus united through insurance in groups of greater complexity, stability, and value than any other sort of business or institution makes possible that we owe as much as we do to the indirect influences which the relations of insurers, adventurers, and beneficiaries make possible and effective.

Were any group of nations to begin in a businesslike and practicable way to do what the individual fellow members of a social order have now the means of doing, namely to insure against risks of some insurable sort, we should have a good reason to expect that analogous and beneficent indirect workings would ere long follow from even a modest beginning in the art of international insurance.

The vast and unexpected transformations which, as the experience of the nineteenth century showed, insurance has introduced into the social order of individual peoples are of a type so much needed in the mutual relations of various nations that no opportunity should be neglected to make such a beginning in this new art of international insurance.

And since the present war seemed to me, and still seems, to furnish a great, although so tragic an opportunity to make such a beginning, I could not forego the chance which the moment offered to indicate, as I tried to do in my book, the general nature of this opportunity as I then saw it. First sketches of novel plans are very generally crude. The details of my own first statement of a mode of beginning international insurance were, as I myself said, wholly tentative, and were meant to be subject to a thorough revision. For such revision there has still been no sufficient time. But I already see aspects of the subject which need, as I believe, some recognition.

And I still believe that if insurance "of the nations, for the nations, and by the nations" once appeared in a practicable form, it would thenceforward not "vanish from the earth," but would tend, more than any international influence has yet tended, to "make the community of mankind visible," and so to further, gradually, perhaps slowly, but powerfully, the cause of peace.

Among the critics of my book there are, (despite all the objections to my plan which have been urged, and despite all the difficulties that lie in the way of introducing into international relations the principle of insurance,) so friendly counselors, who have said: "If we could but see, or devise, some definite procedure whereby a beginning could be made in the insurance of any risks that are common to several nations, then, were this procedure such as, if proposed and undertaken, would involve a feasible and practicable business of international insurance, however modest this beginning, we should be even now quite willing to look with favor upon the discussion of the enterprise."

In fact, for such critics, it is precisely the way of beginning international insurance, on however limited a scale, that they most want to have explained. It is for such readers and critics of my plan that the present article is written.

Since the present war began, I have met with a good many expressions which have come from authoritative sources, and which have related to the ways in which so destructive and widespread a conflict, especially if it continues long, is likely to affect the future conduct of the various forms of insurance which already exist. Said, in effect, in a letter to me, a man prominent in his own part of the insurance world: "By its very nature war tends to impair, and in the long run to destroy, all sorts of interests which, apart from war, have constituted or have determined insurable risks."

Such comments seem to be obvious enough. They are just now, as I believe, frequent. But they so far leave unanswered the question: "What shall be done, or can be done, to protect, after the close of this war, those vast common interests which the insurance organizations now have in charge, but which wars, and, above all, great wars, tend plainly and dangerously to assail?" It is precisely this question to which my present discussion offers at least a partial answer.

The experts in each special branch of insurance must discover for themselves and must define in their own way the relations which war in general, and this war in particular, may be expected to have to the interests which they represent. But there is one type of problems, common to a number of distinct forms of insurance, to which I may next direct attention.

The problems to which I refer are those presented by the sort of insurance business which is called reinsurance. These problems are certain to be very considerably affected by the results of the present war. Some of them are already much affected. This, as I learn, upon inquiry from experts, is especially the case in some regions of the fire insurance field. But problems of reinsurance also play their part in life insurance and in marine insurance.

And at or after the close of the present war, large alterations and readjustments will be needed to adapt the future conduct of reinsurance to the new conditions that will result from the vast and widespread destruction which the war has already produced, and will continue to produce until it ends, and perhaps long after it has ended.

Without trespassing upon the special field of any expert in insurance, it seems reasonable for a layman to venture a mere hint regarding some of the ways in which this effect of the war upon the future conduct of reinsurance may be expected to show itself.

At any time, whether in peace or in war, an underwriter who has already undertaken to carry a given risk, and who regards this risk as altered in its probable value by events that have happened since he made his contract, may, like anyone else who has to face a problem which involves his own risks and fortunes, seek to make a new contract with a second insurer, who, for a consideration, based upon a new estimate of the risk as it appears in the light of the new facts, shall undertake to carry and to fulfil an agreed portion of the obligations which the first underwriter insured.

Such reinsurance may take place in exceptional ways, and may be confined to some one case or to some few individual cases. Reinsurance contracts of this sort are comparatively familiar in marine insurance, and often come to be mentioned in the newspapers of the day when some vessel is long overdue, and when those underwriters who first insured her now go into the market to reinsure their risks. Such reinsurance contracts, when thus confined to individual cases and made subject to no general prior agreements among the various underwriters concerned, may more or less closely approach the character of mere wagers.

Reinsurance contracts possess, however, the character and the social and financial value of typical insurance transactions when they are made systematically, not merely because an underwriter desires not to carry longer a risk previously assumed, but in accordance with general agreements whereby various underwriters combine to carry in union some class that includes several, sometimes many, different insurance undertakings.

This is the case if underwriters A and B agree in advance that A may at pleasure, or subject to certain rules, reinsure with B such and such of the risks that A undertakes to carry; or, again, if A and B agree that of some class of risks which A assumes B shall be bound in advance to carry, for a suitable consideration, such and such a proportion. There are companies—some of them especially prominent in the fire-insurance field—which devote themselves mainly to various types of reinsurance.

It will be noticed, on the basis of such facts, that reinsurance has already become, in a perfectly natural way, and quite apart from any philosopher's speculations, a business which has a wide international extent and importance; although, as yet, no group of nations has taken part in the conduct of reinsurance.

But as soon as we give a little attention to this side of our problem, we stand face to face with the fact that a perfectly definite form of genuinely international insurance has already come, through the course of evolution, very near, not only to general practicability, but to actual existence. The nations therefore already have at hand an opportunity whose preciousness, as I believe, can hardly be overrated. Let us briefly consider what this opportunity is and implies.

That the State may, under certain conditions, undertake to insure its subjects or some class of its subjects, against various sorts of risks, is already a principle well recognized; although, of course, the expediency of state insurance in this or in that special form is a topic that involves many matters of controversy. Most of the forms of modern social insurance involve a greater or less approach to using the State as an insurer of its own subjects. At the beginning of this war our national Government undertook to carry for our shippers some of the special risks to which the war has subjected our commerce. To speak of state insurance, then, is not to mention a wholly strange idea.

If, however, there exist, as has been for years the case, forms and plans of reinsurance which involve interests that are already international in their scope and extent, and in the variety of the problems and interests concerned; and if, at the conclusion of the present war, the whole business of reinsurance, in adjusting itself to the needs and demands of the future, will have to solve problems that will deeply concern the underwriters of many nations; why should not these international problems of the future of reinsurance, involving, as they necessarily will do, the future conduct and agreements of insurance corporations belonging to many peoples, be put at once under the care of a suitable international organ?

That is, why should not we make, and promptly make, a beginning at the international conduct of the business of reinsurance? I refer especially to so much of this business of reinsurance as will in fact, at the end of the present war, demand, of and for the underwriters of different nations, readjustments, new contracts, new agreements among existing corporations belonging to various peoples; while these new problems and contracts will be too complex and too difficult to be readily and adequately and advantageously met by individual agreements among the many widely distributed private corporations that have to deal with the now rapidly changing situation of the whole insurance world, and that will have to deal with this situation in the future.

What sort of international organ would be suited to deal with these problems of reinsurance? The answer is furnished, I believe, by the International Board of Trustees, which in my book I have defined and proposed as the general organ for conducting this sort of insurance.

The choice and formation of this Board of Trustees would involve no new and strife-breeding treaties among the various nations. The board, when once constituted, would have no political powers or functions whatever. Its conduct of the trust funds committed to its care would need no supervision from any arbitration tribunal. No diplomatists would have any voice in its doings. Its funds themselves could be protected, and the longer it existed the more varied and effective this perfectly peaceful self-protection would become, if the board were at the outset constituted as, with reasonable probability, it could be constituted.

Its business would consist, in general, in selling various sorts of policies to the nations which, for any reason, chose to have dealings with the International Insurance Trustees. Nations that made trust agreements with the board could withdraw from them at pleasure, in a perfectly peaceful way, by the expedient of surrendering, upon terms determined by previous agreements, the policies that they had come to possess. The Board of Trustees would have a strong interest in so planning its policies and in so administering its international business as to retain and increase its reputation as an insurance corporation deserving of patronage, and able to offer policies which the insuring nations would find advantageous to themselves.

In my book I have in general defined the nature, constitution, and possible functions of this International Board of Insurance Trustees. My critics have doubted whether I could name a set of insurable risks, common to various nations, and sufficiently attractive to induce a group of nations to do a practicable business with the board when once it had been formed.

My present article points out that, from the end of the present war, there will be a constant increase and variety of reinsurance plans and contracts needed by the private insurance companies of various nations. If the conduct of this new reinsurance business is not put under the care of an International Board of Trustees, the business, of course, will in one way or another come in time to be done.

But, apart from international cooperation, directed to this end, such business will depend upon special agreements made amongst individual corporations belonging to different nations, and will be subject to complications and to competitive hindrances such as must rapidly increase under the new conditions. New and large investments of private capital will be called for, and, for some time, will be harder to obtain, to organize, and to adjust to current requirements than was the case in the conduct of these larger undertakings of the insurance world before the war.

At this point, if only these new problems of reinsurance receive the attention due to the international scope, and to the vast importance of the commercial interests involved, it becomes possible to bring into existence a corporation whose functions, at the very beginning of its life, would be those of a "treaty company" undertaking reinsurance.

Its first contracts might be made, on the one hand, with those already existing private corporations which in any nation desired to reinsure some of their existing or future risks, or which needed to find a systematic way of readjusting their business to the new conditions.

On the other hand, the contracts of this new treaty company from the very outset might in part be made with those nations which, for the sake of aiding their own underwriters in dealing with the manifold and complex problems of the new era, decided to undertake, in whatever way they found suited to the new conditions, the reinsurance of risks which their own insurance corporations had already undertaken to carry, or which these insurance corporations desired in future to undertake and to reinsure.

Such a business, or part thereof, may actually come to constitute the task of some new private corporation which will be formed in the near future, after the present war. There will no doubt be new "treaty companies." Some of them will do an international business. They will be needed. They will also need large new investments of capital in order to carry on their reinsurance business.

What I propose is that this possible new reinsurance corporation should actually begin its life as the international board of insurance trustees which, in my book, I have in outline described, and have proposed. At the outset, although not for any very long period, I propose that the functions of the Board of Trustees be provisionally limited to this perfectly practicable activity of reinsurance.

The reasons why such a reinsurance board of trustees would have ample reinsurance business with which to begin its task have now been indicated. The motives which would at first tend to make such international reinsurance attractive to the individual nations have also been sketched.

The individual nation would at first be induced to take out policies with the international board by the desire, or by the actual need, of aiding its own underwriters to adjust their business to the complications of the new life after this war, or at any rate in some near future time. The board itself would be an entirely new sort of international organ. It would have as its most important task that of finding and of making practicable still other forms of international insurance. Its indirect influence would from the very beginning far outrank in importance its direct accomplishment. Its mode of development would be guided by experience.

At no point in the growth of its work would any fundamental transformation of human nature be needed as a condition prior to its possessing a genuine, a peace-making, and a potent influence. Once having been constituted, with international reinsurance for its first enterprise, it would gradually discover new enterprises, and would increase both its direct workings and its indirect furthering of the cause of humanity by each of its new enterprises.

It would stand in opposition to none of the other peace-making influences which may come to take part in international affairs. It might well tend, in the long run, to transform international relations as, in our recent history, insurance has transformed the social life of individual nations. I submit that the time is ripe for the beginning, in this form, of international insurance; and that the prospect is impressive.

After forming this general plan I submitted it to my colleagues, Mr. W. B. Medlicott and Mr. H. B. Dow, Lecturers on Fire and Life Insurance respectively in the Graduate School of Business Administration at Harvard. I have to thank both of them for valuable suggestions with regard to reinsurance, and for encouragement regarding the general ideas involved. Mr. Medlicott, in particular, is my authority for laying stress upon the international importance which reinsurance has already acquired in his own field, and for the high organization which the business in question already possesses. While I thank my colleagues for their guidance as to special facts, and for their general approval of the spirit of my idea, I alone am responsible for the principal proposals contained in this paper.

Date Due